Judging Delinquents

LAW IN ACTION

A series edited by
Sheldon L. Messinger,
Center for the Study of Law and Society
University of California, Berkeley

Judging Delinquents

Context and Process in Juvenile Court

Robert M. Emerson
University of California, Los Angeles

Aldine Publishing Company / Chicago

First published 1969 by
Aldine Publishing Company
529 South Wabash Avenue
Chicago, Illinois 60605

Second Printing, 1970
Third Printing, 1973
Fourth Printing, 1975

ISBN 202-23001-5

Library of Congress Catalog Number 70-75047

Designed by Chestnut House

Printed in the United States of America

For Pam

Preface

The juvenile court has elicited the interest and criticism of lawyers, social workers, and criminologists, but has received relatively little attention from sociologists. This seems to reflect a more general shortcoming of sociology—a paucity of research on legal institutions. Fortunately, recent studies have begun to rectify this situation (e.g., Blumberg, 1967; Cicourel, 1968; Skolnick, 1966). This book seeks to add to this growing sociological literature on the operations of legal institutions. It describes some critical aspects of the functioning of the juvenile court, an institution charged with judging and treating delinquents. To this end, it analyzes the nature of the court operation, the handling of delinquents, and the court's functions in relation to the wider social and legal system.

This study reflects two distinct sociological heritages. First, it presents an *institutional analysis* of a juvenile court. One basic component of such an analysis involves description of the social context within which the juvenile court functions. In this way this book considers the nature of the court's relations with the various local institutions in its working environment and the consequences of these relations for its internal operations.

But in addition, the juvenile court movement has historically been associated with the introduction of rehabilitative programs into the punitively tempered criminal law. And to this day, the juvenile court represents one of the major areas of involvement for such helping professionals as social workers and psychiatrists in the criminal law. These features provide the second focal point for institutional analysis—the conflicting ideologies and purposes built into the court and the ways in which they are resolved and worked out in the practical matter of judging and dealing with delinquents.

Second, this study grows out of the current *societal reaction* approach to deviance (e.g., Becker, 1963; Kitsuse, 1964). This approach views deviance as the product of the response of official agents of social control to perceived norm violations: "deviance" involves acts and actors reacted to and labeled as such, usually by these officials. In line with this general perspective, this study seeks to shed light on some of the processes by which youths come to be identified and officially labeled "delinquents."

The following analysis attempts to combine the institutional and societal reaction approaches. This means that it is concerned with the ways in which the juvenile court's judgments and responses to the troublesome and disturbing behavior of youths are influenced by the external context and internal dynamics of the court operation.

However, it is necessary to emphasize the limited sense in which this is a study of labeling reactions to delinquents. The juvenile court represents but one of several "screenings" through which a youth must pass before he comes to see himself, and to be seen by others, as a "delinquent." This study does not directly analyze screening stages prior or subsequent to court involvement. Prior stages are considered only to the extent that decisions made there act as constraints on the court process itself. Hence the practices and decisions of the police and other enforcers in selecting cases for court action are considered only insofar as they influence the court's handling of these cases. Furthermore, although this study analyzes how the court responds differentially to cases judged to be of different kinds, it does not consider the consequences of such differential court action ("labels") for the youth involved beyond the court itself. Instead, it highlights the juvenile court's distinctive role in the labeling process, particularly in reviewing judgments and decisions made earlier and in changing the legal and social status of those accused of wrongdoing.

In sum, this study focuses on how a particular legal institution defines, reacts to and deals with the cases brought to its attention, whatever the inherent biases of this sample and whatever the ultimate consequences for youths so handled. It describes the processes that produce differential case outcomes—outcomes whereby some delinquents emerge from their court encounter firmly identified as future criminals, while others escape unharmed, not regarded as "really" delinquent despite the formal adjudication to this effect.

This book is based on research conducted at a juvenile court in a large metropolitan area. Field work began at the end of January 1966, continued on an almost daily basis through July of that year, and resumed at a less intensive level from September 1966 through May 1967. The technique of participant observation was complemented by informal interviews with court staff, usually focused on problems connected with cases that had been observed previously. After initial observation of the various phases of court activity, research centered on the progress of individual cases through the stages of court processing. Cases were followed from the preliminary complaint in the clerk's office, during initial and subsequent handling by probation staff, and finally throughout the courtroom proceeding.

At all stages of field work, special effort was made to observe interaction between delinquents and court officials. Particular attention was devoted to two settings—formal courtroom proceedings and more informal encounters between probation officers and delinquents and their families. Significantly, observation of the latter was facilitated by the lack of privacy characteristic of probation operations at the court: all probation interviews were conducted in one of three large, unpartitioned offices shared by three to four probation officers. Privacy was almost unattainable, and probation interviews, routinely held in this open setting, ordinarily allowed direct and easy access.

Furthermore, regular attempts were made to elicit judgments and expectations related to case dispositions. Court staff were continually probed about their analysis of particular cases and the problems that each presented. Probation officers were often asked what outcome they wanted and/or expected, as well as what they thought of particular delinquents and their offenses. Police officers, truant officers, Child Welfare Department workers, and others with some official standing in cases were approached informally wherever possible with questions about background and outlook. Here acquaintanceship with the probation staff often provided a means of establishing quick rapport. Finally, on many occasions informal discussions were held with judges shortly after the morning's sessions. Explicit statements about the grounds for decisions, factors that had been considered, and perceptions of the problems presented by cases were sought. Many afternoons were spent sitting around probation offices sharing in gossip about the day's cases and about delinquents, lawyers, criminals, courts, and probation work in general.

Following this six-month period of intensive field work, more selective observations of court activities were made at least one day each week. Special attention was given to cases regarded as unusual or interesting by court personnel and to the work of the court clinic. Formal and informal interviews were held with members of the clinic staff, all case conferences held in conjunction with the court were observed, and psychiatric reports were studied and discussions held with their authors, although it proved impossible to observe psychiatric interviews directly.

While the research reported here is essentially a case study, an effort was made to overcome some of the inherent limitations of this approach by observing other courts and related institutions in the area. Of most significance, prior to the major study weekly observations, covering a period of about five months, were made of the juvenile sessions of a neighboring municipal court. A period of six weeks was also devoted to participant observation with two juvenile officers working in a central district of the city. Finally, a suburban court and several adult criminal courts were visited. These observations provided a sense of the comparative nature and context of the court actually studied.

The limits of a conventional case study were also expanded through brief research into the operations of those agencies having regular and important business with the court. Interviews were conducted with policemen appearing in the court (contacts established during earlier work with juvenile officers proved very helpful here). Brief observations and interviews were conducted at the Child Welfare Department, Children's Mental Hospital, and the Harris School. Frequent interviews and more informal conversations were also held with agents from these and other institutions when they appeared in court. Particularly important were contacts with the succession of public defenders who worked regularly in the juvenile court, as well as with truant officers, school officials, and again the police.

Finally, it is important to emphasize the basically exploratory and preliminary nature of the research and analyses which follow. No effort was made to quantify observations, and only the most general statistical data are cited. Furthermore, the analyses presented in the following chapters are intended to be illustrative and suggestive and are not advanced as established conclusions. As a whole, this book should be understood as an initial attempt to make sociological sense out of the activities of a single institution charged with responding to disturbing and "deviant" behavior by youth.

Field work cannot be conducted in any institution without the cooperation and assistance of its members. This study is no exception. I would like to express my gratitude to the staff of the juvenile court for so willingly accepting the continual presence of an inquisitive sociological observer. I would particularly like to thank the judge of the juvenile court, who freely opened all aspects of court affairs to study and who always made time to discuss its activities.

The analysis that follows grew out of and reflects the insights and criticisms of many teachers, in the widest sense of that term. Irving Zola provided constant aid and encouragement throughout the period of field work and during the writing of the initial drafts of this manuscript. Joan Emerson read and commented on the many versions through which this study has passed, always contributing valuable suggestions. Sheldon Messinger's editing and criticism shaped the final manuscript, drawing out much that had been implicit and contributing new insights too numerous to mention. Parts of this study also benefited from the suggestions and criticisms of Everett C. Hughes, Lewis A. Coser, Larry Rosenberg, Erving Goffman, Egon Bittner, and Arlene Daniels. Finally, my initial observations of juvenile courts were carried out as a joint project with Jon Davies. Many of the following pages reflect his sensitive and perceptive reactions to court events.

Most of the period of field work investigation and analysis was supported by a National Institute of Mental Health training grant (NIMH-8116). Later writing was completed during a Russell Sage Foundation residence in law and sociology, and benefited from the aid and support of the Center for the Study of Law and Society, University of California, Berkeley.

Finally, I would like to thank my wife, to whom this book is dedicated, both for her aid and for enduring the trials of authorship.

R. M. E.

Contents

xiii

Judging Delinquents

I

The Dilemmas of Treatment

These initial chapters describe the nature and consequences of the juvenile court's efforts to implement "treatment" as an organizational goal. Chapter 1 presents the general setting and internal organization of the court, emphasizing the balance between treatment and legal concerns with restriction and control within this organization. Chapters 2 and 3 explore the nature of court relations with the political, enforcement, and welfare institutions that make up its organizational environment, relations that tend to contradict and deflect court pursuit of treatment. These chapters serve both to introduce the institutional setting of the juvenile court and to describe the social forces that set the terms on which the court judges and responds to delinquents.

I

The Setting and Structure of the
Juvenile Court

Juvenile court personnel are committed to several different and conflicting orientations toward delinquency and its control, orientations summarized in the "social-agency" and "legal" images of the juvenile court (Dunham, 1958). The legal image highlights the juvenile court's restraining, controlling, and punishing functions, functions that demand some guarantee of due process safeguards. The social-agency image orients activities toward providing "help" and "treatment" to delinquent and other disadvantaged youths. In this light, "the purposes of the juvenile court are to understand the child, to diagnose his difficulty, to treat his condition, and to fit him back into the community" (Dunham, 1958, p. 513). This chapter outlines the juvenile court's commitment to these dual orientations as background for the analysis of court efforts to implement its treatment goals and the consequences of these efforts in the following chapters.

THE CONTEMPORARY SETTING

The juvenile court under study is located in the central district of a metropolitan complex of over two million people in the northern United States. The central city itself has a population of almost 700,000, of which about 215,000 fall within the jurisdiction of the juvenile court.[1]

1. These figures, as all those in this section, are taken from census tract data for the 1960 census.

The juvenile court's jurisdiction covers the business and financial districts, several large state and federal government complexes, and all of the central shopping area. There are also several hospital and medical complexes, a number of colleges and associated student apartments and dormitories, and two wealthy residential areas. It also encompasses those sections of the city that provide its nightlife—bars, theaters, nightclubs, and shows, its most disreputable slum area, and its "vice" center, where derelicts, addicts, prostitutes, and the transient poor wander among rooming houses and bars. Finally, the court's jurisdiction includes a number of clear-cut ethnic settlements: a large and established Italian district, a small Chinese community, and a large part of the Negro ghetto interspersed with small pockets of Jewish, Irish, and Italian families.

Census material on the jurisdictional area indicates the relative importance of slum and ghetto. Of the total population of 215,000, 73 per cent are white and 27 per cent are nonwhite, mostly Negro. It should also be noted that about 84 per cent of the total nonwhite population of the city (and over 90 per cent of this is Negro) falls within the court's jurisdiction. Finally, the population within the court's jurisdiction consistently falls below the citywide average in both education and family income, again indicating the predominantly lower class character of the area.

Fifty-nine thousand or 28 per cent of the population within the court's jurisdiction is under 18. This provides a large part of the clientele of the court, which has jurisdiction over offenders up to the age of 17. But since the court hears all cases arising from offenses committed within its area, without regard to the offender's place of residence, it also handles a considerable number of children both from other parts of the city and from the suburbs. These cases usually involve shoplifting in the major downtown department stores, but they may also arise from incidents in the "red-light district" of the bars, movie theaters, and penny arcades, and in a newer "beatnik" area of coffee houses and discothèques.

Several comments must be made about the general character of the political and institutional life of the city. First, there is an extreme consciousness of ethnicity, despite the fact that all significant foreign immigration ceased more than fifty years ago. This is largely a legacy of the city's patterns of immigration, whereby the established native American groups retained control of the important public institutions long after they had been outnumbered by foreign immigrant populations. This has resulted in a history of ethnic hostility, resentment, and conflict, often coinciding with the religious split between the Catholic Irish and Italian immigrants and the Protestantism of the native American population.

Politics is one of the prime arenas of expression of this ethnic consciousness. The newer immigrants tend to be represented in the Democratic party, which is predominantly lower class and Catholic, and dominated within the city by the Irish. The Republican party, in contrast, is heavily middle class and Protestant, with its main support in suburban and rural regions outside the area of the central city. Within the city the political system is presently dominated by the Irish (with the support of other immigrant groups) and the lower and lower-middle classes.

While the Democratic machine is no longer as powerful as it once was, city politics continue to emphasize personal followings, often along ethnic lines. This places great value on jobs and favors as rewards and resources in the political game. The flavor of local politics is well illustrated by the comments of a former member of the state legislature:

> The fact . . . that the whole legislature is run on a personal basis leaves a lot of room for back-scratching and for "put this man on and I'll see that this man gets in that department," or "I know so-and-so up in this department that's looking for a job and maybe we can work him into another job but at the same time, if I do that for you or for your cousin up there, why don't you do something for my friend down here?" I think there's a good deal of that.[2]

In general, ethnic rivalry and personalism rather than bureaucratic professionalism typify local politics and local governmental institutions.

2. From an interview reported by a political scientist writing about the local political scene.

COURT POWERS AND PROCEDURE

The court under study operates under statutes embodying the ideological thrust of the juvenile court movement. Its purpose is distinguished from that of the criminal court:

> as far as practicable, they [children 7 to 17] shall be treated, not as criminals, but as children in need of aid, encouragement and guidance. Proceedings against children . . . shall not be deemed criminal proceedings.[3]

The court is exhorted to treat children brought before it with the same kind of "care, custody and discipline" that they would receive from good parents. Ordinary criminal procedure is modified to implement this purpose. Finally, the court protects the youthful delinquent from criminal stigmatization with private hearings and with rules insuring confidentiality of court records.

The geographic jurisdiction of the juvenile court extends over the central sections of the city. The court hears all complaints arising from violations of criminal law and local ordinances within this area when committed by children between 7 and 17. These complaints for delinquency arise not only from violations of laws that apply to adults, but also from offenses against laws applicable only to children. A child can be judged delinquent as an "incorrigible child," for example, for "refusing to obey the just and reasonable commands of his parents."

All cases begin with a complaint brought against a child.[4] Most complaints are brought by the police, although they may be initiated and signed by an injured or threatened party, including the victim of a particular offense, or, in the case of a complaint for "incorrigibility," the parents. Complaints may also be brought by

---

3. State statutes.
4. For a recent comprehensive survey of legal procedures employed in dealing with juveniles, see *Harvard Law Review*, 1966; pp. 775–810. For comparative juvenile court procedure, see *ibid.*, pp. 790–801.

school officials (for school offenders) and truant officers (for truant cases only) .[5]

2. Once the complaint has been approved by the clerk, it is turned over to a probation officer who interviews parent and child very briefly in order to complete the court's standard face sheet. Information entered on the face sheet includes basic demographic material about the child and his family (age, race, religion, plus items on parental education, employment, and income) and information about the child's prior court record, school and church contacts, jobs, health, home behavior, hours, associations, and interests. Some inquiry may also be made into the circumstances of the offense, although probation officers often rely solely on police accounts.

3. The child is taken into the courtroom for arraignment following completion of the face sheet. Here the probation officer outlines the complaint against the child. The judge then informs parent and child of the right to counsel and to the appointment of a public defender if necessary. If a lawyer is desired, the case is continued for hearing at a later date, generally at the convenience of the police officer. If no lawyer is desired and there is no other request for a continuance, the full hearing on the complaint follows.

State law provides the juvenile court with wide discretion to establish procedures for hearing and adjudicating delinquency complaints. Formally, the hearing is not to inquire into or determine the child's guilt or innocence but to establish his status as either delinquent or not delinquent. In practice, the juvenile court extends this protection by prohibiting pleas of delinquent by any child unless represented by counsel. A lawyer, however, may "admit to a finding," i.e., agree to accept a finding of "delinquent" on the facts alleged in the complaint. In this case the

5. In addition to delinquency and "school" complaints, the court also has jurisdiction over neglect petitions, alleging that "a child is without proper care (discipline, attention) ." Legal custody over the child is transferred to the state if the petition is successful. The juvenile court can also hear two kinds of criminal complaints against adults: those charging "contributing to the delinquency of a minor" and those involving neglect of minor children (in conjunction with the care and protection petition). In these adult matters the juvenile court has concurrent jurisdiction with municipal courts.

judge makes the equivalent of a "guilty" finding and turns to the question of disposition.

Although the juvenile court partially relaxes the usual rules of evidence, hearings afford many procedural safeguards. The complainant, generally a police officer, acts as a prosecutor, presenting his case with the help of available witnesses. Defense counsel may cross-examine all witnesses, and where there is no counsel, either judge or prosecutor asks the child and his parents if they have any questions regarding the testimony. After the prosecution has finished, the defense may present its case. A lawyer may call witnesses, but often the only one is the child himself. If without counsel, the child will be asked whether there is anything he would like to say about the incident. At any time, the judge may cross-examine or question witnesses; it is court policy, however, not to question children who refuse to testify about the alleged offense.

After all the evidence and statements have been heard, an adjudication of either "delinquent" or "not delinquent" is in order. But just as in adult criminal courts where convictions are nearly always obtained, very few juveniles find their contact with the juvenile court terminated at this point with a judgment of "not delinquent": during 1966 only 7 per cent of all complaints led to findings of "not delinquent". (In a small number of additional cases, "dismissed without finding" represents an equivalent verdict. See Appendix.) In a very basic sense, then, once a complaint has been brought against a youth, the court almost routinely assumes jurisdiction over him.

One factor that distorts the rate of dismissal of complaints deserves further consideration here, since in effect it involves a court practice of holding adjudication in abeyance. Certain cases may be "continued without a finding" for indefinite periods. No adjudication of delinquency is made, but this is kept as an open possibility while a probation officer informally supervises the youth for several months. If the child behaves during this period, the complaint will be dismissed and his record kept unblemished. (Thus, "continued without a finding" represents a contingent finding of "not delinquent" and is the most lenient court response for dealing with delinquent children.)

The decision to handle an accused youth as a "juvenile offend-er" may also lead to the dismissal of the delinquency complaint at this time. State law provides that where the child is over 14, "and the court is of the opinion that his welfare, and the interests of the public, require that he should be tried for said offense or violation," the court may dismiss the delinquency complaint and criminal proceedings may be initiated. In practice, the juvenile court invokes this "juvenile offender" option very infrequently, as judges are reluctant to use it unless all "treatment" attempts have failed, or, as one judge noted, "unless it's an extremely vicious crime." One of the primary expressions of traditional en-forcement and punitive goals in the juvenile court, this option frequently is sought by the police in "serious" cases.

Once a finding of delinquency has been made, the court must decide on disposition.[6] In this it relies heavily on the probation officer's report, which is derived from his initial interview and outlines briefly the delinquent's background, general behavior, family situation, and school record. Where a case appears suffi-ciently clear-cut, this information will be adequate, and the pro-bation officer makes a recommendation for disposing of the case, almost always probation. If there is a lawyer in the case, he will also be permitted to make an argument on disposition, and this may agree or disagree with what the probation officer has recom-mended. However, when confronted by some problem or diffi-culty, the probation officer will request that disposition be post-poned until he has had an opportunity to make a more thorough investigation of the case. This may require contacting other agen-

6. A delinquent has a legal right to appeal both finding and disposition, although this right is rarely invoked. It should also be emphasized that the Supreme Court's guarantee of constitutional rights to juveniles covers only those legal proceedings leading up to the adjudication, and no consideration has yet been given to issues connected with disposition. Moreover, the language of the *Gault* decision would seem to suggest that constitutional guarantees might be reconciled with the treatment goals of the juvenile court by continu-ing to allow maximum discretion at the stage of disposition: "The problems of pre-adjudication treatment of juveniles, and of post-adjudication disposition, are unique to the juvenile process; hence what we hold in this opinion with regard to the procedural requirements at the adjudicatory stage has no neces-sary applicability to other steps of the juvenile process." *In re Gault,* 87 S.Ct. (1967) , 1445, footnote 48. See also p. 1436.

cies involved in the case, visiting the home and parents, calling upon relatives, and/or making a variety of arrangements upon which a desired disposition will be contingent, such as gaining the youth's admittance into a special program or a boarding school.

Referral to the court clinic or to the Children's Mental Hospital for psychiatric diagnosis and recommendation is frequently used to evaluate difficult cases that have been "continued for disposition" in this way. Generally the judge initiates this course of action and will give great weight to the psychiatric report.

Probation and commitment constitute the two main disposition alternatives. There are two general forms of probation. First, there is *straight probation* where a probation officer supervises the child on a fairly regular basis. A more intensive form of probation involves attending the Boys' Training Program, a privately financed afternoon recreation-education program run by the court. Probation officers connected with this program supervise these cases. Second, the court can place a child on probation under a *suspended sentence*: a formal commitment to the Youth Correction Authority is suspended, with probation supervision ordered in the interim. Because appeal can be taken only when the suspended sentence is initially imposed, the delinquent can later be committed to the Youth Correction Authority at the discretion of the court. A suspended sentence is generally revoked if the delinquent commits another offense, but may follow when the probation officer brings the child to court for some lesser violation of probation.

Commitment is the most drastic disposition open to the court. The court has statutory power to commit children found delinquent to the Youth Correction Authority, which then reviews the case and assigns it to the most appropriate institution. Actually this decision is routine, because while there is only one institution for girls, boys are usually assigned to institutions strictly on the basis of age. The Youth Correction Authority has the right to refuse to commit a child, although it rarely does so. The YCA's most important power is over the delinquent's date of release, as the court sentence to the Authority is an indeterminate one. Commitment thus takes the case out of the court's hands.

The juvenile court may also commit truants or school offenders to the County Training School. This school is run on a semimilitary basis, but puts more emphasis on academic school work than do the state reform schools.

Finally, the juvenile court may terminate contact with a child in a number of ways. Commitment obviously has this effect, for even when released from the Youth Correction Authority, the delinquent is supervised by a parole officer from that agency and not by the court. In addition, when a child turns 17, the court loses jurisdiction over any new cases, although probation may extend beyond this age limit. Probation, either "straight" or under a suspended sentence, is generally terminated at the end of the designated period upon a favorable report from the probation officer. The probation officer, however, may also make an unfavorable report and request an extension of the probationary period. In cases that have been continued without a finding, the complaint is simply dismissed at the end of the continuance period, again subject to a favorable probation report. Finally, under certain circumstances the court will dismiss entirely past or current findings of delinquency against a youth. This is routinely done to give a youth a "clean record" in order to qualify him for enlistment in the armed forces.[7]

INTERNAL ORGANIZATION OF THE JUVENILE COURT

Within the juvenile court one can identify three positions with distinctive legal and organizational duties: judge, probation officer, and clinic staff. These figures make the decisions that determine the outcomes of delinquency cases and, in this process, reflect the differing formal orientations discussed previously. In addition, the public defender comes to work so closely with the court staff that he can be treated as part of the same organiza-

7. In general, state statutes seek to limit the significance of records for delinquency, prohibiting use of adjudication as delinquent in any court proceeding except in a subsequent delinquency hearing or in imposing criminal sentence, and prohibiting disqualification from state or local public office because of such a record.

tional system. By considering the role of each in the court, along
with their conception of their duties and responsibilities, one can
get an overall view of the more concrete goals and operating
ideologies of the court.

Judges

There are three judges regularly associated with the juvenile
court, two part-time or associate judges and the full-time judge
who is the dominant figure in the institution. The chief judge
determines the procedural rules applicable to the associate judges,
controls the hiring and advancement of court personnel, including probation and secretarial staffs, and sets general policy guide-
lines for probation work. The institution is very truly "his court."

All judicial appointments to the juvenile court are made by
the governor of the state for the life of the appointee. The annual
salary for the chief judge is somewhat in excess of $20,000 and is
equal to the standard salary for judges of the lowest level, municipal courts. Associate judges sit when requested to do so by the
chief judge. Under the current regime, each associate judge sits
one day a week and on additional occasions when needed. They
are paid on a per diem basis.

All of the current judges (and most of the previous ones) have
been involved in the practice of both law and politics. All have
graduated from local law schools, been admitted to the state Bar,
and had private practices in the city. The two associates judges
continue to devote most of their time to these practices, while the
chief judge is prohibited by law from engaging in private legal
practice. All have also participated actively in local politics, generally within the Democratic party. Although all three judges
now serve on the boards of charitable and service agencies concerned with children, none had been concerned with delinquency
or child welfare prior to appointment to the court. Legal and
political contacts rather than activity in social welfare secured
their appointments to the bench.

The judges exercise the ultimate legal authority of the court.
They conduct all hearings, make all findings on the basis of the
facts presented, and decide on all temporary and final disposi-

tions. The juvenile court is allowed great latitude to determine its own operating rules and procedures, which are set in general terms by the chief judge. This judge is clearly the dominant fig- 'ure in the processing of delinquency cases, not only because of his legally superordinate position within the court, but also because he sits much more often and hence hears the great majority of cases, including all those regarded as "serious" or controversial.

The chief judge also serves as principal administrator of the court, an area in which the associates have no powers. His duties here involve hiring, organizing, and overseeing court staff. But the judge does not so much directly supervise the probation staff as work out policies the higher probation officers are charged with implementing. The judge also takes charge of planning the court's budget and staff and developing or carrying out new programs.

From this it should be clear that the judges, and particularly the chief judge, occupy the crucial formal decision-making positions with regard both to individual cases and their disposition, and to procedural, administrative, and program policy. It is therefore crucial to consider the terms in which the juvenile court judges see the court, its functions and its goals.

To begin with, the judges explicitly acknowledge that the juvenile court is a judicial tribunal, essentially concerned with judging violations of the criminal law and operating by means of often coercive authority. At the time of the study there was some difference of opinion, however, on how far traditional legal protections should be extended in juvenile matters. The chief judge insisted on an extensive set of procedural guarantees securing the child most of the constitutional rights accorded adults in criminal trials, including the right to refuse to testify or answer questions about the alleged offense. The associate judges, however, followed this procedure only with reluctance, as the prior court practice had been to question the child about his offense. But overall, an effort was made to give the child the full benefit of his constitutional rights in a situation where it was by no means clear that the granting of such rights was required by law. For at that time it was not certain that higher courts would reverse juvenile court decisions on these constitutional grounds.

Since then, however, the U.S. Supreme Court has ruled (*In re*

Gault, 1967) that a child and his parents must be told the charges
against him, have a right to an attorney, may confront and cross-
examine his accusers, and may not be forced into self-incrimina-
tory statements or confessions. The current judge anticipated the
Supreme Court's extension of constitutional rights to children
appearing in juvenile courts, a decision in accord with his own
convictions in these matters. Court sessions observed after the
Gault decision were no different than before.

However, the judges' conviction that the basic purpose of the
juvenile court is to "rehabilitate" and "help" children who are in
trouble in practice dilutes commitment to the legal model. Thus,
while the judges acknowledge that the juvenile court is a legal
tribunal, they generally see this as secondary to their duty and
function of helping children. The nature of the proffered help
may vary widely: the chief judge conceives of help in much more
psychiatric and therapeutic terms than do his more traditional
associates. But all recognize the desirability of providing a number of special services, such as special medical attention, remedial
reading, or speech therapy, along with "supervision" and some
"casework" by the probation staff.

Characteristically, the conflict between these social agency
functions and the juvenile court's legal functions is resolved ideologically by emphasizing the separation of finding and disposition: the child is given an impartial hearing on the facts of the
case against him, and only after a finding of "delinquent" has
been made does the court begin to function as a social agency,
now operating with a different set of rules and purposes.

Finally, juvenile court judges are ideologically committed to
law enforcement and community protection. This finds expression in the conviction that children should not be led to believe
they can violate the law with impunity:

> The judge explained in some detail how he tried to get the depart-
> ment stores to overcome their reluctance and bring more of their shop-
> lifting cases into court. "We want them in. Some of the most serious
> cases are shoplifters. . . . If they break the law two or three times
> without getting caught, they think they can get away with it. . . . It
> hurts them in the long run [not to be brought to court]."

Similarly it appears in the strong feeling among all court personnel that a child who commits too many offenses must be dealt with severely. This feeling is epitomized in the ideology "three strikes and you're out"; that is, commitment should automatically follow a set number of court appearances (although not necessarily three). Judges explicitly recognize that this is not treatment, yet feel obligated not to let juveniles "get away" with too many offenses and to protect the community from their future depredations.

In summary, judges dominate the court scene. They are its official representatives and exercise the ultimate decision-making power over cases brought before it. The judges identify themselves as public and judicial figures and feel a sense of responsibility for the use of their legal power. But they also seek to help children in trouble and distress. Hence the competing orientations of the juvenile court come to focus on the person of the judge and on his decisions about the cases before him. The judge must first conduct the legal hearing into the "guilt" or "innocence" of the child and then decide on disposition, a decision that will require balancing or evaluating the conflicting claims of treatment, enforcement of the law and community standards, and prevention of possible future serious offenses.

Probation Staff

Probation officers are appointed by the chief judge of the court, subject to standards set by the Board of Probation and to its confirmation. Standards have recently been raised with a growing pressure for professionalization within probation. Now every probation officer must have a college degree and either an M.A. in social work or two years of experience "in a related field." Salary begins at $6,800 per year and reaches a maximum of nearly $10,000 in ten increments.

During most of the study, twelve probation officers worked directly in the court, while four others assisted with the Boys' Training Program. The latter appeared in court once or twice a week and handled some general probation chores, but devoted most of their time to the noncourt activities associated with their after-

noon program. The regular court probation staff of eight men
and four women probation officers was headed by a chief probation officer and an assistant chief, who handled a variety of administrative and supervisory tasks. In practice the women functioned as a semiautonomous unit but adhered to the general
framework of court probation policy.

Probation officers in the juvenile court were generally lower-
middle class in background. Seven of twelve were Irish. There
were two Negroes, both appointed very recently, despite the high
proportion of Negro delinquents. In general, the probation staff
showed minimal professional training and experience, usually in
fields more related to law than to social work: while only one of
the male probation officers (the assistant chief) had a social work
degree, four had legal training in night law schools, including
two from police backgrounds and two others who previously
served as parole agents with the Youth Correction Authority. Professional qualifications were somewhat higher among the women
probation officers: three held advanced degrees in psychology, social work, and law respectively, and the fourth was a registered
nurse.

Male probation officers spent somewhat more than half their
working hours at the court, overseeing the rather mechanical
tasks involved in getting cases in and out of hearings as "officer of
the day" or appearing in the courtroom on cases assigned to them.
Each of the six regular men probation officers was assigned a district, and handled all cases that the court supervised from that
area. They spent the rest of their time working "on the district,"
visiting families and delinquents, checking on the records and
behavior of their probationers with other officials, and hearing
probationers' "reports" in offices provided by local settlement
houses. In contrast, the senior probation officer in the girls' unit
assigned cases without regard to district. And in general, woman
probation officers made few home visits, holding almost all their
interviews with probationers in their court offices.

The probation officer occupies an ambiguous position in the
overall structure of the juvenile court. On the one hand, he performs the routine chores which keep the court operation going.
His court work provides his occupational identification and elic-

its a great deal of commitment on his part. On the other hand, the probation officer has low professional status within the court itself, relative to both judges and clinic personnel. Furthermore, he is the organizational subordinate of the judges: probation officers hold their jobs at least partially at the discretion of the chief judge, who may dismiss an officer "for cause," subject to review by the Probation Board and who also directs and evaluates their work. However, the probation officer's frequent contact with delinquent and family, his commitment to court work, and his practical knowledge and experience tend to offset this low professional and hierarchical standing.

One expression of probation officers' strong occupational identification is antipathy toward social work and social workers, despite some formal adherence to casework theory and techniques. This antipathy largely reflects the probation officer's commitment to *authority* in his role as a public official.[8] The probation officer feels *outside* social work exactly because he works in a court setting where he must deal with controls and administer legal sanctions. He distrusts social workers, and frequently criticizes their excessive leniency and permissiveness with children. For example:

> A woman probation officer was very upset with a settlement house social worker for not detaining a girl the court had a warrant out for. She complained bitterly: "Asinine little social worker . . . She identifies with the child so much. . . . Granted you have to get their confidence, but the kids will run all over you if you go that far." This settlement house had done nothing about sex and drinking on the premises, refusing to call in the police because "they felt this was nonprofessional." Finally: "That's why I can never understand why she believes everything these kids tell her. I believe practically nothing unless I can verify it."

8. Similarly, handling authority within a relationship of professional trust is a constant problem for social workers in the probation field (Ohlin, Piven, and Pappenfort, 1956, pp. 211–25). These authors comment on the general alienation of social-work–trained probation and parole officers from social work in general, as well as the "partial alienation from the social work profession which practitioners [in parole and probation] trained in social work frequently experience under the pressure of solving their immediate work problems" (p. 217, footnote).

Similarly, although probation officers talk of their work in terms of "helping" and "supervising" children, social work skills are generally ignored in practice. In place of technical and professional competence, the probation officer identifies common sense and knowledge of local community byways as the fundamental requisites for his work. Hence the indispensability of practical experience in probation work receives constant stress. In addition, probation officers emphasize getting to know and to be known in the local community. Common ethnicity and knowledge of local customs and practices contribute to this goal. This belief finds expression, for example, in the official policy of staffing an Italian area with an Italian probation officer. But knowledge of the local community serves not only as a means for obtaining the trust and cooperation of the families of delinquents, it also helps establish personal ties with the various officials and agencies in the district. These connections are felt to lie at the core of probation work, for they both promote exchange of information and favors with community agents such as the settlement houses, schools, and police, and keep the probation officer in close touch with developments in the community.

This particularistic, "common-sense" approach underlies the probation officer's conception of his relationship with delinquents. "Respect," balanced by deserved fairness, must be maintained. As one probation officer commented on what delinquents should think of him: "Mr. Sullivan'll give you a break but he"ll make you toe the line." Establishing respect requires adopting an authoritarian and disciplinarian stance toward delinquents, not a therapeutic and counseling one.

As a consequence, "treatment" becomes an expedient and somewhat provisional consideration in handling delinquents. One probation officer commented:

> The first time a child appears in court no stone should be left unturned "to find out what the problem is and to set up a plan to do something about it." This might include medical or neurological tests, visiting and talking to the family. If the kid comes in a second time, you should check the case over and see if you have missed anything. The third time you begin to wonder. The fourth time the kid should be sent away.

And the chief probation officer noted:

> Of course, the only time you have to knuckle down to the legal part is when the kid might be a danger to someone or destroy property. Then we have to keep him under wraps.

Like judges, probation officers feel youths should not be allowed to "get away" with breaking the law or the rules laid down by the court. The probation officer's primary responsibility, however, is to the judge and not to the public or any outside agency. Hence it is generally more important for him to consider how the judge will react to a recommendation or to a report on how he has handled a case than it is for him to worry about what the public might say.

Lawyers in the Juvenile Court

As noted previously, all accused delinquents in the juvenile court are allowed to obtain legal counsel and are advised of their right to do so on first appearing before the judge. Since there is rarely any question that the youth and his family qualify as indigent, the court staff almost automatically assume that the public defenders will be appointed in cases where legal counsel is wanted. One lawyer from this office is regularly assigned to handle all juvenile court cases. Generally this lawyer is new to the staff and draws this assignment as a low pressure introduction to defense practice. The juvenile court is seen as a desirable setting in which to "learn the ropes" of court work, both because of its informality and because it is felt that ineptitude and inexperience will not have severely detrimental consequences for the client.

During the sixteen months of observation at the juvenile court, four different public defenders handled cases on a regular basis. One was assigned to "cover" the court three to five days a week. Ties between the public defenders and the court staff, particularly the probation officers, naturally grow quite close, and, as will be seen, public defenders come to function in close cooperation with the probation staff. For this reason, the public defender can be looked on as a kind of adjunct to the regular court staff.

Although private attorneys do not make it a regular practice to

represent cases in the juvenile court, and no such lawyer was observed handling more than a single case, private lawyers do
appear fairly frequently in the court. For the most part private
counsel is procured at the initiative of the accused or his family.

It is particularly striking that both public defenders and private lawyers feel awkward and uncomfortable about working in
the juvenile court setting. In the first place, this reflects the inability of the lawyer with experience in the criminal law to function as he normally would in adult matters. As various studies
have noted, most practice of the criminal law involves negotiation between defense and prosecuting attorneys wherein a defendant is allowed to plead guilty to a less serious charge than the
one he originally faced (Sudnow, 1965; Skolnick, 1967). In the
juvenile court, however, "deals" of this nature are very infre-
quent. One basic reason for this is that there is no independent
prosecutor involved in court proceedings; the police or other official complainants conduct their own cases and are less willing to
compromise their desired outcome. Beyond this, in the juvenile
court there is no automatic or necessary relation between charge
and disposition. Disposition is left to the discretion of the judge,
and while the nature of the delinquent act may influence his
decision, the formal charge does not. Reduction of the charge
therefore generally confers no benefit to the accused. Conversely,
since there is no formal plea of guilty, the police have nothing to
gain by reducing the charge.

A second source of awkwardness in practicing law in the context of the juvenile court arises from the apparent irrelevance of
legal talents and skills. As in adult criminal courts, in the majority of cases there is little or no dispute over the "facts" of the
offense. Cases tend to be straightforward, and defenses directed at
overturning the evidence generally appear to be hopeless and
futile. Defense strategy therefore usually concedes the delinquency of the client but tries to minimize the penalty. However,
given the general inability of the lawyer to bargain for leniency,
there is little he can do in pursuit of this end. Legal "defense"
comes to primarily involve making a "pitch" on behalf of the
youth, a presentation depicting the youth as the kind of person
who should not be sanctioned too severely.

Finally, the lawyer experiences difficulty in applying the adversary model to the juvenile court setting (Skolnick, 1967). For the court's constant "treatment" and helping rhetoric obscures any adversary elements in the proceeding. It is difficult, for example, to view a probation officer as an adversary when he holds himself willing to take any "reasonable" course of action to "help" the youth involved. The effect of this stance appears in the following comment:

> A private attorney in juvenile court on a case noted that there was little an attorney could contribute in this setting. "What can a lawyer say? The probation officers know better about the kids. . . . They aren't out to get them." He usually tried to get the best deal possible for a client, but this procedure had no value in a juvenile court, because the probation officers were not out to get the kids. And the lawyer's presence might even destroy the informal atmosphere, if he felt compelled to appear to earn his fee: "You have to put on a show, a presentation for the client."

Under these circumstances the attorney begins to feel doubt about pushing too hard to "get a kid off," particularly on technical grounds. (See also Platt, Schechter, and Tiffany, 1968.) As a public defender commented: "To tip a case over a technicality, so what? . . . I'm not sure it will help the kid."

Court techniques for coopting lawyers behind treatment efforts add to the lawyer's confusion about functioning in the juvenile court setting. The court regards counsel as unnecessary and superfluous in the helping activities considered central to court operations. Hence the court routinely seeks to transform this role into one more congenial to a treatment enterprise, encouraging lawyers to work closely with all court personnel. As the judge commented, "We try to help them all we can." To this end the court makes available to lawyers all records, including the face sheet, prior delinquency record, probation interviews, and psychiatric reports. Probation officers will discuss a case's prospects with the lawyer, communicating court perceptions of the issues and problems, and the outcomes under consideration. In this way the lawyer is drawn into the court's efforts to deal with the case, and constrained to conduct his thinking and suggestions along these more "constructive" lines. As the judge described the focus of these pressures on lawyers to make a "contribution" to the court's efforts to handle cases:

> First of all, they can explain court procedure to their clients so that they know what's going to happen. Then they don't come in here scared to death. Second, they can get information in many cases we can never get. . . . People will tell lawyers things they would not tell members of the court, especially myself. . . . [Such things might include the nature of employment, troubles in the home.] Lots of parents come in here and tell us nothing but lies. Lawyers can get a lot more than we can, and it would be a great benefit to us if we could get them to realize that we are not going to use it to hurt but to help their clients.

The Court Clinic

The juvenile court clinic is formally under the administrative control of the state department of mental health. The director of one division of this agency oversees the operation of all court clinics within the state, including the juvenile court clinic. The department pays clinic salaries and receives clinic reports. The clinic is staffed, however, by the private child guidance clinic, which provides both its director and the psychiatric personnel. During the first year of its operation, clinic staff included a director, four psychiatric residents in child psychiatry, and a social worker. The director worked half time, the residents twelve hours a week, and the social worker full time at the clinic. The following year the number of residents rose to ten, although their working time was halved.

The psychiatrists working in the court clinic almost without exception had been or were being trained in an orthodox school of child psychiatry. Aside from the director, who supervised the general training and court work of about half the residents, all regarded their time at the court primarily as a learning experience. Most invested minimal time and effort in their court work. This tended to maintain their distance from court staff. Their professional standing as psychiatrists, their commitment to doctrines and techniques of Freudian psychoanalysis foreign to the general court approach to delinquency, and their lack of roots in the local community further increased this distance.

Responsibility for the daily routine of clinic operations fell to its social work staff, expanded from one during the first year of operation to two with the assistance of two student trainees during the second year. As only the social workers operated full time in the clinic, they monopolized most administrative tasks and contacts with court staff. Since the part-time directing psychiatrist retained formal decision-making authority, however, this generated a number of administrative tensions, particularly in case assignments, coordinated planning with the court, and meeting court deadlines for reports.

The diagnosis and treatment of delinquency cases referred by the court constitute the clinic's formal responsibilities. In practice, however, the clinic's work becomes almost entirely diagnostic. Hence while the clinic averages about 400 referrals annually, only 6 in the first year and 25 in the second year were continued for treatment.

Diagnosis begins with the assignment of a social worker and a psychiatrist to the case. Ideally the social worker should interview the parents and obtain a social history on the family before the psychiatrist sees the child, but this is not always possible. The psychiatrist interviews the child one, two, or rarely, three times, and then confers with the social worker before writing up the report that goes to the court containing diagnosis and recommendation. Occasionally the psychiatrist may be called in to talk with the judge about special problems posed by a case.

The clinic and the individual therapist decide which cases to accept for treatment. Most delinquents in treatment are seen every other week, sometimes for slightly less than the standard fifty minutes. In some cases a social worker may regularly see the parents, although social workers also treat a number of children directly.

The juvenile court clinic operated on a rationale developed by Dr. Paul Williams, the creator and director of the statewide court clinic system. He views the court clinic as a means of bringing psychiatric care to the lower classes. The doctrine that therapy

can only be voluntary is countered by the belief that legal authority can maintain stability and continuity in the therapeutic relationship:

> The lack [in traditional applications of child psychiatry to delin-
> quents] might be expressed as something which would hold the case
> together while the therapeutic efforts proceeded. . . . It seemed indi-
> cated . . . that with children given to anti-social acting out, and
> whose families were not organized towards the constructive use of
> help, some kind of operational authority was needed in conjunction
> with any therapeutic effort—an authority which would have effect
> upon both the child and the parents.[9]

This authority is to be provided by the court, and more particularly by the probation officer in line with his rehabilitative activities. In effect, court authority is to provide the structure and controls lacking in the personality of lower-class and delinquent children. In the rhetoric of psychiatry, "The essence of Court Clinic
treatment is in the application of psychotherapeutic techniques
to offenders within the ego-supportive setting of the Court and
Probation." [10]

This program has been implemented in the court system in
such a way as to minimize conflict with legal authorities. In the
juvenile court situation, where treatment is formally acknowledged as a primary goal, this implementation has been easier
than in adult criminal courts. (The court clinic program was in
fact initially directed toward juvenile cases, and has preserved
this emphasis.) Clinics are established only in sympathetic sur-
roundings and on terms that recognize the predominance of the
judge and the legal function of the court.

In the juvenile court, efforts were continually made to maintain cordial relations with the judge and to provide him with
"support in his decisions" when faced with trying and perplexing
cases. Good working relations were also facilitated by the clinic
practice of deferring to court selection of its cases. Hence judge

9. From an article by Dr. Williams explaining the court clinic program,
October 1962.

10. Quoted from a court clinic circular, "Treatment of Offenders," October
1965.

and probation officers initiated all clinic referrals independently of any clinical opinion, with the result that cases were selected for diagnosis with reference to the concerns and standards of the court, and not those of psychiatry.

And in general, the clinic defined its role as provision of expert service and consultation, and not as advocacy of a rigorous therapeutic approach to delinquency. Gradual educative influence through continuing cooperation with court personnel assumed importance in clinic members' perception of their function. Court-determined issues framed the diagnostic effort, and recommendations were usually drawn from the alternatives posed by court personnel. Hence psychiatrists coming into the court clinic had to learn to understand the court's concerns in particular cases and the alternative courses of action considered within the realm of possibility:

> One of the residents commented that the main difference between working in the court clinic and the child guidance clinic was diagnosing cases with a view to making suggestions to the court. He was not bothered so much by the need to convey psychiatric information to nonpsychiatric personnel as by the necessity to suggest a concrete course of action. He felt "pressure" in the court setting to "describe that aspect of their behavior that gives some suggestions of how to deal with them." At child guidance the pressure was to describe the "psychodynamics" of behavior.

This pressure is clearly seen in the negative reaction of court staff to clinic reports which dwelled too heavily on psychodynamics, and in their demand for "realistic" and "practical" recommendations about what to do with cases.

While most clinic effort was oriented toward the judges as decision-makers, relations with the probation staff crucially shaped the actual diagnostic process. For the probation officer had a continuing interest in cases, and had to be consulted both to discover the court's concerns and outlook and to confirm a possible recommendation. In addition the clinic staff was encouraged to use the probation officer as the authoritarian figure supplementing their attempted therapy. The official clinic ideology provided that the probation officer control the child while the psychiatrist develops a more open and helping relationship with him. This concept derived directly from the conception of the court clinic as dealing with lower-class delinquents without inner controls. As the director of another court clinic formally stated the theory:

> Most of our patients have weak super-egos and are in dire need of control. The probation officer represents authority. The parents, who have only poor authority, usually welcome his assistance and even the offender himself feels often more comfortable when he does not have to decide. The psychiatrist remains non-directive while the decision-making role is delegated to the probation officer who however may ask the psychiatrist's help in formulating decisions. But the patient is not made aware of this.[11]

In summary, while the clinic represented the psychiatric approach to delinquency within the juvenile court, it did so primarily through the role of technician and consultant. In this way, the psychiatric approach remained somewhat marginal to the court's day-to-day operations, which basically proceeded in more traditional terms. This is not to say that the clinic's role in these operations was unimportant, but rather that it was not made in terms of the framework and logic of psychiatry. The juvenile court retained a distinctly legal focus, with psychiatry functioning to help implement primarily legal goals rather than working to realize explicitly therapeutic goals.

CONCLUSION

The setting and structure of the juvenile court suggest an inherent dualism between legal and social agency models of that institution. On a statutory and procedural level the court revealed elements of both models. Similarly, the working ideologies of judges and probation officers contained strongly legal and restrictive commitments along with the ideals of treatment and help. The clinic was formally committed only to treatment, but it functioned on court-defined terms which partially blunted this com-

---

11. From a paper by a psychiatrist explaining the differences between voluntary and court clinics.

mitment. In general, despite the court's strong support of the treatment ideal, the legal component of court functioning remained strong. The juvenile court sought to both judge and help, control and treat, enforce the law and "rehabilitate" the delinquent.

In conclusion, it will be useful to compare the nature of the juvenile court described to other such institutions. In the first place, the statutes governing the juvenile court are among the more progressive and treatment-oriented in the country. They provide wide jurisdiction over almost all cases involving minors, impose few procedural restrictions on the judge in line with the ideal of maximizing his ability to respond in helpful terms to the cases brought before him, and outline a number of alternative ways of promoting treatment and "rehabilitation." However, the juvenile court appears to be highly unusual in comparison with many other juvenile courts in its concern with the legal and constitutional rights of delinquents. Prior to the *Gault* decision, the court guaranteed legal rights not then required by higher courts. These include the rights to counsel, to confront witnesses, and to avoid self-incriminating testimony, as well as safeguards against admission of guilt. The current chief judge established these procedural guarantees in order to implement personal convictions about court procedure formed during his practice of criminal law. Following the *Gault* decision, however, all juvenile courts will be required to observe most of the procedural safeguards that were recognized in the juvenile court during the whole course of study. In this sense, finally, it is fair to say that the juvenile court placed itself in the forefront of a movement toward procedural changes that will become common policy in the future, and undoubtedly instituted procedures that at the time provided an unusual amount of protection to children accused of delinquency.

Aside from procedure, the juvenile court appears to differ from similar institutions in metropolitan areas with regard to personnel and their background. Although the situation has been changing rapidly under the new judicial regime, the probation staff shows a lower level of professional qualification than is characteristic of the larger and more progressive juvenile court systems. Specifically, probation officers generally are not social workers, and do not conceive their activities in social work terms, in contrast to juvenile courts studied elsewhere (Cicourel, 1968; Matza, 1964).

This lack of professional standing partially accounts for the probation officer's relative subordination in the decision-making process. In contrast with some juvenile court systems, the judges, particularly the chief judge, actively guide and determine the decision-making process and do not simply function as figureheads perfunctorily validating decisions made previously. For this reason, the formal hearing, presided over by the judge, assumes great significance in the determination of case outcomes (compare with Cicourel, 1968, p. 64).

While most treatment-oriented juvenile courts have psychiatric clinics, the overwhelming importance of psychiatrists in the juvenile court clinic is somewhat unusual. Many such clinics tend to rely on psychologists and psychological testing, with psychiatrists in relatively short supply. In the juvenile court clinic, psychologists play almost no role, and psychiatrists routinely deal with all cases, a situation attributable to the proximity of major training facilities in child psychiatry.

Finally, in the period under study, the juvenile court was undergoing definite innovation and change. As will be seen in greater detail in the following two chapters, staff was expanded, new programs added, relations with agencies modified or dropped completely, and new ties with other agencies established. An unusual sense of movement and change pervaded the juvenile court, reflecting the energetic administration of a new judge, committed to contemporary ideas of treatment and possessing sufficient political savvy and power to implement changes. The juvenile court, then, was studied amidst expansion and revitalization after years of stagnation. Psychiatry, introduced directly into the court's daily operations after years of antagonism and resistance, provided much of the impetus for this revitalization. In this sense the processes of innovation involved an attempt to institute previously obstructed programs and policies that have become established and accepted practice in many other juvenile courts.

2

Relations with Political and Enforcement Agencies

While staff members clearly recognize the juvenile court's legal duties and functions, they view their primary task as "helping" delinquent youth and devote a great deal of effort to implementing this goal. The task of "treating" delinquents, however, takes place within the peculiar institutional setting confronting the court. Chapters 2 and 3 analyze the nature and consequences of the court's adaptation to this setting. This chapter describes the court's relations with political and enforcement institutions, Chapter 3 the court's relations with significant treatment resources. Both emphasize the interplay between these external relations and court treatment efforts. On the one hand, a treatment orientation commits the court to goals that shape the nature and direction of its relationships with these environing institutions. On the other hand, the very process of reaching some working arrangement with these institutions deflects and subverts treatment goals.

This analysis must begin by considering the meaning of "treatment" to the court. First, "treatment" emerges as an issue for the court on the concrete level of possible ways of responding to particular cases. Thus the problem for the court is not to decide between punishing or treating a particular delinquent. Rather it is to identify the alternative courses of action open to it and to choose the one that both satisfies the various interests represented in the case and affords the best chance of "helping" the youth involved.

Second, although "treatment" is a relative term, reflecting the differential desirability of the alternatives open in any particular case, court personnel recognize a general order of preference. Most desirable are those alternatives regarded as "pure treatment." These include various kinds of "placements," each again valued more or less highly. Placement institutions providing psychiatric therapy are held in the highest regard, although most group homes and religious and charitable boarding schools are also viewed favorably. Other placement alternatives include private foster homes, mental hospitals, and residential schools for retarded children. Finally, psychiatric therapy on an outpatient basis, whether from the court clinic or another source, represents an extremely desirable form of treatment.

Below these "pure treatment" alternatives are the various routine procedures used by the court to deal with delinquent youths. These include probationary supervision and efforts to get the youth accepted in special programs, generally of a recreational, educational, or corrective (e.g., speech therapy) nature. While these programs are regarded as beneficial to the delinquents involved, they both serve acknowledged control purposes and exercise only minimal influence over the youths' lives.

Finally, the various institutions run by the Youth Correction Authority provide the least desirable alternatives, although even commitment to these institutions may on occasion be described in therapeutic terms. Westfield, the reform school for boys under 12, is quite favorably regarded as providing at least a partially effective treatment program. But the other reform schools are generally described in purely custodial and restraining terms. Hence, to commit delinquents to these institutions represents an essentially controlling and punitive measure and effectively writes off these youths as "unsalvagable" and future criminals.

Since the legally prescribed alternatives for treating delinquents are restricted to routine probation and Youth Correction Authority commitments, the practical implementation of court treatment goals has required gaining access to the desirable treatment programs and facilities, particularly placements and psychiatric services. The court has employed two general strategies to this end. First, it has sought to develop its own programs. The Boys'

Training Program and the court clinic represent successful endeavors of this nature, although other efforts, including a foster home system and a group home for hard-to-place delinquent boys, have failed. Both the unavailability of financing and the resistance of established agencies tend to undermine and limit court projects of these kind. The court's foster home program, for example, terminated in the face of strong attack from established adoption and foster home agencies, while a recent group home project met defeat in part because of threatened intrusion in the domain of the Youth Correction Authority.[1]

Because of the difficulty of developing independent programs, the juvenile court must expand and cement relations with institutions that possess either desired resources or access to them. Historically, for example, settlement houses supplied and paid members of their own staff to serve as the court's first probation officers, and for many years the court relied almost exclusively on settlements and private charities to provide facilities for "helping" delinquent children. Since that period the court has always tried to avail itself of treatment facilities already existing in the community, initiating its own programs only when these facilities are unobtainable or inadequate. Thus, the court obtained its own court clinic only when faced with shortage of psychiatric facilities in the community.

Consequently, a thoroughgoing commitment to "treatment" pushes the juvenile court into developing working relations with community institutions which control existing "helping" resources. This in turn integrates the court into this local institutional complex. While many traditional judicial bodies have been structurally isolated from such external ties, such isolation is possible for the juvenile court only if it can restrict itself to narrowly adjudicative functions. Hence, the social-agency image of the juvenile court undermines the legal image by cutting down

1. Miller has emphasized the role of interinstitutional conflict in undermining the efforts of a delinquency prevention program:

> There is much conflict over the issue of proper procedure among the different groups which maintain varying orders of responsibility for delinquency prevention. This conflict results in a lack of coordination and mutual blocking of efforts. . . . (1958, p. 23) .

the court's distance from the network of institutions that can provide the resources to implement its treatment goals. This subjects
the court to a variety of institutional and community pressures
from which a more conventional judicial body would be isolated.

Court integration into the local institutional system takes place
through a process of mutual exchange of services, benefits, and
favors. For it is by means of a series of concrete and recurring
"organizational exchanges" (Levine and White, 1961) that the
court orders its relations with institutions whose cooperation it
must obtain in order to expand its treatment alternatives. In
terms of such exchange, cooperation with existing treatment facilities is less costly and more rewarding than attempting to obtain
the funds and services necessary to start independent court programs.

However, court relations with this institutional complex, shaped
by the process of organizational exchange, modify the court's internal functioning. The rest of this chapter describes the juvenile
court's relations with two segments of this institutional complex—
the political system and enforcers—as they shape and change its
internal operation, particularly its efforts to implement its treatment goals.

While organizational exchanges expand the number and nature
of alternatives available to the court, they also influence the
selection of a particular alternative in any given case. In this
sense the juvenile court mobilizes a number of parties around a
particular juvenile "trouble case," [2] the case outcome representing a negotiated settlement with the court acting as mediator and
arbiter between these various interests. However, to focus attention on the individual case and the negotiative processes surrounding it would lose sight of the overall patterns of negotiations in
which the individual case is the basic unit. For the court is able to
bargain for a certain service or advantage from an institution on
behalf of one case and repay its obligation in its handling of a
completely different one. The outline of the overall nature of the

2. The fundamental significance of "trouble cases" in legal processes was first
emphasized by Llewellyn and Hoebel (1941) in their study of Cheyenne law.
For a recent statement of the advantages of approaching the anthropological
study of law through trouble cases, see the analysis by Laura Nader (1965).

court's relations with other organizations in Chapters 2 and 3 thereby provides a framework within which the course of any individual case may be analyzed.

THE NATURE AND CONSEQUENCES
OF POLITICAL TIES

Politics pervade the juvenile court. Political patronage determines court staff, as judgeships are generally rewarded to protégés of the state governor and probation positions in turn provide patronage resources for the judges.[3] The court depends on funds from local government to conduct its day-to-day operations to a much greater extent than local criminal courts, which can defray a large part of their operating costs from sums collected in fines and court fees. Judges, probation officers, and court clerks continue to participate in political party affairs more or less actively. Political events and figures provide regular fare for informal discussions in the probation offices and judges' lobby.

The necessity of maintaining institutional viability in a changing community reinforce these "natural" and inherent political connections, increasing court dependence on political figures. For example, urban renewal in the central city area threatened the court with a declining caseload. The decline in the number of cases handled undermined any attempts to expand personnel and services. When the judge of the municipal court with jurisdiction over the city's Negro ghetto expressed interest in eliminating his large caseload of juvenile cases, the judge of the juvenile court seized the opportunity. A bill transferring jurisdiction over these

3. For example, consider the following field notes relating to political pressures on the judge regarding appointments to probation positions at the juvenile court: I asked the judge whether there was political pressure applied to the court to get probation jobs when openings appeared. He replied, "Oh yes. But there's so much of it you don't really have to take it. There are so many that no matter who you take you're going to make someone mad."

The chief probation officer commented on the current vacancies on his staff and then told this anecdote. Once a member of the city council had come to the judge and asked him to appoint a friend of his as a probation officer, saying he would get the council to budget special money to pay the salary of this new position. The judge had not gone along with the proposition.

cases was rushed through the legislature with strong backing from
the attorney general's office. In less than one month the transfer
was completed. However, several months later segments of the
Negro community protested against the change and filed a bill to
return jurisdiction to the local court. The legislature held hearings on the measure and heard the transfer condemned as dis-
criminatory against the local Negro community. But the judge of
the juvenile court mobilized sufficient political backing to insure
defeat of the bill in committee, thereby protecting this acquisi-
tion of additional cases.

In a somewhat similar vein, the juvenile court vigorously lobbied in support of legislation to create juvenile courts in several
of the other large cities in the state. Such a measure would have
enhanced the court's preeminence as the leader of a reinvigorated
juvenile court system.

Moreover, court efforts to expand and add resources specifically
to implement its treatment ideals strengthen primary political
ties. For example, the court submitted a legislative bill giving it
authority to commit children directly to state schools for the mentally retarded. This would have given the court great autonomy
in an area of treatment where its efforts had previously met constant delay and refusal. Other political forays involved areas that
only peripherally touched the court, but served to obligate organizations closely tied to court treatment efforts. For example, the
court helped pass a bill allowing the Child Welfare Department
to provide assistance to mothers and their infants leaving the girls'
reformatory. The court also supported the regional council of
child psychiatrists in its efforts to require qualified child psychiatrists in community mental health centers. All of these efforts
involved lobbying with key figures in state government.

Political connections also allow the court to directly expand its
own treatment resources. In this way, the judge obtained a court
clinic during the first year of his tenure, despite the expense involved and prior, longstanding, and urgent requests for clinics
from other courts. The judge's political connections with the director of the Department of Mental Health also proved crucial
at the beginning of the clinic's second year when he was able to

have restored funds earmarked to pay the salary of additional psychiatric residents but cut by the Department of Mental Health, even though the director of the court clinic program had been unable to do so.

A second attempt to expand treatment alternatives through political means involved a court project to establish a residential treatment center for boys on an abandoned military site. The success of this project came to hinge on the decision of the public commission that had assumed control over the site. The judge approached a number of high state officials, eventually the attorney general and the governor, in an effort to obtain backing for his proposal, but the necessary support was not forthcoming.

The strengthening of primary ties through continual use of the political system became particularly marked under the regime of the current judge. This regime has revitalized the juvenile court by aggressively initiating new programs and contacts. In this revitalization, the judge has drawn heavily on his knowledge and connections in state politics, acquired during a decade of activity in the state Democratic party. The contemporary court therefore has much more extensive dealings with political bodies and agencies than in the past.

These political associations heighten court sensitivity to community outlooks and pressures. One reflection of this is the community and ethnic consciousness of court personnel, noted earlier with particular reference to the probation staff. Again, this appears in the fact that politically important segments of the local community, rather than the city's social agencies and social welfare professionals, provide the juvenile court's primary "constituency." This primacy found clear expression in the dispute over filling the latest judicial vacancy on the juvenile court. The city's social agencies lobbied vigorously for the appointment of someone from or sympathetic to their professionally oriented circles. But over their loud objections the appointment eventually went to a political figure, a close adviser to the governor.

Court sensitivity to political pressures, however, does not mean that the court is responsive to the whole community. In general, the politically unrepresented, a high proportion of the court's clientele, lack effective voice in court affairs. At present, for example, while its caseload is heavily Negro, the makeup of the court's staff continues to mirror the political dominance of the Irish and Italians. But this sensitivity does mean that the court responds, although only partially and somewhat belatedly, to changes in local power. Thus, in order to consolidate its hold over juvenile cases from the Negro ghetto, the court has had to find allies in the Negro community. In fact the court has obtained the backing of newer, professional middle-class Negro groups to counter the opposition of the conservative, old guard Negro leadership to its expansion into the ghetto. This has produced both greater sensitivity to pressures from these Negro "community leaders" and a rise in Negro court personnel.

Orientation to the politically represented community, however, has other important consequences for the juvenile court's operations. For it subjects the court to generalized pressures for punitive and restrictive handling of delinquents. This tendency results from the interplay of influences from local groups, politicians, and the press.

On one level, pressures on the court are characteristically restrictive and punitive rather than therapeutic in nature because "public opinion" becomes aroused primarily by "crime in the streets" and threats to public order. Hence local demands are for control and punishment, not for treatment for sick or unfortunate children. This tendency at least partially reflects the organization and expression of such "community sentiment" by politicians and the news media. The press tends to play up sensational and brutal crimes and to encourage response to "criminals" on punitive terms. Periodic press-inspired crime waves, for example, give rise to a variety of demands for heavy penal sanctions against offenders. But in addition, many local politicians seem to feel that they can make greater political capital out of opposing "crime in the streets" with a "get tough" policy than in advocating the rehabilitation of offenders. Particularly when crime or delinquency becomes a hot issue, punishment and restriction seem to provide direct, simple, and convincing solutions. Hence, when concern with the problem of delinquency becomes pronounced, the politically oriented tend to denounce "leniency" and the "coddling" of criminals, and to urge harsh punishment for violators.[4]

In general, then, close political and community ties tend to increase court sensitivity to general pressures for control and punishment of delinquents by increasing susceptibility both to politicians representing and trying to anticipate community sentiment and reaction, and to anticipated community demands which may receive political support.[5]

The judge of the juvenile court, however, can resist successfully many of these pressures. That he is able to do so reflects both the minor nature of many offenses by delinquents and insulating mechanisms in court structure. One such mechanism is the exclusion of the press from court hearings, along with the withholding of the names of juveniles arrested or appearing in court. This allows the court to operate in considerable secrecy, such that most court decisions have extremely low visibility in the community at large. The result is protection against moralistic demands from the press and the public for harsh sanctions, and hence considerable latitude for the court in disposing of individual cases.

While general pressures from political and community sources tend to be restrictive, if a politican or other "community leader" (e.g., minister, social worker, politically established lawyer) becomes involved in a specific case, he is apt to urge consideration for the delinquent and support a lenient disposition. Such figures appear in the court either formally or informally in the role of *sponsor* for the accused delinquent (Matza, 1964, pp. 125–28), attempting to "get him off." Such appearances represent favors performed for constituents or charges, and receive greater consideration to the extent that the court must be concerned with local community and political sentiment.

On specific cases, therefore, political and community pressures

4. It should also be noted that strong racial overtones are involved in these cries for harsh penalties for delinquents and other offenders against law and order, as it is implicitly assumed that these violators are Negroes. For example, the increasing crime rate in the city was often attributed to the growing numbers of Negroes migrating to the city.

5. The judge on several occasions commented that particular cases or decisions could possibly "blow the lid right off," indicating his underlying sense of threat from this direction.

are not necessarily restrictive. But whatever their direction, the court incurs greater obligation to act in accord with these pressures because of its increased dependence on political figures, resulting from its efforts to sustain itself as a viable organization and to implement treatment goals. Furthermore, while such case-directed pressures are not uniformly punitive, they provide no direct support to the court's treatment policies. For political efforts to "get a kid off," while they may be compatible with and rationalized in terms of therapeutic goals, grow out of the exigencies of political and personal relations. Hence, such efforts have no necessary or consistent relation to "treatment," although on occasion they may produce lenient dispositions that coincide with the dictates of such policies.

In summary, even though the juvenile court is inherently a political institution, its sensitivity to political demands and to community reaction, possible as well as actual, is accentuated when it is forced to use political contacts in order to obtain new services and favors. For the court's treatment implementation efforts tighten and reaffirm its political and community obligations, which in turn increases the degree to which it has to take into account possible political and public reactions to its dispositions of cases. But mere sensitivity to political and community pressures automatically determines neither the direction nor the overall impact of such pressures. While the political system in particular tends to generate and express restrictive and punitive demands more easily than treatment ones, the insulation and low public visibility of concrete court dispositions prevent such generalized demands from restraining its decisions in most cases. Moreover, often political and community intervention on the level of the specific case seeks leniency—to "keep the kid on the street."

Political and community pressures, then, basically influence court operations. If the court can often resist demands emanating from these sources, and can sometimes play off one group or politician against another, it can never completely ignore them. As a result these pressures shape many aspects of court functioning, particularly when translated into a fundamental concern with "trouble," as will be discussed in Chapter 4.

RELATIONS WITH ENFORCERS

Political pressures of a restrictive nature on the juvenile court are characteristically nonspecific and diffuse. Concrete pressures for restrictive and punitive decisions arise rather from those agents immediately concerned with the maintenance of community order and the enforcement of its laws—the police and the schools. This section will deal with the juvenile court's relations with these two institutions.

Two characteristics of these institutions underlie their importance for juvenile court operations. In the first place, the police and the schools constitute the two most important local institutions routinely concerned with controlling the behavior of children (e.g., Werthman, 1964). While children comprise the sole concern of the schools, they are incidental—but not by this fact unimportant—to the operations of the police. Moreover, both police and schools have special agents dealing with delinquency problems, agents who in the course of their work come into regular contact with the juvenile court. Consequently they come to develop strong ties with court personnel, particularly with probation officers. This increases their influence on the nature of the court's operations.

Second, through its relations with these agents the juvenile court establishes connections with institutions having important ties with the local community. School agents deal with trouble arising in connection with the local neighborhood schools, which are by far the most important communal institutions dealing with children. The relationship of the police to the community is more diffuse and not channeled into one central institution. Many people with some kind of trouble or complaint often turn to the police in the lower-class neighborhoods that cover most of the juvenile court's jurisdiction. In effect, the police mediate between the troubles, gripes, misdeeds, and complaints of the local community, its inhabitants, and many of its unofficial institutions, and the formal legal structure,[6] in exactly the same way that the

6. Cumming, Cumming, and Edell (1965) emphasize police performance of this kind of function in lower-class communities:

truant officers and adjustment counsellors mediate between the court and the most important local child-concerned institution, the school.

It is this mediating function that makes relations with these institutions and their agents so important for the juvenile court. As an institution responding to the troubles and misdeeds of children, the court cannot afford to cut itself off from the lay community and its institutions. The police and school agents provide this crucial connection with the ongoing affairs of the community.

The Police

Within the city the police are organized around local station houses. Three such district police stations cover the area of the city within the juvenile court's jurisdiction. Based in each of these local police stations are several (usually two) "juvenile officers" with patrolman rank but operating in plainclothes and charged with investigating all cases and complaints involving minors. These juvenile officers occupy marginal positions on the police force, as working with "kids" and their misdeeds has low priority among policemen oriented toward making "good pinches" of dangerous criminals (Skolnick, 1966, p. 118; Westley, 1953, p. 36).

The juvenile court serves as a judicial body supervising (and hence in many cases, legitimating) official actions undertaken by the police in enforcing the law with respect to the misdeeds of juveniles. The court derives its fundamental power over the police through this right to review and dispose of all delinquency complaints that they initiate. Formally the court stands as overseer of police actions, and the current judge is strongly committed to holding the police to the rule of law. This is most directly relevant in the legal standards of evidence imposed on the police. Prior to the current judicial regime police officers were allowed to present cases in outline, because no witnesses, not even a com-

---

poor, uneducated people appear to use the police in a way that middle-class people use family doctors and clergymen—that is, as the first port of call in time of trouble (p. 285).

plainant, were needed to prove the alleged offense. Now the judge requires that the police prove all the necessary elements of the alleged offense. This and other procedural requirements undoubtedly make it more difficult for the police to make a complaint "stick" in court and demand greater effort in preparing cases, particularly in arranging for the appearance of witnesses.[7]

But as several studies have emphasized, police decisions to invoke formal criminal sanctions arise out of the contingencies of their day-to-day work, particularly out of those activities that have been described as "peace-keeping" (Banton, 1965; Bittner, 1967a, 1967b). Thus Bittner has argued that officers patrolling skid row "do not really enforce the law, even when they do invoke it, but merely use it as a resource to solve certain pressing practical problems in keeping the peace" (1967b, p. 710). Similarly, police-initiated delinquency complaints are more often products of attempts to control juvenile misbehavior and "troublemakers" in order to "keep the peace" in the community rather than abstract decisions to enforce a particular criminal statute. This feature of police operation demands consideration in more detail, since it exercises fundamental influence on police relations with the juvenile court.

Peace-keeping activities loom particularly large in police dealings with juveniles.[8] The juvenile officer, who does no patrol work and who only by chance witnesses the actual commission of offenses, spends most of his time checking out complaints that concern juveniles. Many of these complaints bear only superficial resemblance to "crimes," are distinctly minor in nature, and are taken even less seriously because they involve children. Faced with this kind of "beef" about juvenile disturbances, problems or misbehavior, the juvenile officer uses his wide discretion to seek informal settlement of the "trouble" by mediating between the

7. It could also be anticipated that this policy would lead the police to rely more heavily on informal means for dealing with juveniles and their misconduct, hence completely avoiding the court.

8. The following comments are based on six weeks' observation of two juvenile officers working out of a district police station. This station handled an area now within the jurisdiction of the juvenile court (regarding cases involving juveniles), but at the time of field work was under the jurisdiction of the municipal court.

parties involved. In a typical case, a man called the station to complain that several boys were breaking his garage windows. After talking to the man and making a few perfunctory inquiries in the neighborhood, the juvenile officer located the culprits. But since he regarded the incident as too inconsequential to merit official action, he settled the case by getting the boys' parents to pay for fixing the windows and by calling the boys down to the station with their parents for a stern lecture.

The juvenile officer's job is not so much to solve "crimes" committed by juveniles as to handle often legally ambiguous complaints involving juveniles. The juvenile officer seeks both to satisfy the complainant and to keep the youth from making further trouble. Given this emphasis on settling trouble cases within the community, not on abstract law enforcement, the policeman's power to arrest provides a strategic weapon to be used to cajole and threaten juveniles into better behavior. Arrest and court action thus become threats for influencing behavior and, like most threats, are more effective in this respect when posed rather than actually invoked.

In these terms the decision to initiate court action is the product of the failure or inappropriateness of mediation and informal settlement. Mediation efforts may fail when the complainant-victim refuses to settle the case and insists that the police take formal action or when the accused juvenile or his parents resist compromise. But many court complaints grow out of police judgments that informal settlement is an inappropriate means for dealing with the particular case. Thus, youths are more often arrested and brought to court for felonies than for misdemeanors. Furthermore, the police may avoid informal settlement when they think the offender deserves tough treatment. This can occur in what would otherwise be an inconsequential encounter except that the policeman feels that his authority has been assaulted, as by inappropriate behavior on the part of the youth (Piliavin and Briar, 1964, p. 210). But this also occurs when a youth gets into recurring trouble, particularly after he has been given "breaks" through informal settlements of previous offenses. The following excerpt, for example, reveals police attitudes toward a youth that would clearly rule out any attempted informal settlement:

In the probation office a policeman was talking about a boy who had been stealing handbags in his district. He grabbed them from young and old alike—no one was safe on the streets. The policeman bemoaned the trouble this youth was causing the police: "This Taylor kid—he's killing us."

In such cases the police want the youth "off the streets," i.e., out of the community where his misconduct is producing a constant stream of complaints from citizens. Under such circumstances they actively encourage injured parties to take out court complaints, even on inconsequential matters, trying to get a youth into court and committed to reform school.

The nature and occasions of police use of the juvenile court grow out of these peace-keeping and control activities. Pressure for court action to support and reinforce these activities accompanies and underlies police-initiated complaints. It is for this reason that police pressure on the court's handling of specific cases tends to be restrictive and punitive: interest in *controlling* troublesome behavior takes precedence over any concern with *changing* such behavior. "Rehabilitation" is peripheral to police concerns; while they may initially accept therapeutic efforts to change a youth's behavior, they quickly reassert the priority of control and restraint on any sign of conflict with their procedures for controlling delinquents.

Other contingencies of police work, however, may lead to different sorts of police pressure on the court. Specifically, the police require court support of the informal bargains which characterize their processing of many cases. Much work done by juvenile officers relies on a system of informants and confessions (Skolnick, 1966, pp. 112–38). The juvenile is typically promised more lenient treatment either for confessing to prior offenses so as to "clear" police records or for naming those responsible for other offenses. The police consequently have an interest in insuring that the court will go along with the bargain on the case. Within the structure of the juvenile court this particularly requires the cooperation of the probation officer who makes the recommendation on disposition. The policeman must therefore enlist the backing of the probation officer behind the recommendation that will support his end of the bargain. The difficulties of so doing and the dangers from failure are clear in the following case observed while studying several local juvenile officers:

> Juvenile Officer Koller had apprehended an escapee from reform school, Freddie Black, who had committed numerous car thefts since his escape. In most cases an escapee is returned directly to the Youth Correction Authority and hence to reform school. But Koller had taken out a number of new delinquency complaints against the boy, preventing any such automatic return. A new hearing was then scheduled, and with the boy's prior record and additional criminal offenses trial and incarceration as a "juvenile offender" became a strong possibility. Koller, however, had obtained Freddie's admission of responsibility for 35 or 40 car thefts in the police records in return for the promise to oppose any such recommendation for criminal trial. He therefore wanted Black adjudicated delinquent, but then recommitted to the maximum security Youth Correction Authority institution rather than to the relatively open reform school from which he had earlier escaped.
>
> Koller talked about his conversation with Freddie in detention. He had warned the boy that they might treat him as a juvenile offender and have him sent to prison. "I think that jolted him a bit. He was upset. . . . I told him to tell the truth about what he'd done since he'd been out [all the stolen cars], and he wouldn't go to prison." He had told. Then the case had been arraigned before the judge of the municipal court and the situation explained to him. He had apparently been favorable to Koller's idea. But at the actual hearing there was no guarantee that this judge would be sitting. Any judge might hear it and decide to try the boy as a juvenile offender. Koller would then be hurt in his relation with the boy [who would not understand his inability to control the situation]. Freddie would say, "Koller, you're a louse!"
>
> Koller therefore approached several of the court's probation officers and explained the problem to them, getting their help in placing the case before the right judge. This was worked out, and the case eventually disposed as Koller had planned.

Not only could court action have discredited the juvenile officer in the eyes of the particular delinquent, but, more importantly, it could have damaged his reputation within the local community so that other delinquents would come to distrust him and refuse to "cooperate."

In most police-initiated cases, therefore, the juvenile court encounters pressures for dispositions dictated by the contingencies of police work activities. There are no obvious reasons, however, why the court should heed such pressures, for its wide discretion in hearing and disposing of police cases clearly gives the court dominant power in dealing with the police. On closer examination, however, a number of factors can be identified that draw the court toward at least partial dependence on the police.

The police gain influence over the court by reason of their intermediary position between court and local community. As the juvenile court cannot afford to isolate itself, it must make some effort to maintain good working relations with the police, as well as with other community agencies. This point has been emphasized by Freidson in his analysis of factors influencing the official rate of identified deviance:

> The social distance of defining agents from the lay community obviously restricts access to cases to be identified. And the isolation of a defining agency from other agencies or agents also restricts access to possible cases to be identified (1966, pp. 83–84).

Access to cases is particularly critical for the juvenile court because expansion must be justified by need, best demonstrated by a rising caseload.[9] Discretion to initiate or refrain from initiating court cases consequently provides the police with important leverage *vis-à-vis* the juvenile court. The police could simply refuse to bring any but the most unavoidable cases to court. Such a policy is likely if the police come to feel that the court is run by softhearted social workers from whom they could expect no consideration for their more punitive interests in cases.

9. This was clearly demonstrated in the judge's description of his negotiations with various political bodies to increase the number of court probation officers. After expansion of the juvenile court jurisdiction to include the largely Negro area of the city, the Board of Probation had suggested that his probation staff be increased by eight. He himself had asked for six additional probation officers from the city council, and had eventually been granted four. Here the judge commented: "Whether I get those other two [probation officers, cut from his request] depends on what the caseload settles at."

Furthermore, because of its commitment to a treatment ideology, the court sees itself as a delinquency prevention agency. In order to realize this goal its personnel must not only have cases brought to them, but also influence the kinds of cases police bring in. Thus the court staff feel that they have a greater chance of preventing serious future delinquency if young offenders are regularly brought to court for supervision. This concern becomes particularly relevant in light of the fact that younger children are exactly those most likely to be released by the police with a lecture and "a kick in the pants." Therefore the court encourages the police to bring in more cases of young offenders, in return incurring some obligation to them.

Again, the police have the power to bring "bad cases," and on occasion court staff complain about cases they feel the police should not have brought to court. And in general, the court relies on the police to sift out inappropriate and time-consuming cases. In this way the court counts on the police to control and direct individuals who try to take out complaints on their own initiative. This is particularly relevant in "incorrigible child" complaints, which frequently involve parents taking the initiative in complaining about the behavior of their child. When such parents come directly to the court to make the complaint, the court requires them to contact the juvenile officer in their district police station first, who can then handle the case in court (*if* he feels it is merited). Not only does this procedure use the police as a means of culling out complaints by amateurs that are considered inappropriate or unfounded, but it also allows the case against the child to be conducted by someone familiar with the procedures of the juvenile court. This tactic reinforces the established position of the police within the court, particularly their near monopoly over the right to initiate delinquency complaints.

Finally, the court occasionally seeks special services from the police, thereby incurring specific obligations to them. One such instance occurs in neglect complaints. Sometimes the court discovers facts that indicate a neglectful family situation and will try to start court action. A neglect petition requires both an initial complaint and a long-term investigation by a "neutral agency" (i.e., one other than the complainant). Since all private agencies in the city avoid court cases, the Child Welfare Department is the only possible neutral agency. In order to prevent disqualification of the department as the neutral agency, the court gets the police to investigate the family situation and to file the neglect complaint if circumstances warrant it.

Police-Probation Relations

The factors discussed so far reflect on the general court need for close ties with the police. But there are a number of contingencies arising specifically out of the work situation of the probation officer that increase his ties with the police, particularly with juvenile officers. This then complements police officers' dependency on the court and probation officer for getting desirable outcomes for their cases. Probation officer and police come to establish firm working relationships, based on a system of mutual dependence and cooperation, that facilitate effective performance of their respective tasks.

One factor promoting this cooperation is the probation officer's sympathetic outlook toward the problems of the police. In part this results from close similarities in the probation officer's approach to his work and the goals of the police. For the probation officer shares the policeman's concern with preventing and punishing serious breaches of public order and with enforcing a number of conventional social standards on what are often recalcitrant populations. This in turn reflects a common lower-middle class Irish background, as well as a tendency for probation officers to be upwardly mobile policemen (two of the court's probation officers came from police backgrounds). It also reflects a common nonprofessional status in a field increasingly preempted by professionals.

In addition, under certain circumstances a probation officer may become dependent on the police officer in order to get the outcome he desires on a case. For example, a probation officer may want to "drop" (i.e., get committed to the Youth Correction Authority) a juvenile whom he has on probation or with whom he has had some experience in the past. The probation officer is concerned that a police officer present a "good case" against such a boy, so that he will be found delinquent and the recommendation to commit can be advanced. Thus bitter comments are frequently heard when a police officer has "blown" a case, i.e., done his job so ineptly that a "guilty" youth is found not delinquent. This might occur, for example, if the police went ahead with a case without having witnesses needed to prove some basic part of the complaint present to testify.

But this is only one reflection of the more general process whereby police and probation officer are drawn together by common problems of competent performance in presenting and conducting cases during the actual hearing. Police officers are generally in charge of getting all those involved in proving the complaint into the courtroom, and then directing the prosecution during the actual hearing. This effort has to be closely coordinated with the work of the probation officer who handles the delinquent and his family. But in addition, the probation officer relies very heavily on police accounts of the facts and circumstances of the alleged offense and of the background and general reputation of the child. In order to "look good" before the judge the probation officer must have a clear idea of the facts of the case and an idea of the probable outcome, all of which can be obtained on short notice only from the police officer involved in the case. For it is the implicit duty of the probation officer to find out all the circumstances of an offense and to bring them to the attention of the judge where relevant to a decision. This is particularly true where the court must decide whether to hold a juvenile in detention, a situation where the probation officer must uncover and report all relevant background materials.

Even greater dependence arises in the course of probationary supervision. In the first place, the probation officer's work with probationers effectively parallels that of the police officer, in that his main concern is with enforcing rules to control behavior and with preventing the juvenile from "making waves" or causing trouble that might reflect on the way in which the official (and the court) is carrying out his job. Thus, in dealing with a juvenile population, the probation officer faces many of the same problems as the police officer, not only preventing outbreaks of trouble but also doing so in such a way that one's official authority is not challenged.

Second, in carrying out his supervisory tasks, the probation officer is heavily dependent on a variety of community sources for information about the activities of his probationers. In this way the police provide channels of information not only about offenses that have yet to come to the attention of court officials, but also about behavior that foreshadows further delinquent misconduct. A probation officer wishes to learn when one of his boys is drinking frequently, taking drugs, or hanging out with a gang known to engage in serious delinquencies. The following case demonstrates how the police can provide probation officers with this kind of material:

> Juvenile Officer Roche came up to a probation officer in the hall and asked if a boy was his [case at the Boys' Training Program]. This probation officer said no, he was Casey's [another probation officer] case. Roche then reported that this boy was hanging around the North Street coffeehouses "with the homos and barbiturate boys." Casey should be told about this. Probation officer made sure he had the exact name of the particular coffeehouse to relay to Casey.

Furthermore, police knowledge of local youths and their regular activities and hangouts may help the court locate a delinquent wanted on a warrant or a boy who has run away from home.

Mutual support between police and probation appears in several other areas. In the first place, probation officers establish particularly close relations with the police and juvenile officers working in their district. One expression of this occurs when juveniles are arrested by the police. By law the probation officer must be contacted to make the decision on whether the juvenile shall be held in detention or sent home prior to his arraignment in court. If the juvenile is on probation already, his regular probation officer is contacted. If he has not had previous contact with the juvenile court, the police are required to call the probation officer listed "on duty" for that month. But as a probation officer explained: "But usually the police have certain ones they call. . . . Like I get the calls from Station A" (in the neighborhood he had "covered" for a number of years).

There are a number of striking demonstrations of the close relations that grow up between court personnel and the police. In the first place, probation officers recognize police interests in cases and will generally discuss possible recommendations with the officer on the case prior to the hearing, clearing any unusual course of action with him before presenting it to the court. For example:

> Probation Officer Collins received the case of two suburban boys from "good families" who had been arrested in the city for stealing a car after having a few drinks at their high school hockey game. Collins talked to the boys several times and decided "they're half decent." He decided to "give them a break" and try to have the charges against them dismissed. His first step in this direction was to consult with the policemen who had picked the boys up: "I asked the police whether they would mind dismissing it and they said they did not care."

Second, the probation staff makes a special effort to guide the police and their cases advantageously through the court. The most striking instance of this occurs in the handling of shoplifting cases from the big department stores. In such cases, the police, the stores, and their detective forces are particularly liable to civil suits for false arrest (see Cameron, 1964, pp. 28–29). The police seek to prevent this by getting the court to make findings of "delinquent" in all shoplifting cases or, more exactly, to avoid all findings of "not delinquent." Thus, in shoplifting cases where the evidence is weak, most judges will continue the case without a finding rather than make an adjudication of "not delinquent." In turn, the probation staff will guide cases away from judges who may not conform to this practice:

> It was a busy morning for the court, and the hall was crowded with cases waiting to get into hearings. For the first hour only Judge Rose was sitting, and although "store complaints" are usually heard early so the store detectives don't have to spend all morning in court, none of the half dozen in this morning were taken before him. At one point a PO suggested to the assistant officer of the day that they start getting the store cases in before Judge Rose, but the assistant officer of the day answered: "No, Joe [assistant chief PO] wants Judge Craft to hear those." I asked the OD why this was, and he replied: "He

dumped a couple civil suits on them [the department stores]. He found a couple not delinquent." These store cases were not in fact heard until Judge Craft came in very late that morning.

Finally, turning back to the court in general, all personnel, including judges, act in ways that support the authority of the police in situations where this authority is threatened. For example, when dismissing police charges, judges often emphasize that they do so because of the stringent requirements of the law, lecturing the youth and warning him not to misbehave in the future. He thereby defends the police action, acknowledging the defendant's "real" guilt while denying his legal guilt. Again, the judge may dismiss the complaint because of illegally obtained evidence, but then praise the police for taking necessary even if illegal action. Finally the court protects the official and personal integrity of the policeman who appears before it. To accuse the police of lying or prejudice is almost inevitably to bring down the wrath of the court.

In summary, several factors promote mutual dependence and close cooperation between the police and the juvenile court. While the police are subject to court authority in the disposition of all their official actions, the court occupies a position where police cooperation and trust make performance of its tasks easier. Dependence on the police thus arises out of the court's need for access to the community for cases and information, and for special services in selecting and initiating certain kinds of cases. It also reflects the need to coordinate activities within the same operating legal system. Yet, police-court relations are subject to a basic strain: the court has great discretion in deciding cases initiated by the police and has a formal obligation to oversee and control police activities. But its obligations to the police tend to make it difficult for the court to maintain an independent stance toward them. This conflict is reduced in two ways: First, daily contacts with the police are mediated through the probation staff, while the judges maintain more distant relations. Second, while imposing legality and proper rules of evidence, judges conduct court hearings in such a way as to protect the legitimacy and authority of police actions even when they violate these very standards.

The Schools

The public school system has developed two distinct kinds of institutional arrangements for dealing with troublesome students, both of which regularly utilize contacts with the juvenile court. In the first place, there are several specialized agents concerned with order and control within specific schools. Such agents include the traditional truant officer, employed by the city school department and handling all problems of school attendance in one district, and the "school adjustment counsellor," a Youth Correction Authority agent located in one school to deal with "predelinquents" and more generally with the recurring difficulties presented by in-school troublemakers. The position of truant officer has provided an avenue of mobility for a number of juvenile officers from the police force. The job closely resembles that of the police, as a great deal of time is spent patrolling the district, with minimal contact with the particular schools. Adjustment counsellors, most of whom are reputed to be former teachers, function much more within the school structure, handling not only many of the discipline problems traditionally delegated to the assistant principal, but also all contacts with outside agencies and services. In this regard these agents are responsible for placing difficult students in remedial and special programs.

Second, the juvenile court has close ties with the Harris School, a small special public school for boys in the middle grades (about sixth to eighth grades) who have been expelled from the regular school system for various kinds of misbehavior. The Harris School performs almost purely custodial functions, with the daily classroom routine organized around maintaining a minimum control over boys regarded as severely delinquent and as incapable of learning. This school in fact constitutes the dumping grounds used by the regular school system to get rid of troublemakers felt to be uncontrollable in a normal classroom setting and too young to be legally expelled from school. The principal of the Harris School has long-standing ties with the juvenile court, having worked as a temporary summer probation officer on a number of occasions. On a first-name basis with all court personnel, he makes frequent use of the court to support the disciplinary regime of his school.

In general, as in the case of the police, these school agents file court complaints only after initial attempts to correct the problem have failed. Delinquency charges are a last resort used after a period of unsuccessful pressuring and bargaining. A "truant," therefore, is not simply a child who has refused to go to school, but one who has resisted all efforts to help and encourage him to overcome this problem. As one truant officer said when asked when he took out a court complaint for truancy: "Only when it's impossible. You try everything and get nowhere. . . . The only time's where nothing works. Then you have to do something." A truancy complaint thus represents a request that the juvenile court take corrective action toward a previously tackled problem of control, a request either to use its authority to get the child to conform or to get rid of him. In line with the first expectation, the court must provide an additional and realistic threat to a tenuous situation of control; in line with the second, it must eliminate an inveterate troublemaker. Either case represents an appeal to the court's coercive and incarcerating powers.

A striking example of this appeal for supplemental control from court authority appears in the "informal hearing" frequently arranged for the truanting child who resists the truant officer's remedial actions. Such hearings, now limited almost exclusively to truancy cases, have no official standing, and are conducted by the chief probation officer at his desk. For example:

> Principal of the Harris School brought in two boys with their parents, and got the chief PO to talk to one of them about his school behavior, including causing disturbances and skipping school. Typical of the lecture: "Would you like me to bring you into court? Have the judge send you away to training school? . . . You're going to go to school, and when you're in school you're going to sit in your seat, and you're not going to move." Boy and parents were allowed to leave after this talking-to, no official action being taken.

Such informal hearings are a special service provided to truant officers with particularly close working relations with the probation staff. In effect such hearings provide the truant officer with an additional sanction to use in pressuring the child to return to school, but one that retains intact the still more potent sanction of the formal court hearing.

Court cases initiated by other school agents grow out of similar contingencies of institutional control. While complaints from the Harris School and adjustment counsellors frequently involve a specific delinquent act occurring within the school setting, such as an assault against a teacher or another student, formal court action again represents an appeal for supportive action in dealing with what is felt to be a long-standing control problem.

As with the police, obligations incurred toward these school agents render the juvenile court more amenable to granting their appeals for restrictive and coercive support in handling problem cases and "troublemakers." Again, the court's desire to acquire cases at an early stage of misbehavior, in order to implement an effective treatment program, provides a primary basis for such obligation. The significance attributed to "school problems" as indicators of future delinquency accentuates court pressures to "get cases early." Thus the judge of the court emphasizes the desirability of identifying "trouble" at an early stage, and views the schools as the ideal institution to perform this task. School agents are therefore entreated to bring before the court as soon as possible children who are "school problems." And school cases where remedial action seemed indicated long before clearly disturb court personnel. For example, a truant officer who had taken no action against a child who had been truant more than seventy days during the previous school year was severely criticized by both judge and probation officers. The court encourages the schools to bring cases to its attention. The judge feels that the schools are particularly well situated to make early identifications of "trouble" that reflect mental disturbance, and has encouraged action in such cases by making the juvenile court clinic available for psychiatric evaluation and treatment of such school "problems."

While firm working relations develop between court and all school agents, those with truant officers tend to be the closest. One reason for this is the truant officer's unique power to initiate "school complaints" (which have a statutory basis distinct from delinquency complaints). Under certain circumstances, school complaints take on special value to the court staff. For example, only a school offender can be committed to the county training school. Court staff consider this school a much higher quality institution than the reform schools operated by the Youth Correction Authority. Hence in certain delinquency cases, often involving younger boys, where commitment appears unavoidable, the court would prefer to commit the delinquent to the training school rather than to a YCA institution. But since adjudication as a delinquent precludes such commitment, the court must seek the truant officer's cooperation in order to obtain a complaint against the youth for truancy. On the basis of this complaint, the youth can then be committed to the county training school as a school offender.

CONCLUSION

While this chapter has not dealt directly with the processing of cases, the juvenile court's relations with political and enforcement institutions both determine the fundamental conditions on which this takes place and influence the direction of particular case outcomes. For in the process of adapting to its working environment the juvenile court becomes susceptible to the pressures of these institutions for particular kinds of dispositions. These institutional ties and obligations therefore influence the court's orientation and hence the purposes with which it attends to cases. More particularly, the juvenile court's sensitivity to the seriousness of delinquent offenses and to the degree of "trouble" characteristic of the actor and his situation reflects its dependence on politically organized parts of the community and its working relations with enforcers.

Furthermore, the nature of the court's external relations has a number of more immediate effects on case outcomes. In the first place, individual case outcomes are products of the concrete negotiation which occurs within the framework of these relations. Moreover, these negotiations are influenced by the court's close connections with the world of enforcers, for these connections predispose court personnel to accept the views of these agents about the delinquent involved and to respond to cases on the terms presented by these officials. These and other aspects of the court processing of delinquency cases will be analyzed in Part II, following consideration of the court's relations with another set of crucial institutions, treatment resources.

3
Relations with Treatment Resources

In contrast with its unavoidable contacts with enforcers, the juvenile court's relations with those institutions that control access to "helping" services and facilities are distinctly discretionary and negotiated in nature. Bargaining and mutual exchange implicit in the court's dealings with police and schools become explicit in relations with treatment resources. For the court such exchanges offer the stategic advantage of using existing community resources to pursue its treatment goals. But diversion of such resources to meet the court's requests may prove costly for the resource institution. Often this cost will be counted prohibitive unless offset by some service obtained from the court in exchange. Consequently, contacts between the juvenile court and the institutional system of treatment resources are funneled through those agencies that need the exchange services the court can provide.

This funneling process takes place within the context of (and helps maintain) the fundamental "institutional division of labor" between private and public service agencies. Cloward and Epstein, among others, have discerned a widespread "disengagement from the poor" by private social agencies (1965, pp. 623–44). This has been associated with a commitment to a "psychologically oriented private casework approach" that selects "motivated" and high status clients, passing on to the public agencies the harder-to-work-with, "resistant" ones. Cloward and Epstein list a number of manifestations of this "referral" process whereby undesirables are shifted to public agencies:

Private residential treatment institutions for juvenile delinquents, having made "errors" in intake, "pass on" their difficult cases to the public training schools; settlements and community agencies arrange to have public detached street workers assigned to the more difficult juvenile gangs; family agencies abandon so-called multi-problem families to welfare departments; private hospitals shrug off the chronically ill patients to the back wards of publicly supported custodial hospitals. Thus the public programs have tended to become the repository for the poor; private agencies have abandoned the neediest segment of society as their chief target (p. 626).

These tendencies are particularly marked within the city under study, especially within the child welfare complex. The private agencies, more highly professionalized and able to select clients, both avoid difficult and undesirable cases and shift those that have proved more undesirable than anticipated to the public agencies. The result is that the public agencies function largely as repositories for the rejected. As a caseworker from the Child Welfare Department, the main agency the court works with, described the nature of his caseload: "All the cases I get are trouble." This is because the Child Welfare Department receives most of its cases from other agencies who have decided they can no longer do anything for them. Many of their referrals come from the city Board of Public Welfare, and are of this nature. The Child Abuse League and Family Service refer cases they feel "cannot benefit from their work." In sum, "a great deal of our cases are cases that other people have looked at and decided they can't do anything for . . ." Or they are "too complex" (i.e., involve too many problems), requiring a great deal of work, and are referred for these reasons.

Nearly all juvenile court contacts with the world of child care and service are mediated through public agencies occupying this kind of position within the institutional division of labor. The following analysis will highlight the consequences of this characteristic institutional division of labor for the two most court-contacted agencies. the Child Welfare Department and the Children's Mental Hospital, and for their relations with the court.

THE CHILD WELFARE DEPARTMENT

The court's relations with the Child Welfare Department, that branch of the state Department of Public Welfare charged with the care and custody of neglected and orphaned children, are dictated by its need for "residential placements." Placement alternatives range from state institutions (as for the disturbed or the retarded) to privately run boarding schools, group homes, and foster homes. Access to public institutions is severely restricted and is generally considered undesirable; hence the court prefers private placements. Private institutions, however, particularly those with psychiatric services, charge very high fees. Few families of delinquent children, and practically none of those of the more pressing cases, can afford to pay even minimal costs of private placement, and the juvenile court itself has no money to make such payments. As a result, the court's only access to these desired placements is through the arrangements it can make with the Child Welfare Department. The Child Welfare Department has access to almost unlimited state funds for placing neglected or orphaned children in such private institutions. It is the Child Welfare Department's control of and access to these funds, and hence to the important private placements, which makes relations with this agency so critical for the court and its treatment commitment.[1]

The Child Welfare Department, however, has no legal obligation to pay for court placements. By statute the department can

1. The actual number of cases referred by the court to CWD for placement is generally very small. For example, the total number of boys referred to CWD during a six-month period was about fifteen. The number of girls referred was much lower. Thus it is probably a question of a maximum of forty cases per year. Yet these cases have an importance out of proportion to their number. In the first place, these cases are selected out of a much larger population where the court feels placement would be desirable, but thinks it futile to waste the time and effort because the child's record is so bad that placement would be impossible. In this sense those cases pushed for placement epitomize the court's treatment aims. Second, a tremendous amount of work is devoted to these cases, particularly in conducting negotiations with homes, child, and family. In this very concrete sense of investment of time and effort, these cases also take on significance beyond their numerical proportion.

pay for the placement of only those children in its custody. Under ordinary circumstances, the agency gains such custody only over orphaned children or, alternatively, over children found in need of care and protection, generally after a lengthy court proceeding. But the department may also assume custody through a "voluntary referral," where the parent signs over the child's care to the agency in an agreement terminable by either party with 24-hour notification. This "voluntary referral" process enables the juvenile court to transfer formal custody of cases to the department and hence to secure their placement in a residential treatment institution.

This placement procedure, however, places the juvenile court under heavy obligation to the department. In discharging this obligation the court aids the agency in a number of ways. These can be considered in terms of emergency, sanctioning and "dumping" services.

Emergency Uses of the Court

The juvenile court provides two general sorts of services to the Child Welfare Department in emergency cases. First, the department frequently faces a situation requiring an emergency placement. When a child runs away from or causes a disturbance in one of the homes used by the agency, and the home refuses to let him return, the agency must immediately resume his care. While working out another placement, a time-consuming and arduous process under most circumstances, the department must find a "short-term" or emergency placement, i.e., some residence that will temporarily house and care for the child. But regularly used group and foster homes are extremely reluctant to take children on a temporary basis. Consequently, the agency routinely turns to the juvenile court to make emergency placements. An agency worker takes out a "runaway" or "incorrigible child" complaint against the youth. During the period of the continuance (regularly requested to allow the public defenders to enter the case on behalf of the child), the worker requests that the child be temporarily committed to the Youth Correction Authority Detention Center. Although this is entirely a matter of judicial discretion, judges routinely grant this request. Holding the youth at the detention center both provides an emergency placement and gives the worker a period of grace in which to look for a permanent placement. As one child welfare supervisor noted ironically: "We would be in tough shape if we did not have the YCA (detention center) as an adjunctive service."

The second kind of emergency situation in which the Child Welfare Department turns to the juvenile court involves what might be called psychiatric crises. The Child Welfare Department has no psychiatric facilities directly at its disposal. In cases of children with recurrent but manageable psychological problems it can avail itself of the psychiatric services of other agencies. The juvenile court, for example, regularly allows the department access to the court clinic for psychiatric diagnoses. Similarly, the Child Welfare Department can go through regular channels to get its children admitted to public mental hospitals for treatment, although this is a tedious process highly unpredictable in outcome (chiefly because the agency has to demonstrate the child's illness and negotiate with the hospital to accept him). These procedures are totally inadequate, however, in cases of sudden psychological disturbance or mental breakdown requiring immediate action. The tendency for such psychiatric emergencies to involve crises in the institution's relations with the child, rather than simply a sudden deterioration in mental condition, accentuates the inadequacy of routine procedures. In such emergencies the Child Welfare Department turns to the juvenile court and its power to commit children temporarily to mental hospitals for psychiatric observation. Such cases are rushed before the court, the disturbance and its psychological nature established to the court's satisfaction, and the child ordered committed for 35 days' observation. Even if no permanent psychiatric help is found during this time, at least the period of respite allows the crisis to cool off.

Appeal to Court Sanctions

The most clear-cut appeal to coercive sanctioning by the juvenile court occurs with the threat of court action to facilitate work with "problem families." The Child Welfare Department seeks both direct and indirect support from the juvenile court for casework efforts with such families. The threatened court action, a neglect or care and protection proceeding, determines the legal custody of the children (assumed by the Child Welfare Department if the petition is successful) and the criminal responsibility of the parents for neglecting or abusing these children.

Often the Child Welfare Department is not directly concerned in the casework effort, but becomes involved because of its access to the juvenile court. In such a situation a private family-help or child-care agency or a public welfare agency has begun working with a family whose children are not receiving a generally acceptable standard of care. When a family does not respond to such "help," court action in the form of a care and protection petition may be threatened to compel cooperation. The Child Welfare Department may be asked to intervene as part of the process of carrying through with this threat. A department worker specializing in such matters described the process as follows:

> Often a petition would be initially mentioned by an agency which wanted the Child Welfare Department to check and see whether it was merited. He would go and visit the home and try to get them to accept help. No care and protection petition would then be taken out if they cooperated. But if he received no cooperation, and the people told him to get the hell out, "I call the agency and tell them, 'Go ahead and take your care and protection.'" But most cases could be worked out voluntarily.
>
> Similarly, the Public Welfare Department often contacted Child Welfare before filing a care and protection petition; "they like us to evaluate it before they take it out." If a need for help were found, the highly preferable solution was to work something out voluntarily. Sometimes the petition would be filed and then some arrangement reached, in which case he would ask the court to dismiss it, something they almost always did.

Similarly, the agency may use the threat of court action to support its own attempts to do casework. Moreover, a threatened neglect petition may be used to deal with families where casework has failed. For example, such court action may be threatened to compel parents to "voluntarily" sign over custody of their children to the agency, thereby saving the bother of a hearing and permitting quicker action on a case:

> Johnson noted that he only really had to threaten court action in cases where the parents just "don't care" about the children or receiving help. Here you might tell them: "Look here, if you don't sign this paper to give us custody of the children, we'll bring court complaints against you and take them away. You know you'll lose in court, and neglect convictions carry a maximum penalty of one year in jail and a $200 fine." Johnson emphasized that he did this just with those families "you can't work with," and that it was a way of saving the court appearance and fight by getting them to give up their children voluntarily. "It saves some work."

Finally, court complaints, either for runaway or incorrigibility, may be used in order to bring court authority behind efforts to control the behavior of youths in the Child Welfare-dominated Boys' Home.

The Court as a "Dumping Ground"

The most important court service provided the Child Welfare Department is that of eliminating agency cases that have proved persistently difficult or unmanageable. The court performs this function by permanently commiting department wards to the Youth Correction Authority and hence to reform school. In this way the Youth Correction Authority comes to serve as a vitally needed "dumping ground" for cases judged hopeless or uncontrollable by a public agency with little or no discretion in selecting and expelling its clients.

The need for a dumping ground grows out of contingencies surrounding one kind of typical career through the agency. Most wards move in and out of a number of foster and group homes before leaving the custody of the agency. Initial placement of a young child in a "good" foster home, one with few other children and some parental affection, may not work out. Placement in a less desirable home, where the parents are motivated by agency payments and hence take as many children as possible, often follows. Such a placement is often necessitated by "behavior problems," and these tend to find little or no tolerance in these homes. Hence as a youth grows older and becomes harder to place for these reasons he is moved to progressively less desirable foster homes. Finally he will be placed in group homes, at first temporarily and then on a permanent basis. Here again he tends to move from the "better" group homes to those that are more tolerant and accessible, crucial considerations if he has accumulated a record for frequent and serious misbehavior.

The case of a 12-year-old boy brought to court as a runaway well illustrates this kind of career movement and the problems it poses for the Child Welfare Department. This youth had been thrown out of a series of foster homes because of insistent curiosity about sex and open masturbation. The following excerpt occurred during a court conference, involving court, clinic, and Child Welfare Department staff, seeking to come up with a new treatment plan for this case:

> The department worker commented on the difficulties of finding a foster home for a child like this, with sex problems and a history of shifting from one home to another: "Now we're going downhill. . . . With these tougher kids—hard-to-place kids—you have to place them in a home that may not be the best home, but she will tolerate him so he has to be placed there. With a boy like Gino, especially if there are young girls in the family, the foster mother comes to feel he's going to do something to the girls and she can't tolerate it." Hence it becomes almost impossible to find a place that will take the boy.

Given the limited possibility of foster-home placement in this case, the conference decided to seek a group placement. Even this would be difficult, however, for group homes as well will not tolerate a boy engaging in these kinds of sexual activities. Hence, in all likelihood, his future will involve transfer from one group home to another, moving from the more to the less desirable ones.

At the very bottom of the system of group homes is the Boys' Home, dominated by the department, which pays for most of its residents. The Boys' Home serves essentially as a Child Welfare Department satellite, housing those older boys who have been rejected by the rest of the system of residential placements. The Child Welfare Department worker attached to the Home explained how its wards ended up there:

> That's simply this—some foster mother says "Out!" You get some boy 13 or 14, he's clipped $20 from her purse, or was masturbating in the bathroom and the little daughter saw him—any type of acting out which on second thought looks pretty normal. Anything like that will get them kicked out.
> RE: And it's hard to find other foster homes for this type of kid?
> Peters: Most of the kids at the Home have been pillar to post for several years. . . . They've been bouncing in and out of homes for years.

Most cases where the Child Welfare Department seeks commitments to the Youth Correction Authority involve residents of the Boys' Home, because the Home serves as the agency's repository for its most difficult and unplaceable cases. There is literally no place to send a boy who causes trouble at the Home except the Youth Correction Authority. In other words, the Home serves as a way station through which the general system of child placements funnels its most trying cases to the court and ultimately to the dumping grounds provided by the reform schools. As the department worker assigned to the Home noted:

> We need the court. Because you see, the kids that go to the Boys' Home are not adjusting anywhere else. . . . They're too old for foster homes. They've been around—dead-endies.

"Dead-endies" is exactly right. These youths have reached a dead end in the system of placements. They have been sent to an institution established specially for their kind, but even this institution must have somewhere to dump those it cannot handle. The court then helps perform the important function of ridding both the Home and the entire agency of elements which have proved indigestible.

This transfer from the care of the Child Welfare Department to court and reform school—the dumping process—is initiated by filing a complaint against the youth, either for incorrigibility or runaway. A department supervisor rationalized this dumping process and described the procedure in these terms:

> Supv.: There may be a boy in a group home who gets too disruptive. (In such a situation the only thing that can be done many times is to go to court and take out an incorrigible child complaint to get the boy incarcerated where he can be controlled.)
> RE: You mean you use the court and the YCA as a way of dealing with kids who get too disruptive—
> Supv.: Yes, as a resource for a closed setting. This court recognizes that we do this and goes along with us.

The following case provides an excellent example of the manner in which this dumping is carried out, as well as a concrete example of the organizational contingencies underlying the process:

> A Negro boy, John Brown, about 15, was a ward of the Child Welfare Department and a resident of the Boys' Home. He was charged with a second boy on two counts of larceny from the person and one count of attempted larceny. In court, the police had the three victims testify about the incidents and then told about the apprehension. Defense lawyer asked a few perfunctory questions. Brown was then found delinquent.
>
> The probation officer reported on the boy's background, which included four previous court appearances and an appeal of a commitment to the YCA that was still pending. Defense lawyer made no statement on disposition, but rather let the boy's natural father make an appeal for another chance. The judge turned this down because, he said, the boy had not cooperated in a previous effort to help him. He then checked with the Child Welfare Department worker associated with the Boys' Home about the circumstances of this, finding out that Brown had been turned down for all the placements they had tried to get for him when he ran away in the middle of the effort. Judge then committed the boy to the Youth Correction Authority.
>
> Before the court session I had talked to the Child Welfare Department worker about this case. He said he was just going to sit there and keep quiet and let the boy get committed, because "there's nothing you can do with him." I asked why this was.
> Peters: We can't hold him. He needs controls. (He then joked about "therapeutic controls" at the Youth Correction Authority.)

RE: Where do you want him sent—Stanman School?
Peters: I know where I *don't* want him to go.
RE: Where's that? Back to the Home?
Peters: Yes.
RE: Why's that?
Peters: He wouldn't stay two days.
　Again after the session I commented to Peters that he had hardly said a word.
Peters: That was a sure shot. (All he had to do was sit back and let things take their course.)

It must be emphasized that the commitment of children in Child Welfare Department custody demands the cooperation and acquiescence of court personnel, particularly the judge. Harmonious relations between agency and court in fact hinge on such requests receiving a sympathetic hearing in the court. Hence the tension and near hostility that marked earlier court relations with the department derived in large part from the refusal of the previous judge to commit such children. The following comment presents the current judge's analysis of this situation:

> The judge mentioned that his predecessor, because of a continuing feud with public welfare, "would not ever commit a CWD child." The Child Welfare Department got a number of cases that they just were not able to handle, going through one foster home after another, and whom they wanted sent to the Youth Correction Authority. But his predecessor had refused to commit these kids. By implication, however, he now cooperated in this goal.

While harmonious relations between the juvenile court and the Child Welfare Department rest on the exchange of placement financing for emergency, sanctioning, and dumping services, this system of exchange is neither exactly specified nor overly rigid. Exchanges follow a general pattern, involving both unspecified obligation and recognition of the legal limits and organizational requirements on the other party. While the general patterns of exchange are clearly established, it is problematic whether any particular request will be granted. Thus, the court expects the agency to try to find placements for a number of its cases, but does not absolutely require that the department come up with something. Similarly, the Child Welfare Department expects the court to be open to the possibility of committing its problem wards to the Youth Correction Authority, but realizes that the court may not feel this is justified in all or even most cases. Both parties become attuned to the organizational and work problems of the other party, and learn to make *reasonable* demands on the other's terms.[2] The court will therefore not ask the Child Welfare Department to find a placement for a 16-year-old dropout with a record of violent assaults, nor will the Child Welfare Department ask the court to commit a 12-year-old girl who has run away from an overly strict foster home. Each organization tolerates the circumstances that make it impossible for the other to fulfill all requests made of them. (E.g., the court will be sympathetic toward the Child Welfare Department's problems in placing any older delinquent boy, while the agency will understand why the court is reluctant to commit most Child Welfare Department wards to the Youth Correction Authority.) In this way the failure to fulfill a certain request need not threaten the sense of mutual obligation that underlies the exchange relationship.

However, as a result of this pattern of exchange control over initiating and negotiating placements for court "delinquents" shifts almost inevitably into the hands of the Child Welfare Department. For the department's power as financer of court placements generates pressures for control over all stages of placement strategy and implementation.[3] The following comments made by

2. The reciprocal of this is the need to cool out "unreasonable" demands. Generally this is easier for CWD, which can pass the buck and lay the blame for the failure of getting a placement on the source itself, if it feels compelled to go through the motions of trying to place an "unreasonable" case. As a CWD worker described this situation: "If I look at his record and I see there have been four or five different approaches to try to correct the situation, I figure it's not worth doing anything more." But there are very few cases of this kind, because "Jim [CWD liaison with the court] turns back most of them that are too way out." But when the court turns down a CWD request to commit a kid it is clear that the responsibility rests solely with the court itself.

3. This financing power also provides the *means* for assuming such control, as the agency can pressure placement sources to deal directly with it rather than with the court. Use of this strategy is clearly illustrated by the following case:

a department worker on one such placement effort reveal of the dynamics of this process:

> Johnson noted that for all cases from the court they tried to find group homes, as these would tolerate worse records and behavior. The one exception to this were two young boys placed in a foster home, but the court "did it themselves," making the arrangements and getting the Child Welfare Department to pay for it. Of course, it had not worked out, as the boys ran away within two days. Johnson felt strongly that this whole affair had been badly handled, and indicated that the agency had now decided not to pay for placements it had not arranged itself. "We are discouraging their making placements and sticking us with the bill." I asked why this was being done, why they did not want the court to make its own placement arrangements. Johnson: "It does not work out." Probation officers were not trained to work at this kind of thing; it was not their job to find the best placement for a child and carry through on it. And *the probation officer "does not have as adequate and realistic a view as we do"* about the possibilities of finding something and of the child's adapting well to it. Because the court plans were often bad and unrealistic there were many complete busts. "We end up with all the headaches and didn't even set it up. You've landed with a lousy situation. Now it hasn't worked out you want me to pick up the pieces."

In general, the Child Welfare Department's efforts to control placement arrangements that the court had once conducted independently reflect its distinctive involvement in the child placement system. Left to itself, the court can concentrate on individual cases, seeking to place a single youth felt to be in particularly pressing circumstances. It has no problem of managing its relations with all placements, and can focus all its efforts on pressuring one placement resource to accept this single case. In contrast, the Child Welfare Department must arrange placements

---

Johnson told of one boy the court had tried to get into the Orphan's Home, but the Home had referred the court to the department, since it knew that agency would ultimately foot the bill. The Child Welfare Department had then made the placement at the Home directly. Johnson noted that most other agencies preferred to deal directly with the department in the same way: "We hold the purse strings, and that makes it damn important to these agencies."

within the limits imposed by the need to distribute large numbers of children within a set number of placement slots and to maintain access to as many slots as possible. On the one hand, the department cannot lightly risk alienating a scarce placement resource by pushing an "unrealistic" candidate likely to act up and cause trouble, because such "unrealistic" and unsuccessful placements threaten all possible placements there in the future. On the other hand, the department cannot adopt the strategy of pushing one particularly deserving (but hard-to-place) candidate, but must put forward the candidate most qualified for the slot in order to avoid losing the vacancy entirely. Therefore organizational efficiency demands selection of the child most likely to be acceptable to the particular placement with an opening. To place a likely "troublemaker" is thus to give a scarce opening to a child not likely to retain it, and to deny that opening to one more qualified who would have succeeded.

The result is to subject the juvenile court to the underlying bias of the child placement system against "delinquents." Any child who has had contact with the court system is perceived as a dangerous troublemaker to be avoided at all costs. Therefore, as the Child Welfare Department assumes control over guiding and arranging court placements, the court becomes dependent on an institution which, in order to protect its own organizational interests, must fully respect these standards and practices regarding "delinquents." The requirement to seek only "realistic" placements, as determined by the prevailing standards of the placement system, thus effectively undercuts court efforts to place "hard-core" cases. Or again, the Child Welfare Department's ties to the placement complex make it less inclined than the court acting independently to take the risks necessary to place a delinquent who may cause trouble. In surrendering initiative and control over the placement process, the court loses the ability to press energetically for the placement of delinquent clients on whom it is willing to take a chance.

Hence in order to pursue its goal of treating delinquents the juvenile court enters into a system of exchanges on conditions which require a partial abandonment of this goal. Or to state the paradox in another way, the juvenile court, originally founded to prevent and treat delinquency, finds it increasingly difficult to pursue this task because of the limited commitment of associated agencies to "prevention" and "treatment."

Finally, the pattern of exchange with the Child Welfare Department further deflects the court's realization of its treatment goals. In committing the agency's most troublesome children to reform school, the court obtains treatment for some cases only at the cost of undertaking actions in other cases which are at best a form of nontreatment and at worst a severe punishment (commitment to a reform school). This results from the fact that the most valuable "commodity" that the court has to offer to the Child Welfare Department is its legal power to subject children (and their parents) to sanctions against their will. This coercive aspect of the court's legal powers, which distinguishes the court from other institutions in the child welfare complex, is a unique commodity much in demand on certain occasions by these agencies. That such power is the court's unique resource means that in becoming engaged in exchange relations with these agencies the court comes to perform functions that are essentially coercive.

The importance of this coercive power appears in the court's relations with a number of other agencies in the child welfare complex. At one point the court was approached by representatives of one of the hospitals in the area with a request for help from the court's coercive powers:

> Two doctors from the Children's Hospital [medical] observed the session today, and for some time afterward talked to the judge in his lobby. They wanted him to agree to let the hospital refer [psychiatric] cases to the court, which would then "deal with it informally" in getting the patient to go to treatment.

Similarly, there are a number of other child-care agencies that turn to the juvenile court for sanctioning and for "dumping" its worst cases. Committing cases to the Youth Correction Authority, however, is a course of action the court generally tries to avoid at all cost. Hence those agencies without the general trust relation to the court and the reciprocity possessed by the Child Welfare Department generally encounter resentment and resistance on the part of the court in response to their requests. The judge, for example, complained bitterly about the frequency with which the Orphan's Home, a private agency running a number of small residential units, brought cases to court:

> The judge was talking to a probation officer about placements. He made a bitter statement against child agencies who refused delinquents. He took the Orphan's Home as an example: "They've been told every time they get a tough case to bring it in here and get an incorrigible complaint. . . . It happens every day of the week" (i.e., an agency coming to court with a case giving it trouble and trying to shift responsibility for it on to the court) .

Court personnel are skeptical when an agency attempts to dump its worst cases on them. Aware that its legitimate coercive power is a valuable commodity, the court guards against its abuse. But because of the special ties Child Welfare Department has been able to develop with the court, it is much more able to overcome the judges' suspicion in such matters.

Yet there are agencies for which this commodity has little value or relevance, but to which the juvenile court must turn for services. Relations between the juvenile court and the Children's Mental Hospital are of this nature. Here there exists no apparently beneficial exchange upon which cooperation and "trust" can be based. It is to the analysis of these more strained relations that I now turn.

THE CHILDREN'S MENTAL HOSPITAL

The Children's Mental Hospital is the sole state residential treatment facility for disturbed children under 16 years of age. The strong psychiatric commitment of the juvenile court would seem to render close cooperation with this institution imperative, but in fact relations have been strained and open conflict has flared on more than one occasion.

By statute, the juvenile court does not possess the right to commit a child permanently to a mental hospital. Rather, its legal power is limited to the right to commit a child for observation and care for a temporary period (10 or 35 days), with the decision to retain the child resting with the psychiatric staff of the hospital. The hospital, in turn, has no obligation to keep any patient unless formally diagnosed as "psychotic."

Two general uses of the Children's Mental Hospital can be identified in the pattern of cases the court commits there. First, there are the "emergencies"—cases where it is felt something must be done immediately with an apparently very disturbed child. The following are typical of this kind of situation:

> An older white boy brought into court late in the afternoon by the Child Welfare Department after a reported suicide attempt was committed to the Children's Mental Hospital on the recommendation of a resident psychiatrist in the clinic.

> A 12-year-old white boy, twitching and groaning when brought into the courtroom, was committed to the hospital for 35 days' observation after the director of the clinic had been called in to quiet him and form an opinion about what to do with the case.

Second, some cases are committed to the Children's Mental Hospital, not so much because of the crisis quality they evoke, but rather because of a conviction on the part of the court of the *probability* of severe mental disturbance. In these cases the emphasis is on both giving the child a "last chance" and getting him in a setting where he can be controlled but still receive psychiatric care and observation. The aim is to get the child "off the street" but in such a way that he will get psychiatric attention.

In either case, the court commits children to the Children's Mental Hospital for 35 days' observation with the hope that ultimately they will be diagnosed as "psychotic" and given long-term care by the hospital. But the Children's Mental Hospital returns nearly every referral with a diagnosis of "not psychotic," labeling most of these "character disorders," thereby dashing court hope of securing psychiatric care. This development must be understood in terms of the treatment strategy followed by the hospital.

The Children's Mental Hospital has maintained a high degree of selectivity with regard to patients despite legal requirements in an apparently contrary direction. The hospital has committed itself to a policy of intensive care for a limited number of patients. Thus, while the unit was originally designed for 160 children, it now generally houses no more than 80 at any one time. The staff believes that any more would render it impossible to create a "therapeutic environment" or to provide adequate staffing. In addition, the hospital staff has restricted its purpose in another significant way: Effective therapy is promoted by giving preference to children with forms of mental disturbance successfully treated in the past. Conversely, those children with symptoms which have not been effectively dealt with in prior experiences are routinely rejected.

The Children's Mental Hospital can achieve this high degree of selectivity over its clientele, despite legal requirements, because of the flexibility of psychiatric diagnoses. The hospital need keep only those cases diagnosed as psychotic; most often it is itself charged with making the final determination in this respect. This power allows the hospital staff to take advantage of the vagueness of this category to reach a diagnosis of "not psychotic" and thus reject most children they want to avoid treating. But in addition, the hospital staff tends to routinely perceive the lower-class delinquent children referred to them by the court as "character disorders," and even anticipates that court cases will be of this kind. The very diagnosis is therefore biased in a direction that precludes retention of such court referrals.

This policy of selectivity produces great strain in the juvenile court's relations with the hospital. In the first place, court cases constitute unwelcome emergencies, as all other cases have been carefully studied before admission, and a course of treatment worked out. As the director noted: "All other than the courts' are planned admissions. Or if not planned at least they are screened. . . . The only admissions we get on an emergency basis are the courts.' "

Second, diagnostic cases referred by courts are hard to fit in to the organization of the unit. Resources have to be diverted from treatment; children have to be placed in programs on a temporary basis, often with disruptive consequences. The hospital is therefore interested in limiting the number of such cases referred from the courts.

Beyond this, the hospital has no incentive to assume the extra burden posed by court cases, generally perceived as disruptive character disorders. The court possesses nothing to offer the hospital in exchange. The coercive and sanctioning services that constitute the basis of the court's ties with the Child Welfare Department have little value for the Children's Mental Hospital. For unlike the Child Welfare Department, which must turn to the court in order to dump its most unwanted and most troublesome cases, Children's Mental Hospital can simply not admit such cases. Similarly, the Children's Mental Hospital can routinely send its disruptive cases to the maximum-security adult mental hospital associated with it for more strict control (and for punishment). Thus the Children's Mental Hospital anticipates no benefits from cooperation with the juvenile court.

Given that it possesses so little to exchange with the hospital, the court has tried to improve its position by threatening to abuse its legal claims on the hospital. In this way it can then exchange *the decision not to carry through on the threat* for some desired service. There are two clear examples of this kind of procedure:

The judge had been carrying on negotiations with the Children's Mental Hospital and its director, Dr. Richards, for some time, but without success. That is, he could extract no concessions from him. After an unsuccessful visit to Children's Mental Hospital, where the staff had complained about their overcrowding, the judge had threatened to commit "the first fifty [cases] that come through the door" of the juvenile court, if the hospital thought they were overcrowded then. He would send them a couple hundred cases indiscriminately, and as soon as one 35-day period was up he would order another one. The hospital director was apparently worried by this, and on one occasion when he met the judge socially said he was sure "you would not hurt us." But the judge insisted he would carry through on his threat unless changes were made.

The case of a 12-year-old boy with a history of mental trouble was referred to the Children's Mental Hospital on an emergency basis, after the court clinic had seen him and decided that he was without doubt psychotic. But after a period of observation the boy was returned with a brief report that he was not psychotic. The court then

had the task of making a decision about what to do with the case, and
requested copies of the material the hospital had compiled on the boy,
including the results of an EEG that had been performed. But these
reports never arrived. The judge became very upset with this, and
issued orders to have all the medical and psychiatric records Children's Mental Hospital had on the boy, and all the doctors who had
been involved, summoned to court. This was communicated to the
director of the court clinic, who in turn talked to the hospital director
about it, and the situation was smoothed over. (Also a general settlement was reached.) The judge reported that "Dr. Richards sort of
came around." I asked if he had really intended to carry through on
the threat. Judge: "I ordered the summonses. And I told Dr. James
they would be served unless something was done on it." He added that
if it had gone through it would have pretty well disrupted the hospital, for one day anyhow.

Some of the problems involved in these relations are highlighted in the compromise agreements eventually reached between the judge and the Children's Mental Hospital, through the
intermediary of the court clinic director. These reflect the desire
of the Children's Mental Hospital to eliminate the emergency
component of court commitments. As the court clinic director
recounted the agreement:

> Commitments will be made to the hospital only after a full psychiatric
> evaluation by the court clinic, during which time the child will be held
> at some place other than the hospital. From now on all "doubtful
> cases—fairly psychotic but not dangerously psychotic"—will be held at
> the Youth Correction Authority Detention Center while the clinic
> makes a full study and final recommendation regarding commitment.
>   A second major aspect of the agreement is to give the court respon-
> sibility for informing the hospital before a case is to arrive, and to
> send all reports, including psychiatric reports and social history, to the
> hospital with the child, because the hospital has complained of not
> getting any material on commitments until long after the arrival.

This arrangement allows the hospital to shift much diagnosis
onto the court clinic. It also means that the hospital would hence-
forth deal directly with professional colleagues, particularly with
the psychiatrist-director of the clinic, so that negotiations would

be handled within the framework of the psychiatric profession. Finally, the Youth Correction Authority Detention Center was to assume the hospital's prior custodial function. In return the court received the implicit promise that more of its cases would be accepted for treatment. (Thus, in the case that precipitated this compromise, the Children's Mental Hospital agreed to take the boy for treatment if he did not get along in the reform school he was sent to.) This settlement also made it more difficult to reject cases referred with clinic sanction, for rejection required official disagreement with fellow professionals. Similarly, the new arrangement undercut the hospital's oft-repeated contention that it returns so many cases because they were referred without proper psychiatric evaluation. In effect the court clinic legitimates the juvenile court's mental hospital commitments, but presumably reduces their frequency. In sum, the court exchanged decreased reliance on its right to use the Children's Mental Hospital for diagnostic and custodial purposes for increased access to its residential treatment facilities. Or, in return for the promise of special consideration for its cases the juvenile court accepted the hospital's definition of the nature of its operations.

CONCLUSION

The contemporary juvenile court is the survival of a reform movement that has lost its vitality.[4] What began as a radical social experiment has become routinized and institutionalized. But institutionalization occurs as part of a process whereby the court adapts itself to its social and organizational environment. In the juvenile court under study, this adaptation has been correlated with changes in the professional affiliation and commitment of the staff, its ethnic composition, and its orientation to delinquency.

The juvenile court was established at the beginning of the twentieth century in conjunction with an upper-class, native

4. For an analysis of social background and implications of the "child-saving" movement that produced the juvenile court, see Platt, 1969.

American humanitarian and philanthropic reform movement, and its early judges were drawn from this tradition. The earlier court staff was also closely allied with local settlement houses and social agencies and frequently went on to further careers in professional social work. Psychologists and psychiatrists were regularly consulted in court matters. Gradually, however, all this changed. The court staff increasingly came to reflect the political power of the city's ethnic groups. The Irish became prominent, and eventually an Irish Catholic was appointed to the judgeship that had come to be regarded by the Yankee Protestants as their traditional preserve. Concurrently with this development, the professional affiliations of the staff grew weaker. This reflected not only the change in training and ethnicity among court staff, but also the increasing professionalization of social work and its related withdrawal from matters concerning courts and delinquency. Ties with political, enforcement, and correctional bodies came to be stronger than those with the world of child welfare.

Finally, this was accompanied by a clear shift in orientation: earlier beliefs in scientifically based techniques, administered in a spirit of benevolent paternalism, gave way to a more openly moralistic, locally oriented, and "common-sense" approach. This shift in orientation can be dramatically illustrated by changes in ideas of the nature of delinquency and the juvenile court. As the first judge of the court wrote in an early magazine article:

> The Juvenile Court is administered on the assumption that the fundamental function of a juvenile court is to put each child who comes before it in a normal relation to society as promptly and as permanently as possible . . .

But forty years later, the traditional enforcement concern of the criminal law pervaded the testimony of the immediate predecessor of the current judge before a United States Senate subcommittee:

> We must educate children to understand that there must be respect for authority. We know that you cannot have order without law and the respect for law. There is no law without the sanctions and penalties for any person who is rash enough to offend the law.

On another level, it can be noted that the original thrust of the juvenile court movement, with its positivist ideology and professional ties, was toward separation of legal institutions dealing with children from the established, politically controlled criminal court system. In these terms, the institutionalization of the juvenile court transformed an experimental agency committed to principles alien both to its clientele and its related agencies, a transformation accomplished by incorporation into the local political, social, and institutional systems. This analysis has described the nature of the court's ties with these various worlds, as it is exactly these ties and the obligations they entail that give the juvenile court its distinctive character.

This chapter in particular has considered the juvenile court's relations with that institutional network concerned with child care. It was noted that institutions at the bottom of this system characteristically face severe limitations on their selectivity of clients. Dealing with the least desirable and most troublesome children, control becomes the dominant organizational problem. Under these circumstances the court's capacity to apply coercive sanctions provides a necessary and even essential service. As a result, the court's ties with the child-care complex are funnelled through those institutions at the bottom of this complex.

In this way the juvenile court serves to link the world of child welfare with the world of juvenile correction. The court performs a crucial "readdressing" function in displacing the "dirty work" of the field of child welfare onto the state reform and training schools.[5] In fact, this is a critical function for the total system of child welfare: the more "desirable" placements can only maintain their desirability and relative exclusiveness through the accessibility of the least desirable ones in which to dump their rejected cases. A similar situation holds with respect to techniques: the permissive casework methods of the high status agencies and facilities depend in some degree on the existence of lower-status custodial agencies who must dirty their hands with authoritarian controls. Thus, while permissive agencies may frown upon the

5. The concept of "dirty work" as a fundamental aspect of the "moral division of labor" within professions has been developed by Everett C. Hughes in his "Social Role and the Division of Labor" (1958, pp. 70–72).

"unprofessional" and coercive style of those handling the system's dirty work, their very ability to employ preventive and noncoercive methods depends upon the latter's taking over those clients who might otherwise make demands on them. The juvenile court reinforces those doing the dirty work in this system, both by supporting their controlling efforts and by transferring the very dirtiest cases to another system (the penal-criminal).

This chapter has analyzed the details of this process. It has argued that in the course of negotiating with other agencies the juvenile court's treatment goals are subtly displaced. "Treatment," as the court visualizes it, is compromised through the coercive and dumping uses made of its power. But even more significantly, treatment is undermined through court cooption into a system of placements biased against "delinquents." As a result, the court finds that it cannot press too insistently for placement or treatment of "hard-core" cases as a condition for obtaining sympathetic consideration in milder and less threatening cases, despite its own conviction that the former have the same or even greater need for "help" in these terms. This, then, completes the process whereby the court funnels the most desirable and promising delinquents out into the child-care system, while transferring the most troublesome cases from this system into correctional and custodial institutions.

II
Case Management and Moral Character

The following chapters describe some basic features of the practices used by the court in dealing with the cases presented to it. Analysis focuses on the categories employed by court staff to carry out their daily organizational tasks—on "the functional units in which business gets done" (Scheff, 1966, p. 179) in the juvenile court. In this respect, the court initially distinguishes cases marked by "trouble" from those without. In subsequently working out solutions to trouble cases, the court relies heavily on its assessments of delinquents' moral character. The role of such assessments of moral character in court management and processing of delinquency cases and the contingencies surrounding these assessments provide the major themes of the following chapters.

4

The Framework of Court Categorization:

Trouble and Moral Character

"TROUBLE"

It was suggested in the previous chapter that youths brought before the juvenile court generally represent "trouble" for some caretaking or control institution. In this sense every delinquent is "trouble" for someone. It may be added here that every delinquency complaint represents a plea that the court "do something" to remedy or alleviate that "trouble." Hence, one fundamental set of problems and demands confronting the juvenile court arises from the pressures and expectations of those initiating court action that "something be done." In this sense the court must work out practical solutions to cases that satisfy, or at least take some cognizance of, the concerns of complainants.

But not all cases represent "trouble" in the eyes of the court; the court does not automatically accept the contentions of complainants. Rather the court makes an independent assessment of "trouble" and of the necessity of "doing something," an assessment that reflects its own organizational priorities and "problem relevances" (Schutz, 1964, p. 235).

These distinctive problem relevances turn on two fundamental features of the court situation. First, the time, personnel, and resources available for dealing with delinquency cases are severely limited. Consequently, court operations are subject to strict econ-

83

omy in the uses of resources and personnel. Second, court personnel have a higher tolerance of "delinquency" than most complainants. Routinely encountering a wide range of youthful misconduct, the court develops a relatively narrow definition of delinquency. This definition generally requires quite frequent and serious manifestations of disturbing conduct before a youth will be categorized as "really delinquent." As a result, court workers often feel that complainants' "troubles" are exaggerated and that the kinds of official responses they seek are inappropriately drastic.

The court thus comes to follow a principle of conservatism in case management. This in turn requires it to separate "serious" cases where there is "real" trouble, from those where the "trouble" is "mild" or "normal," requiring little attention.[1]

The search for "real" trouble emerges as a recurring theme throughout court staff's explanations of their work. For example, the judge described his orientation toward the conduct of formal hearings in the following terms:

> We look for tip-offs that *something is really wrong.* We get some tip-offs just from the face-sheet; truancy, school attendance, conduct, and effort marks. . . . *If you get something wrong there, you know there's trouble.* When you get truancy or bad conduct plus the delinquency, there's definitely something wrong. [Emphasis added.]

Similarly, a woman probation officer in talking about girl shoplifting cases said:

> Shoplifters are the simplest and most promising kind of girls I have. Often they come from good families. But there may also be *"a very serious problem"* involved. Sometimes while taking the face sheet you can see how "serious" it is. But usually these cases are continued without a finding in order to determine if there is any "serious problem." . . . Then again, some are dealt with more severely, "depending on the girl's attitude." For some of the cases are more *"severe"* and have to be dealt with accordingly.

1. Cavan (1966) employs the concept "normal trouble" to describe aspects of barroom behavior. "Normal trouble" involves "improper activities that are frequent enough to be simply shrugged off or ignored" and hence constitutes "a taken-for-granted aspect of the public drinking place" (p. 18). Cases where the juvenile court feels no special intervention is required involve "normal trouble" in this sense.

By this sifting process the court begins to allocate its time, efforts, and resources among delinquency cases. On the one hand, the court locates cases where "something has to be done," where special handling is required; on the other hand, it finds cases which can be "let go." The great majority of the court's cases are of the latter sort—"untroubled"—and require staff to devote only a minimum of time and effort to overseeing and changing the life circumstances of the delinquent. A woman probation officer, for example, commented on the unserious nature of girl shoplifters by noting: "I don't see them any more [after their hearing]." On the other hand, in cases where "trouble" is found, where "something wrong" is noted, the court more actively intervenes, concentrating its efforts and resources for change. Extraordinary measures are taken in managing these cases, and much effort is devoted to working out some adequate remedy.

In general, a case brought to juvenile court under a definition of "trouble" has three possible outcomes. First, complainant and court definitions of trouble may more or less coincide; the court then seeks some satisfactory remedy for the case. Second, complainant and court definitions of trouble may diverge. Usually this disparity reflects a judgment of a lesser degree of trouble by the court, for the reasons discussed previously. In this situation the court initially tries to convince the complainant that it has no power to do anything or that nothing need be done. This may require special efforts to satisfy the complainant, to persuade him not to press for special action, or to induce him to accept some less drastic solution than he originally envisioned.[2]

Finally, the court may feel there is no trouble, but be unable to "cool out" the complainant. In this situation the court may be moved to "do something" even though it feels such action is not really necessary. A course of events leading to such an outcome occurred in the following case:

2. On occasion, however, the court may find itself in the position of pushing a more severe definition of "trouble" and a more drastic course of action upon some other party. This occurs when the court diagnoses "trouble" where the complainant feels there is none and, more frequently, when parents deny serious trouble in the case of their child.

A 16-year-old Negro boy was brought to court for assaulting a fire chief. The previous night the boy's best friend had been knifed during a fight and a fire department "ambulet" called to the scene. When the fire chief directing the operation had refused to let the defendant accompany his critically wounded friend to the hospital in the ambulet, the youth had punched him. As a result, the chief had insisted that the police take out the assault complaint.

In court, a social-worker sponsor of the youth reported that the police had expected the case to be settled with an apology by the boy, but that the chief had refused to drop his complaint. The police officer acting as prosecutor outlined the alleged facts briefly, requested a two-week continuance before the hearing, and concluded by stating, "the boy came here on his own volition this morning," suggesting that bail would not be required. Outside the courtroom, in discussing this continuance with me, the police officer noted: "We let it cool. Let the chief cool off."

When the hearing was finally held, the judge placed the youth on a suspended sentence after finding him delinquent on the assault complaint. At the same time, the judge complemented this relatively severe judgment with special efforts to sooth the fire chief's indignation.

As this case suggests, the strength of a complainant's demands to "do something" may constitute a crucial factor in the court's identification of "trouble." Strong demands create a presumption that "something has to be done" and demonstrate the existence of behavior intolerable to someone with responsibility for controlling the delinquent.

There are two circumstances under which the court routinely identifies "trouble," i.e., two "demand conditions" (Bittner, 1967b, p. 701) perceived by court personnel to require that "something be done." First, a serious offense creates a presumption of "trouble." Because serious cases mobilize strong community and enforcement pressures, they are presumed to require some kind of action, perhaps drastic. Second, "trouble" may be identified in patterns of behavior and social circumstances that are felt to precede serious delinquent or criminal activity. In this way, trivial current activity may be given meaning in light of an anticipated future development of a delinquent career. For example, as one probation officer noted about girl delinquents, "incorrigible can be a prelude to runaway, which is a prelude to prostitution."

Special note should be taken of the fact that under both conditions "trouble" is essentially a *predictive* construct. The fact that a youth has committed a serious offense is of particular interest to the court partly because it suggests that he may well do so again; such a delinquent has shown himself to be the sort of person who might so behave. When current behavior is minor or trivial but the court feels "trouble" is present, it is judging that such conduct, in light of attendant circumstances, is "symptomatic" of involvement in a *delinquent career* that will inevitably lead to more harmful conduct.

"Trouble," then, is an inferred potential for committing seriously delinquent acts. This central dimension of "trouble" is associated with the quality of "dangerousness." "Dangerousness" implies some active threat to the lives or person of others. However, it may represent merely a *potential* for this kind of behavior *in the future*. Thus, even in the face of a complete absence of any prior outburst of seriously delinquent behavior, a delinquent can be regarded as dangerous and his case identified as one of trouble. The issue is: if something is not done about this youth and his social circumstances right now, it is certain that he will commit some serious offense in the future.[3]

This basic concern with "trouble" focuses the direction of court activity in attending to cases brought before it. The courtroom hearing does not emphasize the confined, offense-directed question, "what happened?" Instead, the effort is directed toward establishing, "what is the *problem* here?" The following ex-

3. Note the similarity of these predictive components of "trouble" with the medical concept of illness as a "progressively unfolding disease." As Scheff has argued:

> The medical framework . . . leads one to expect that unless medical intervention occurs, the signs and symptoms of disease are usually harbingers of further, and more serious, consequences for the individual showing the symptoms (1966, p. 51).

The use of the model of disease and necessary medical intervention in the analysis and treatment of many social problems has been emphasized by Korn (1964, pp. 578–87).

tended-case observation illustrates this fundamental orientation toward delinquency cases, as well as the procedures that typically guide initial inquiry into the case:

Two white girls, Jean and Mary, both about 15, had been arrested for shoplifting in a downtown department store. Store detectives told of apprehending the girls outside the store with the stolen clothes in the bottom of a shopping bag. Mary's father questioned the store detective very closely, then turned to his daughter and demanded to know whether she had stolen the clothes. She admitted she had.

The two probation officers with the girls gave their reports. Mary had run away from home several times previously and, in fact, the present shoplifting episode had occurred on the latest of these. She also was often absent and truant from school. But from her interview "she seems mild, well-behaved." Her mother had tried to keep her away from Jean, but without success. Jean, it was then reported, showed a similar record of running away and trouble in school. And she had behaved badly in the office interview: "She seems mean. She was most disrespectful to her mother in the interview at my desk. She asked me if it was any of my business if she was a runaway when she was charged with shoplifting." One probation officer then requested separate dispositions, on the ground: "I think the other girl [Jean] may need something more drastic, with her attitude." Judge refused, and inquired in detail into previous runaways, especially from Jean's mother about why she had not reported her daughter missing. Then questioned the girls about where they had been for the several days they had been away; they said they spent the night in a doorway in a nearby, lower-middle class suburb. Judge also questioned them very closely about a girl they reported they met in a downtown hotel who offered them jobs and a place to stay with her.

Judge then began to concentrate on Jean: . . . "What's the idea of running in the first place?" Jean: "I don't know." Judge: "What's the trouble? Huh? Any trouble at home?" Jean denied this, and was generally sullen and uncommunicative. Judge then questioned Mary, particularly about her school work. Then asked probation officers for their recommendations, which were "continued without a finding" for Mary, "probation" for Jean.

Judge thought briefly and then reacted: "Since they're not going to school and not doing well, I want them held in detention for study. Psychiatrics on both. I want physicals on both too. (Both girls are now crying, as they will be held for another two weeks.) . . . There's something going on with them. I'm not worried about the stealing but that brings it to a head. . . ."

In this case it is clear that very little time was devoted to establishing the facts of the shoplifting complaint. Rather, the court's concern lay in three other areas: (a) the runaway episode, particularly what the girls had done during this time, checking on the likelihood of prostitution; (b) the general behavior and character of the girls; and (c) their home situation. In all areas there are firm indications of "trouble": recurrent running away; at least some likelihood of sexual activity (it was this possibility that led the judge to order a physical exam), perhaps even the beginning of prostitution; frequent conflict in both home and school. As the judge noted, "There's something going on with them." The severity of the probable "trouble" in the judge's mind is indicated by his handling of case, i.e., holding the girls in detention and ordering psychiatric study. (Girls, except state wards, are very rarely held in detention.)

This perspective oriented toward "trouble" and "problems" both grows out of and is reinforced by the court's commitment to "treatment." This commitment broadens court concern beyond the simple allocation of sanctions. In seeking to provide "help" and "treatment," the range of relevant dispositions the court may consider is tremendously expanded. Under such circumstances, the offense in itself provides no sure guide to the kind of response that should be forthcoming. Rather, the court turns to the delinquent himself—to his overall behavior, personality, and family and social circumstances—in order to decide how best to deal with the case. The explanation for delinquency is sought "in the character and background of offenders" (Matza, 1964, p. 3) .

THE RELEVANCE OF MORAL CHARACTER

In seeking practical solutions to cases felt to involve "trouble," the juvenile court is largely guided by its judgments and inferences regarding the nature of the delinquent actor involved. That is, the solution to the problem—what can and what must we do with this case?—generally depends on the answer to: what kind of youth are we dealing with here? This involves a process of inquiry into the youth's *moral character*.

"Trouble" and "moral character" represent sets of categories relevant to two distinct phases of the organizational sorting of delinquency cases. In the initial separation of troubled from untroubled cases, the court comes to distinguish between cases that demand some unusual effort and care—some form of "special handling"—and those it can simply "let go." Assessments of moral character allow a subsequent, second sorting, through which the court specifies what *kind* of special handling is relevant. In this way assessments of moral character differentiate among kinds of trouble cases in such a way as to guide subsequent reponse to the case; they provide explanations of the "trouble" that suggest particular institutional solutions to the case.

If the court decides that there is no trouble in a case, it assumes that the delinquent involved is *normal* in character. If trouble is located, however, character is rendered *problematic*. This initiates more intensive court involvement with the case, as well as more intensive concern with accounting for the youth's behavior. Upon examination, it may be felt that the delinquent is really possessed of normal character despite indications of trouble. As a result, assessments of normal character may occur at either initial or subsequent stages of the court sorting process.

Similarly, damaged character may not be identified on first contact but begin to "emerge" in subsequent encounters. For example, a case may be treated as routine until the delinquent appears in court for a second or third time within a period of several months. Such reappearances cast doubt on the previously assumed normality of character. Initial judgments may fall before a variety of factors. At almost any point in a court career, doubts cast on character may be minimized or dismissed or, alternatively, confirmed and explained as expressions of some discredited kind of moral character. The court builds up experience with an individual delinquent and accumulates a biographical file on him so that its assessments of his character become stable. Yet this view is nearly always open to some modification: while an assessment of poor character is not easily removed, it may at least be reinterpreted as of a different kind.

Court staff distinguish three general kinds of juvenile moral character. First, a youth may be *normal*, i.e., basically like most children, acting for basically normal and conventional reasons, despite some delinquent behavior. Second, a youth may be regarded as a *hard-core* or *criminal-like* delinquent, maliciously or hostilely motivated, consciously pursuing illegal ends. Third, a youth may be *disturbed*, driven to acting in senseless and irrational ways by obscure motives or inner compulsions.

For the juvenile court these categories of moral character provide institutionally relevant means for "explaining" or "accounting for" the patterns of behavior that led to the identification of "trouble." To explain such behavior by fitting the individual case into one of these categories both suggests and justifies particular court actions to deal with it.

For example, to decide that a youth is "disturbed" is to provide an account for his "bizarre" behavior that indicates the need for and justifies psychiatric care and/or institutionalization. Similarly, to determine that a boy is "really" a "hard-core delinquent" explains his past and future misconduct as the product of that kind of criminally motivated actor who can only be dealt with by means of punishment and restraint.

Organizational relevance in turn derives from the correspondence of categories of moral character with the alternative courses of action open to the court. (See also Cicourel and Kitsuse, 1963, p. 74.) The three classes of moral character recognized by the court—normal, criminal, and disturbed—correspond to the following general reactions which the court may try to implement: (a) routine handling of the case: generally probation and the relatively minor obligations and checks accompanying it; (b) incarceration in reform school or some other institution of that nature; and (c) special care and treatment, especially in a psychiatric setting.

The organizational relevance of the categories of moral character recognized by the court becomes particularly striking when examining the formulation of the "disturbed" category. "Disturbed" identifies delinquents who seem essentially irrational, prone to uncontrollable emotional outbursts, and not fully aware of what is going on. Delinquents identified by the court as of disturbed character, however, can be either mentally ill ("sick") or retarded. For the "problem relevances" of the juvenile court, mental illness and retardation constitute equivalent explanations of behavior, and both elicit a common response from court personnel.

On the level of explanation, mental illness and retardation merely identify different psychic causes for generally identical kinds of disturbing and unusual behavior: in retardation it results from an abnormal lack of intelligence, in mental illness from some inner emotional tension or compulsion. Since "retarded" and "mentally ill" are functionally equivalent kinds of explanations for disturbed behavior, "retardation" can provide a completely adequate explanation for what might otherwise be defined as mental illness, and *vice versa*. To consider the former possibility:

A 13-year-old Negro boy, Paul Robinson, was accused of assault and battery on a young, short, blonde female schoolteacher. Teacher testified that she had been correcting papers in her homeroom after school, when she heard a noise at the door and eventually discovered Paul out in the hall. He refused to go home, and at first refused to say what he had been doing there, replying, "What's it to you?" Eventually she found out that he had been kept after school by the assistant principal. But Paul continued to refuse to go home and then threatened her by saying, "I'm going to break you, four-eyes" (referring to her glasses). Teacher then was obviously very nervous and began walking down the hall away from the boy, but he followed her and hit her four or five times on the back and side of her head with his hand. On the stairs he hit her again on the head and kicked her. Outside she found a custodian and told him of the incident. He talked to the boy, who was apparently standing nearby. Custodian started to walk her to the principal's office, but he returned to get the boy's name when he found she did not know it.

Paul's special class teacher, a very young, short, slender man, next testified that the boy had been sent to his class three days before the incident in question, and during that afternoon had been particularly bothersome in class. After class Paul had hit him several times with a stick and thrown a broken soft drink bottle at him when ejected from the school building. It was because of this behavior that the boy had been taken to the assistant principal's office and made to stay after school. Public defender cross-examined briefly, emphasizing that this involved a *special* sixth grade class and asking: "Are you aware of his school record? That he could be classified as emotionally disturbed—a slow learner? That he is retarded?" Teacher replied that he had not been given specific information on the boy when he entered his class, but assumed he had been placed in this class because he was retarded.

A Child Welfare Department worker in the court then asked to testify. Judge asked how his agency was involved in the case. Worker replied it was working unofficially with the family. The boy's IQ had been tested at 59, and they had tried to get him into the Willard School, but had been turned down when this school found the boy had a "potential IQ" of 74. Application had recently been made to a school for retarded children run by the Catholic archdiocese, with the outlook favorable. Judge continued the case for a month to allow the placement to be worked out. Boy was sent home with his mother and the warning: "Try to keep him at home."

In this case the behavior of the attacker is contradictory and inconsistent: the boy made no apparent effort to run away, and his attack appeared to be purely without reason. But all inquiry into the nature and features of the offense terminated with the reference to retardation. Mental retardation provided a motivational picture that adequately explained all the presented features of the offense. Since the boy was retarded, no need existed to establish the motives or reasons for his act (e.g., what had happened with the special class teacher). Absolutely no questions were addressed to him, and the court staff in particular acted as though he were not present. Similarly, the boy's responsibility for the act was so mitigated that the judge did not give him the usual lecture on the wrongness of his offense. This lack of responsibility, for example, was emphasized by the comments of the Child Welfare Department worker after the hearing:

> "He's sick. She [teacher] panicked, and he took advantage of it. . . . He's retarded—you can't blame him." The boy had probably been upset originally by the way the special class teacher had treated him. The special class teaching posts go to those "at the bottom of the shit list." This teacher had been insecure; "he didn't know what he was doing, and set him off. . . . They set off this kid."

Finally, mental retardation is easily established. In this case it required only presence in a special class and verbal report of a low IQ.

Furthermore, "retarded" and "sick" do not describe features of youth's character directly relevant to the court's initial handling of cases. One reflection of this is the fact that not all "retarded" youths are categorized in terms of disturbed character. Some delinquents with low IQ's are considered of normal character. Although a little "slow," they can be managed in ordinary settings. Hence they may be kept in the community on routine probation or with required attendance at the Boys' Training Program. But other retarded children may be considered liable to uncontrollable outbursts of emotion and aggression, and still others subject to strong criminal propensities. Here character is judged to be disturbed, and the case managed accordingly.

In general, then, the court responds primarily to disturbed character as such. In this way it initially handles all disturbed behavior—however explained—in the same way, by referring the case to the court clinic. Only subsequently do the explanations of such behavior—retardation or mental illness—become relevant to case management. Hence, the distinction between "mentally ill" and "retarded," peripheral to the court's initial problem relevances, often becomes central when cases are referred to the clinic. For the clinic faces the decision of whether or not to recommend a commitment to a mental hospital or a school for the retarded and hence must determine whether the youth is "really" mentally ill or "really" retarded. The clinic then attempts to justify and legitimate this decision in negotiating with the selected institution.[4]

4. Here the distinction between mentally ill and retarded is often difficult to make and impossible to prove, even with the professional assistance available to the clinic. It should be noted that while "mentally ill" and "retarded" are not logically exclusive (e.g., a youth could be both), the immediate exigencies of obtaining treatment and placement tend to make them mutually exclusive in practice. As a result the clinic and the court were frequently frustrated in their attempts to negotiate with specialized placement institutions by what one clinic psychiatrist termed "differential diagnosis." That is, a mental hospital would diagnose the child as retarded and refuse to accept him for treatment on these grounds, while a school for the retarded would refuse the same case on the basis of their diagnosis of mental illness. Thus, even the psychiatric diagnosis made by the clinic of "mental illness" or "retardation" remains inclusive and subject

In sum, the court's concern with accounting for delinquent behavior and with moral character is strongly practical in nature. At least initially it can manage cases without deciding whether disturbing behavior is due to mental illness or retardation. Similarly, under most circumstances, "causes" of delinquent behavior, drawn from the common-sense stock of theories of youthful misconduct, are organizationally irrelevant to the juvenile court's practical decision of what has to be done about cases. For the court's response to a case is determined by its judgment that character is conclusively abnormal, irrespective of the "causes" that produced this condition. For example, in the following case, delinquency is ultimately attributed to a "bad home situation." But this "cause" becomes organizationally irrelevant to the management of the case in light of the youth's basically warped character:

> Jeremiah Taylor, a 15-year-old Negro boy, was charged with assault with a dangerous weapon in the yard of the Harris School. The facts were heard, and reports made indicating prior aggressive behavior (see p. 123). The probation officer then reported on the family situation. The boy did not get on at all with his mother and had been living with an aunt. His family situation was clearly "deprived." The probation officer continued: "One thing is clear and that is that no good can come from returning this boy to his mother." In fact, things had probably gone so far with this boy that he was now beyond help himself: "The early exposure to this kind of thing may have been going on so long that it's irreparable. As I say, it's a tragedy and a half. . . . If there ever was a situation that sprang from neglectful attitudes by the parents, this is unfortunately it." Again, "I'm not sure anything can be done about it at this late stage." Boy now seems to have an uncontrollable temper, functions at a very low mental level, and is very emotional and unpredictable. Decision was then made to hold the boy in high bail at the Youth Correction Authority Detention Center while a psychiatric evaluation was made; the court was generally uncertain about whether mental hospitalization or reform school was the best solution.

---

to revision. In disposing of a case, a child is only "labeled" as disturbed or retarded upon successful negotiation of his admittance into a specialized institution committed to treating one kind of patient.

In general, once a delinquent is considered "hopeless"—i.e., is identified as irretrievably criminal or sick in character—concern lies not in how character came to be shaped, but rather in how the youth is presently to be dealt with and controlled.[5]

"Causes" may assume practical organizational relevance, however, in handling cases where there is no basic question about the normal character of the delinquent involved. In this situation, locating causes of delinquency provides the court with points for intervention to forestall any further movement in that direction. In this sense causal explanations are relevant to court action in cases where the possibility of "reform" is still recognized.[6] The reconstructed causes of delinquent behavior become organizationally irrelevant when moral character comes to be regarded as irretrievably spoiled, and some drastic response seems called for.

MORAL CHARACTER AND CASE OUTCOMES

It has been suggested that in the process of disposing of cases, the juvenile court looks for trouble and assesses moral character. But it must be added that a decision on character does not represent the actual outcome of the case; it merely indicates what the court feels should be done. The practical contingencies of placement and treatment mean that frequently the court is unable to implement this most desirable disposition, and hence must compromise and settle for second best, or even worse.

In the first place, the court often decides that a delinquent is "disturbed" and badly needs "help." But this youth may never be admitted to a mental hospital, and therefore never become labeled as mentally ill. For implementation of this desired disposition, based on the "sick" assessment of the delinquent's moral character, requires that (a) the clinic psychiatrists validate this

---

5. Similarly, as the judge in Samuel Butler's mythical "Erewhon" informed a convicted criminal: "There is no question of how you came to be wicked, but only this—namely, are you wicked or not?" (Reprinted in Donnelly, Goldstein, and Schwartz, 1962, p. 254.)

6. Furthermore, causal explanations play a crucial role in insulating moral character from the soiling effects of delinquent behavior. In effect they provide a variety of excuses that diminish a youth's responsibility for misbehavior (see Chapters 5 and 6) and hence help maintain a definition of normal character.

assessment of mental illness, and (b) court and clinic successfully bargain with a mental hospital to accept the youth. Thus the court's initial assessment of disturbed character may not result in psychiatric management of the case because of the contingencies surrounding implementation of the implied decision. In the following case, for example, the impossibility of gaining permanent admission to a mental hospital leads the court to commit a youth regarded by all as "disturbed" to the Youth Correction Authority:

> A youth had been seen in the court clinic a number of times, and had been diagnosed mentally ill. But after failing to arrange a psychiatric placement, the court committed him to the Youth Correction Authority, feeling there was no other alternative. As a probation officer commented: "There's no doubt the kid's disoriented. But what can we do about it?"

Again, contingencies surrounding the actual "solution" of a case may lead to different case outcomes despite common assessments of moral character. For example, the juvenile court may come to classify a boy as a dangerous, criminally motivated person, in which case some penal sanction such as commitment to reform school would seem indicated. But the decision actually to invoke this sanction is influenced by factors such as the boy's home situation and the availability of alternatives to reform school. Thus a boy who is a state ward is more likely to be committed to reform school than a boy judged just as criminally inclined but from a stable home. Commitment follows for the first case because there is no other place to put the public ward.

Conversely, a delinquent felt to be of essentially normal or disturbed character may well be incarcerated in a manner appropriate to a criminal-like delinquent when all other solutions to his case are foreclosed. This occurs in the following case, for example, where reform school remains as the only alternative after a delinquent kicked out of his own home messes up a placement arrangement:

> In the case of Ralph Robinson, both judge and probation officer emphasized how much the mother was to blame for the boy's behavior, feeling that she was very "disturbed" and "disoriented." But he was disturbed also, and hence could not be placed in the same home with

his mother. In addition, the mother was insisting that the court get rid of the boy. Originally the court had worked out a placement for the boy at the Roberts School, but he had run away from there and they could not get him back in. In the face of this situation the court felt compelled to commit the boy to the YCA. As the probation officer stated: "There's nothing else we can do." The boy could not stay at home and had messed up the court's effort to place him. Under these circumstances the only thing they could do was send him to the Youth Correction Authority, even though they did not feel the boy was potentially or actually criminal.

Thus, when a case comes to be characterized by a certain degree of "trouble," the court tries to mobilize additional resources on its behalf. If this can be done successfully, incarceration is avoided. But if it fails, the youth is then threatened with the possibility of commitment to reform school. Such commitment is not automatic, however, for if an initial "placement" cannot be worked out, the case is reevaluated in light of the alternatives of keeping the youth "on the street" or institutionalizing him. It may be decided that the youth is of such character that it is safe to "gamble" on letting him remain in the community. But again, it may be decided for any of a variety of reasons unrelated to moral character that it is impossible to let him return to the community, and the court may therefore order his commitment.

In a certain sense, then, incarceration follows from the inability to mobilize more desirable or preferable resources on behalf of a case. It is here that the court's operations are fundamentally affected by contingencies of social class, for the higher social classes are better able to mobilize the desired resources and hence to avert commitment which would otherwise result (Cicourel, 1968, pp. 273ff) . For example:

A distinctly upper-middle class teenaged girl was brought to court for shoplifting. The judge referred the case to the clinic, which reported that the girl was disturbed and that her offense had been a gesture aimed at obtaining psychiatric care. The girl's family knew many psychiatrists, and she even babysat for psychiatrists' children. When the case returned to court, the complaint was dismissed on the condition that the girl undergo psychiatric treatment on a private basis. Her

family was able both to find a psychiatrist willing to provide therapy
and to bear the costs of such therapy.

In this case both money and connections are crucial in obtaining
the kinds of resources needed to get the court to agree to let the
case drop. In the following instance, money alone is able to prevent certain commitment to the Youth Correction Authority:

> A 15-year-old white boy whose mother was a well-paid nightclub singer
> had constantly appeared in court, accumulating a long record. But
> when commitment to the Youth Correction Authority seemed immi-
> nent, the mother and the boy's probation officer began negotiations to
> send the boy to a private military-like school in a neighboring state,
> with the mother to pay the relatively high fees involved. Even while
> admission to this school was being arranged, the boy got into several
> more scrapes with the law, but these were tolerated by the court until
> everything had been worked out with the school and the boy sent
> there.

Finally, case outcomes may not exactly reflect judgments of
moral character because of the juvenile court's inclination to
"make do," i.e., to exert only the minimally adequate effort and
resources toward dealing with cases. The effects of "making do"
are particularly striking where a delinquent comes to be regarded
as hopelessly criminal yet not dangerous in character. In such
circumstances, despite criminal character, the court perceives no
need for restraint and incarceration. Its concern is then merely to
mark time until the youth passes into the jurisdiction of adult
authorities. For example:

> The judge commented on a 17-year-old white girl in court for prosti-
> tution, a girl the clinic had diagnosed as "one hundred per cent socio-
> path": "This little girl today, she's hopeless. . . . Absolutely no con-
> science. She couldn't have cared less about being in here. We couldn't
> do a thing for her. . . . The best you can hope for in a case like this is
> to put it on probation and let it go. That's all you can do. She's
> completely indifferent about it."

In practice, however, only girls of criminal-like character are considered so unthreatening as to permit this kind of response.

Almost without exception hard-core delinquent boys are felt to be dangerous and hence in need of restraint.

In conclusion, assessment of a delinquent's moral character does not necessarily determine his fate at the hands of the court. But this assessment does play a fundamental role in the process, since it provides the framework within which the court constructs its definitions of what is going on and hence shapes its decisions about what course of action is called for. As a result, actual case outcomes reflect the interplay between assessments of moral character and practical contingencies affecting what has to and can be done about the case. An assessment of moral character may proceed independently of the negotiation and implementation of the disposition associated with that assessment. But it does set the conditions on which the court initially seeks to carry out these negotiations and implementation efforts. Again, success or failure in implementing these decisions leads to reassessments of moral character, as an initial version of moral character must be reconsidered in light of new alternatives. Thus, constant interplay between definitions of what the case is about (moral character) and negotiated case outcomes marks the progress of delinquency cases through the juvenile court.

CONCLUSION

This chapter attempted to reconstruct the general framework within which the juvenile court disposes of its cases. In so doing, the process may have been made to appear somewhat more rational and distinct than it is in fact. For the court tends to grasp cases "all at once"—as wholes—without weighing independently all their separate elements. What, for purposes of analysis, has been pictured as temporally segregated may actually occur simultaneously. Moreover, there is a provisional and tentative quality about judgments of "trouble" and moral character. For moral character is not determined permanently and irrevocably at any one time. Rather, an initial assessment holds "until further notice" (Schutz, 1962), subject to revision as circumstances and issues change while the case moves through the court.

5

The Dynamics of Categorization:
Establishing Moral Character

The previous chapter described the categories employed by the juvenile court as it processes cases, categories based on judgments of moral character. The next two chapters analyze the ways in which particular cases are determined to belong in one of the available categories.

Moral character is not passively established. It is the product of interaction and communicative work involving the delinquent, his family, enforcers, complainants generally, and the court itself. Specific versions of moral character must be successfully presented if they are to be adopted by others (Garfinkel, 1956). Officials, who play the dominant role in this process, both directly communicate their opinions of the moral character of the youth involved and more indirectly make selective reports of incidents and information pertinent to the court's evaluation of this character. In general, the version of moral character finally established is negotiated from among these presented "facts," opinions, and reports.

Two sets of processes affect the court's estimate of moral character. On the one hand, the concerned parties present versions of moral character. On the other, the delinquent may attempt to affect the outcome of this presentation through use of protective strategies. This chapter analyzes presentation processes and Chapter 6 analyzes protective strategies.

PRESENTATION STRATEGY:
PITCHES AND DENUNCIATIONS

Character-related presentations are inextricably linked to issues of disposition. For moral character is established in the process of negotiating a disposition of a case from among the various expectations and demands of the parties involved. In this process, the court determines an outcome not by balancing the relative merits and demerits of possible disposition alternatives, but by attempting to establish a correspondence between a youth's moral character and a particular alternative. As a result, issues of disposition lead to contests over moral character, and parties to these contests, who seek to influence the outcome of a particular case, have to marshal and present evidence to establish a version of moral character appropriate to their desired outcome.

Since the judge is the ultimate decision-maker, such presentations are usually addressed to him, although similar presentations regularly occur more informally outside the courtroom. Thus, a policeman seeking to convince a probation officer of the validity of his version of a youth's moral character or a probation officer trying to establish his view of this character for a psychiatrist or public defender face management and presentation problems similar to those encountered in successfully establishing a delinquent's moral character before a judge.

The practical necessity of marshalling and presenting evidence to convince another of the validity of a particular version of moral character and of the disposition it implies is clearly illustrated in the following case:

> Rodney Knight, a 16-year-old Negro boy, was accused of stealing a handbag from a woman in a subway station. The police told of the arrest, and complained that the boy had given them "difficulties," particularly by using false names, address, and age. The probation officer recommended that Knight be held in county jail under $1,000 bail until the hearing. The judge reacted: "My only problem is the county jail. I can understand the $1,000 bail for this crime—it's serious enough to warrant it. But I'm curious about the recommendation of county jail." Probation officer replied that the boy had a previous record for

use without authority at the municipal court. In addition he had been "uncooperative—information limited" with the police. Judge: "Let me put it this way: Is this something that in your opinion could not be handled at the YCA [Detention Center]?" Probation Officer (hesitating) : "It's a problem of either the one or the other. (pause) I think that possibly the YCA is more of a picnic grounds." Judge: "Are you making this recommendation because of his uncooperativeness, or because of some knowledge you have of his previous conduct?" Probation officer replied that he knew nothing about the boy's prior life and conduct. But another probation officer reported that the municipal court had told him that Knight had not done well while on probation there. The arresting policeman again told of how much trouble the boy had given them.The judge finally agreed to county jail, but with considerable reluctance.

Here police and probation officers have come to share a common assessment of the youth as criminal in moral character, with the probation officer recommending a correspondingly punitive course of action (detention in the adult county jail) . The judge, however, questions this proposal and probes for material about the youth's moral character that could justify it. Such material is provided by the second probation officer in a report of a prior period of probation, which both reveals previous court contact and indicates a "bad attitude" of long standing.

Management problems in the presentation of moral character can be more or less acute, depending on the relationship between proposed character and expected disposition. Cases are settled against the background of what is the "normal" disposition for "cases of this kind," i.e., for delinquents of this kind of moral character. Where the disposition of a case appears routine and unambiguous—where there is no question about the right and proper way to handle the case—moral character is established almost incidentally during the course of the hearing. In part, the proper disposition is obvious because indexes of moral character are similarly unambiguous. Management problems in presenting moral character are accentuated, however, where there is uncertainty or disagreement about what to do with a case. Uncertainty may arise because the delinquent's moral character is unclear, disagreements because of different assessments of that character.

In such situations, evidence must be presented to establish either what moral character is in this particular case, and hence what the proper disposition is, or that one's version of moral character is a tenable one and hence what previously appeared as the appropriate disposition is no longer adequate.

In these terms, there are two substantive types of character presentations. First, the presentation can be directed toward obtaining a more lenient disposition than would initially seem appropriate. In the words of court personnel, such a presentation, depicting character in a favorable light, constitutes a *pitch*. For example, if a probation officer, lawyer, or social worker wants to keep a delinquent with a long record "on the streets," he must present a picture of the sterling qualities of the youth's moral character, both to convince the judge to go along with the proposal and to provide the court with evidence to justify its leniency. Second, one may seek a more severe disposition than could be anticipated by presenting evidence that tends to soil and discredit character. Such a presentation will be termed a *denunciation* (see Garfinkel, 1956, p. 421).

Pitches generally involve attempts to establish character as normal, denunciations as criminal. In certain circumstances, each may involve efforts to establish disturbed character. On one hand, a pitch may present disturbed character in order to obtain psychiatric care as an alternative to otherwise unavoidable commitment to reform school. On the other hand, presentation of evidence of disturbed character may seek basically to discredit a delinquent. Establishing disturbed character may therefore involve either a pitch or a denunciation.

With regard to denunciations, it should be noted that requests for relatively severe dispositions arise at regular junctures in the organizational processing of delinquency cases. Denunciations occur almost routinely in many cases because of the interest of both complainants and probation officers in maximizing their control over a delinquent. Thus, police will undertake denunciations in an effort to get a youth placed on probation rather than merely "continued without a finding." Similarly, probation officers may make denunciations in order to get the judge to place a delinquent on a suspended sentence rather than on probation. In

ESTABLISHING MORAL CHARACTER

both cases denunciation furthers crucial work concerns, serving to obtain closer supervision and control over cases.

A more extreme form of denunciation arises, however, when an official tries to get a delinquent incarcerated. Such a disposition is inherently nonroutine simply because the court regards it as the most extreme reaction to a case, a "last resort" to be undertaken only with great caution. Thus, denunciations initiated in order to obtain a commitment to the Youth Correction Authority are aimed at *totally* and *fundamentally* discrediting moral character, at establishing character as unequivocally and irredeemably of a kind to warrant such a severe sentence. *Total denunciation,* in other words, involves communicative work seeking to establish a correspondence between a delinquent's moral character and that of the kind of person for whom incarceration is an inescapable measure.

Total denunciations regularly come from two sources. First, they are a recourse open to probation officers for dealing with probationers who have spoiled character (see Chapter 8). Second, for a variety of officials outside the court, total denunciation represents a necessary step in ridding caseloads of troublesome cases. In each instance, total denunciation involves an attempt to "dump" a case considered extremely undesirable and burdensome.

Although pitches and denunciations seek to establish diametrically opposed versions of moral character, of necessity they employ similar techniques, focusing on the same critical areas. One such area is the delinquent act, in that it provides the court with crucial evidence for its assessments of moral character. The second area involves the delinquent's general behavior, including his personal and social background. Here the successful establishment of moral character demands construction of a biography out of these materials that is consistent with the proposed version of character. The following two sections will consider each of these areas and some of the presentation problems they involve. Briefly, it will be argued that a successful denunciation will (*a*) establish that the present act is of a kind typically committed by a delinquent of criminal-like character and (*b*) construct a delinquent biography that unequivocally indicates someone of such character.

Conversely, a successful pitch will seek to depict the act as the typical product of a normal actor and thus to establish the normalcy of the youth's biography.

In addition, in constructing a biography, both pitches and denunciations must also concern themselves with the delinquent's "family situation," since the moral character of the youth's family is also subject to evaluative inquiry, with reference not only to biography but also to the issue of reputable sponsorship. A consideration of family evaluations and some problems of sponsorship will lead into an analysis of the special features of total denunciation.

PRESENTATION TACTICS: THE OFFENSE

Court personnel approach and understand delinquent acts in terms that indicate the actors' moral character. As a result, the manner in which an offense is presented to the court may critically affect subsequent assessment of character and disposition of the case.[1] Therefore, a denouncer's or pitchmaker's success depends in part upon his ability to shape and influence the court's understanding of particular delinquent acts. Some basic tactics in this presentation process will be analyzed, following a description of the general framework within which the court understands delinquent acts in organizationally meaningful terms.

Typical Delinquencies

Court personnel regularly deal with a recurring sequence of delinquent acts. In this activity, they come to make certain characterizations about routinely encountered delinquencies and delin-

---

1. Matza has argued that the delinquent offense and its seriousness are reinstituted as a concrete guide to disposition in the juvenile court because of the ambiguity and inclusiveness of the "principle of individualized justice" in this respect (1964, pp. 124ff). But as will be shown here, the delinquent act also retains fundamental significance for the juvenile court as a shorthand means for inferring the moral character of the youth involved.

quents. A given delinquent act is understood in terms of these characterizations; that is, its organizationally relevant meaning derives from its membership in a known class of "typical delinquencies." Typical delinquencies are constructs of the typical features of regularly encountered delinquent acts, embodying the court staff's previous experience with and common-sense knowledge of the situations and setting of delinquent acts.[2] The following comments made by probation officers illustrate the substantive nature of several typical delinquencies:

> *Boy shoplifters:* "Usually it's a very mild type of boy. There are not many seriously delinquent boys." Generally no previous record. Often from "well-to-do families" and taking goods "for kicks." "Usually they're pretty nice children. They give you no trouble." Seldom in court again. "Usually they're not thieves at heart. They're in the store and they succumb to a beautiful display or something that looks good to them."

> *Handbag snatchers:* "These are generally pretty seriously delinquent boys. They're known to other courts or on parole. . . . They're either probationers or parolees. Very aggressive delinquent boys."

As constructs of the ordinary and expected features of delinquent acts, typical delinquencies indicate *the kind of actor* typically involved. This process reveals several dimensions:

1. Typical delinquencies identify typical actors in terms of such *social characteristics* as age, sex, class, and residence.

2. Typical delinquencies provide explanations or "reasons" for the particular delinquent act, including but not limited to the actor's *immediate motives*. These are not incidental but an inher-

---

2. The concept of "typical delinquency" is the juvenile court equivalent of the concept of "normal crime" employed by Sudnow (1965) to analyze the operations of a public defender's office. "Normal crimes" are constructs held by public defenders which indicate "the typical manner in which offenses of given classes are committed, the social characteristics of the persons who regularly commit them, the features of the settings in which they occur, the types of victims often involved, and the like" (1965, p. 259).

The term "typical delinquency" will be used in preference to "normal delinquency" to avoid confusion with those delinquent acts typically committed by youths of *normal character.*

ent and central part of the construct.[3] Thus, a typical motive for a handbag snatch is of the following nature: "Most of them are doing this to get a little stake to get out of the home or to get out of town." Similarly, a middle-class girl shoplifter typically steals because of peer-group pressure at school, a lower-class shoplifter because of need.

3. Beyond typical motives, typical delinquencies also identify the kind of typical actor in terms of *moral character,* because they include a picture of the kind of youth who is apt to be involved in this kind of performance. Implicit in the following comments on "use without authority," for example, is a judgment of the moral character of the kind of delinquent typically involved:

> "Kids (in for "use without") work out pretty well on probation. . . . Usually aside from this one weakness they're the nicest kids. They're good at home, behave in school—they wouldn't steal a dime. . . . Usually they're pretty nice type kids. Easy to work with." [4]

In contrast, "handbag" cases typically involve actors of criminal-like character—"very aggressive delinquent boys."

Since each typical delinquency implies an actor of a certain kind of moral character, typical delinquencies as a whole may be grouped into one of three classes depending on whether they imply actors of normal, criminal, or disturbed character. However,

3. While not emphasized, such motives seem basic to Sudnow's normal crimes. Note the very explicit "explanations" in terms of motive contained in the following comment by a public defender on child molesters (Sudnow, 1965, p. 259):

> "These sex fiends usually hang around parks or schoolyards. But we often get fathers charged with these crimes. Usually the old man is out of work and stays at home when the wife goes to work and he plays around with his little daughter or something. A lot of these cases start when there is some marital trouble and the woman gets mad."

4. As this comment suggests, typical delinquencies also prescribe the appropriate *reaction* to make to such an actor in line with the anticipated future outcome of the case. These features stand out even more sharply in the following comments by a probation officer about normal girl shoplifters:

> "I don't see them any more [after the hearing]." They are given continued sentences along with a lecture by the judge, which frightens some of them. They are required to send in their report cards and write a letter from home about what they are doing until the continuance ends and the case is dismissed. "A lot of those from the suburbs are like this."

it must be emphasized that typical delinquencies so classified *crosscut particular formal offense categories*. Typical delinquencies in fact describe the features of "familiar" social performances and situations routinely encountered *within* a given legal offense category. Hence, a single offense category may include a number of typical delinquencies, each implying an alternative version of moral character.[5]

To consider a concrete example, the court recognizes three distinct social events as possible occurrences within the formal offense category of "assault." On the basis of the implied moral character of the actors involved, these can be termed typical normal, criminal and disturbed assaults. First, a typical normal assault involves a "fight" and highlights the following features of the delinquency situation: the scene is usually a street; the combatants are children, usually boys but sometimes girls; fists or weapons picked up in the heat of battle are the rule; both parties appear to have contributed to the incident. In such cases, while there may be fairly serious injury, the "offense" itself is considered minor, growing out of an often childish disagreement between youths well known to each other. "Fights," then, are perceived as natural incidents usually involving normal actors.

Second, an assault may involve circumstances that indicate

5. Comparison here with the categories of "normal crime" Sudnow has described in the operation of the public defender's office is instructive. "Normal crimes" follow the formal offense categories, grouping within each such category a number of different social situations. Sudnow reports that the "normal child molester" category, for example, encompasses both "middle-aged strangers" who hang around parks and school yards, and "lower class middle-aged fathers" whose wives have accused them of playing around with a younger daughter (1965, pp. 259, 260). This classification reflects basic organizational contingencies of public defense. Briefly, in determining that a given case reveals the features of a normal crime, public defender and prosecutor agree that it is appropriate to employ a set "recipe" to guide the reduction of the initial charge in return for a guilty plea (Sudnow, 1965, pp. 262–64). Categories of normal crime, then, embody *equivalences of culpability* that warrant invoking formulas of complaint reduction as part of the process of obtaining the defendant's "cooperation" in pleading guilty. The juvenile court, however, responds to cases on the basis of common moral character, not of equivalences of culpability for a particular act. Thus, in distinguishing between different kinds of moral character, typical delinquencies differentiate between character-relevant types of illegal performance that would be grouped within one guilt-relevant category of normal crime.

criminal character. Such criminal assaults involve attacks on strangers and nonpeers with robbery as the apparent motive. Criminal assaults are typically "muggings," where a lone male, often a drunk or homosexual, is grabbed, roughed up, and relieved of his money by a small group of older, tough delinquents, in a public but deserted area. Criminal assaults are often described as "vicious"; they are regarded as extremely serious, for potentially they involve murder.

Third, typical disturbed assaults occur without apparent robbery motives, but generally in similar settings. The victim, previously unknown and not robbed, is assaulted for no apparent "reason." Here the violence may be interpreted as an irrational outburst of aggression or hostility. Disturbed assaults too indicate viciousness, often even more dangerous because of its gratuitous and unmotivated nature.

Finally, when court personnel describe the typical handbag snatcher as of criminal character and the typical "use without" as of normal character, this does not mean that only delinquents of such character commit these offenses. Rather, such statements reflect recognized *frequency distributions* of typical actors within particular offense categories. For example, when handbag cases are held to involve "pretty seriously delinquent boys," the court indicates that it expects *most* handbag snatches to involve criminal-like as opposed to normal or disturbed delinquents. Similarly, although the court may distinguish typically normal, criminal, and disturbed shoplifters, to characterize "shoplifters" as "easy to work with" indicates that most shoplifting incidents will involve delinquents of normal character.

In summary, by determining that a particular delinquent act is typical of a certain class, the court embeds the act and its author in its common-sense knowledge of delinquency situations.[6] Thus the court is able to understand the act and to assess the character of the actor. The court makes its initial formulation and carries

6. Gluckman has described a similar use of constructs of typical patterns of wrongdoing by Barotse judges in weighing evidence and deciding cases. He notes: "There are social stereotypes of how thieves, adulterers, and other malefactors act. If the witnessed actions of a defendant assemble into one of these stereotypes, he is found guilty, though the judges prefer direct evidence to convict" (1955, p. 359).

through its response to the case in these terms. Consequently, typical delinquencies, although identified in terms of offense categories (e.g., shoplifting, assaults, handbags), actually distinguish between typical actors of different moral character, motivation, and future potential.

Distinguishing between Typical Delinquencies

Efforts to establish moral character are fundamentally constrained by the nature of the categories of typical delinquencies. Someone committed to a particular version of moral character must demonstrate that the present act reveals features belonging to the class of typical delinquency that implies an actor of that moral character. To consider the example of an offense of assault: denunciation requires demonstration of the features of a typical criminal assault (a "mugging"); a pitch, those of a typical normal assault (a "fight").

It should be noted that there is an inherent selectivity in what gets reported about offenses in the juvenile court, a selectivity that can make highly problematic the nature of the court's ultimate interpretation of any given offense. For the meaning of delinquent acts emerges only from secondhand reports on "what happened," and such reports involve an inherent "truncating" of the original fullness and complexity of the event (Cicourel, 1968, passim.). For example, in one case the police reported in the courtroom that damage done to the complainant's car windshield was not consistent with a shot from a BB gun (p. 159). This report greatly influenced the court's verdict of not delinquent. However, in conversation after the hearing, this policeman noted that the damage was consistent with a pellet from a "pop gun." By withholding this information the policeman completely transformed the court's perception of "what happened" in order to obtain the outcome he desired.[7]

7. In following this course of action, the officer seemed guided not so much by dislike of the complainant-"victim" as by a desire not to "interfere" (and hence have the court interfere) in what he regarded as strictly a personal feud between two families.

If court determination of "fact" is susceptible to modification in this way, the significance it attributes to an act for an actor's moral character is even more subject to the influence of truncated reports. In particular, very minute details of what took place during and after the offense can determine in what class of typical delinquency an act will be placed. Some of the possibilities here emerge in the following case:

> Two older girls who had run away from home and been caught shoplifting in a department store claimed they had spent the night in a doorway. The judge seemed reluctant to accept this story, and asked the arresting officer if the girls had been "clean" when he caught them. The policeman said no, and added that the blond girl had been wearing eye make-up and had her hair done up.

Here it can be noted that a typical normal runaway by girls involves staying away from home and living on the streets for a day or two following a family argument. This fades into a more criminal-like runaway, where the girls become involved in prostitution. Hence it becomes critical to determine where the runaways spent the night, and the court routinely questions runaways about this and other topics pertinent to living "on the streets." The answer here that the night was spent in a doorway arouses the judge's suspicion. He then attempts to gauge the nature of this runaway episode by asking the police officer about the girls' appearance at the time of arrest (on the assumption that had they indeed stayed in some doorway they could not stay "clean," while if they had been in an apartment somewhere they would have). The policeman's answer is ambiguous in this respect, since he reports that they were clean, but that one girl was heavily made up, a possible indicator of prostitution. Nonetheless, the circumstances of this inquiry clearly suggest how one minute aspect of a report may shape the perceived nature of a delinquent act (i.e., determine the class of typical delinquency in which it will be placed).

This case suggests, then, that establishing the typical nature of any particular act involves not only demonstrating the coincidence of its features with those of the desired class, but also *dis-*

tinguishing these features from those of classes implying actors of other forms of moral character. For example, assaults may indicate typical actors of either normal, criminal, or disturbed character. To establish that a particular delinquent is of criminal character, a denouncer must demonstrate not only the features of a typical criminal-like assault, but also the absence of features indicating normal and disturbed assaults.

Given this requirement, one can analyze act-centered procedures for establishing moral character by identifying those dimensions of typically understood acts that are employed to distinguish actors of normal, criminal, and disturbed character. Or again: analysis can focus on the qualities of an act that make it seem criminal (or disturbed or normal) to court personnel. In brief, it can be suggested that the court assesses as criminal those delinquent acts carried out in ways that evince *a high degree of commitment to illegal activity*.[8] Normal acts in contrast indicate a fundamental commitment to conventional life styles and norms. A number of indexes are routinely employed by the court to gauge these kinds of involvement.

In the first place, stealing becomes the product of a normal actor where its purpose can be made to appear as personal gratification of some immediate need or desire characteristic of children. Normal shoplifting, for example, involves theft of a single item of minor value but with distinct appeal to youth. Objects of normal shoplifting should reflect the social value of consumption, possessing primarily display and ornamental value for the taker. Girls should steal clothes, cosmetics, records, etc. With normal boy shoplifters: "You seldom see them take expensive things—expensive rings, cameras." Rather they steal clothes, sports equipment, candy, and the like.

A normal "use without" is similarly perceived in terms of immediate personal gratification. Cars are the recognized center of teenaged social activity. Thus it is understandable that boys without cars might steal one, enjoy it, and ditch it. As a probation officer described this conception of "joy-riding": "It means

---

8. This is indicated by the very language used by court personnel; they often speak of "involvement" in delinquency, making such statements as: "There seems to be some involvement here."

nothing. The kid just takes the car for a drive around the block. He probably doesn't even think of it as stealing; he thinks of it as just borrowing the car for the night."

In contrast, stealing appears criminal where it reveals qualities that suggest a basic or continuing commitment to illegal activity. More concretely, where the purpose of the act suggests that theft is a way of making a living, and not of merely obtaining immediate personal gratification, criminality is assessed. In shoplifting, for example, theft of nonchildish goods distinguishes the criminal for the normal delinquent. The case of a 14-year-old Negro boy who appeared in court for stealing three expensive dresses from a small women's store illustrates this perspective. To the court, this act suggested that the child had been sent into the store by an adult with a list of items to steal.

Similarly, "use without authority" becomes criminal in nature where the evident purpose is not "joyriding," but something of a more instrumental nature. Any indications that the car is to be kept permanently, or sold or passed on to another party, tend to indicate a high degree of involvement in a criminal way of life.

A second indication of commitment to illegal norms and lifestyles is a delinquent's willingness to cause injury and harm to others in achieving his illegal end. In these terms, an act becomes criminal when it appears that the actor intentionally risked "serious consequences" in committing it. Any act involving violence appears criminal because violence is regarded as too disproportionate a means for achieving even an illegal end. Most shopliftings tend to be seen as normal, for example, because they involve little or no harm and risk. Handbag thefts, however, are usually criminal, since the act of knocking over a little old lady to take her handbag displays a willingness to steal no matter how serious and harmful the consequences.

In extreme form this willingness to disregard possible serious harm to others makes a key contribution to the quality of "viciousness" in delinquent acts. A vicious act shows a complete and needless disrespect for the safety, rights, and lives of others while pursuing illegal ends. Such a delinquent is felt to lack all social and moral *conscience;* his actions appear completely unrestrained. "Viciousness," then, evidences commitment to illegality for its own sake, and vicious acts come to represent the prototype of criminal activity.

Both pitches and denunciations must deal with the intentional harmfulness of delinquent acts. Denunciations must highlight the great harm resulting from the act. Where no harm actually occurred, emphasis must be placed on the great likelihood that it would have but for some chance factor or outside intervention. More important, harmful consequences, whether actual or only potential, must be made to appear intentional. For such demonstrated intent links the harm directly to the actor's character. In many offenses this occurs almost inevitably: in an armed robbery, for example, a high risk of danger and injury appears inherent in the delinquent's intended act. It is for this reason that such an act seems intrinsically criminal to court personnel. Under these circumstances the burden of proof is on any pitchmaker to demonstrate the act's normalcy. In this situation the pitch must isolate the act's dangerousness from the true character of the delinquent, generally by mitigating his responsibility for it. These possibilities are illustrated by the following comments on a youth who shot a man in the course of a holdup and subsequently tried to commit suicide:

> The judge noted that the basic problem he had to consider was the danger the boy might pose to the public. This judgment in turn depended on whether the clinic psychiatrists interpreted the shooting as part of a wider pattern of dangerous personality traits. For example, if the psychiatrist told him that the boy had shot because he was "afraid," "that he didn't mean to do it," and that it was not likely to happen again, he would be willing to "take a chance on him" and not transfer the case to the criminal courts.

However, other kinds of offenses do not appear dangerous or harmful. Shoplifting and car thefts are of this character. Here the burden of proof shifts to the denouncer. Often a kind of commonsense parallel to the tort doctrine of criminal negligence may be employed here. For example, the police may increase the discrediting implications of stealing a car by describing the culprit's driving as extremely hazardous, noting very high speeds, great risk-taking, and actual damage that resulted. Moreover, emphasis is routinely placed on the fact that such driving occurred in the deliberate attempt to escape police pursuit. In so presenting car theft (in itself harmless) as deliberately reckless, a kind of substitute connection is established between possible serious harm and the youth's intentioned activity.

Finally, the technique and style used in committing a delinquent act provide the court with important indicators of the degree of involvement in and commitment to criminal as opposed to normal life-styles. In the first place, the use of professional or sophisticated techniques for committing the offense suggests both exposure to criminal ways of doing things and criminal purposes. The court closely attends to the use of special tools or instruments or of expert knowledge in the commission of a crime. In this way, for example, the court inquires into the techniques of car theft, for use of a master key rather than "popping" the ignition indicates a criminal rather than a normal typical delinquency:

> A 13-year-old Italian boy was charged with use without authority. The owner had not left the key in the car, and at the station the boy admitted using a master key to get the car going. He claimed he had found the key, with several others, in a plastic bag near a local church. The judge questioned the youth very closely about how he had started the car, and where he had obtained the keys. The boy continued to maintain that he had found them. Finally the policeman volunteered: "It was my understanding that he was seen in the company of two other boys in the same parking lot earlier that night. But he's keeping it all to himself."

Similarly, in the following case of "breaking and entering," possession of "professional" burglar tools completely undermines the lawyer's attempt to present the offense as inconsequential act of a normal delinquent:

> A 16-year-old Negro boy was accused of trying to break into a church social center at night. The night watchman there had heard him and called the police, who had caught him on the roof with wirecutters and other tools in his possession. The judge looked these over carefully. The police reported: "He said he had been drinking and did not know how he got up there. . . . He wouldn't say anything."

The judge found the boy delinquent and asked for the probation report. PO noted that the boy had been committed to reform school on a school complaint, had been in trouble several times there, but had been released when he turned 16.

Public defender then made his argument on behalf of the boy. He indicated that the boy had been into no trouble for nearly three years. Probation officer interrupted to say that this was not quite true, since there had been several recent parole violations. Defender continued: "I think this is another case of idle hands where this boy has nothing to do. I—" Judge: "Idle hands? How can you say it's a case of idle hands when he went out buying these tools? These are professional tools. It's not just a kid breaking into a place with a crowbar. These are professional tools. . . ."

Professionalism can also be indicated by the technique used to commit the offense. In handbag thefts greater criminal expertise is indicated when the purse-snatcher comes up suddenly from behind and surprises the victim. Approaching from the front may warn the victim and increase the chance of identification. Thus a psychiatrist wondered whether a boy he was evaluating "came up and grabbed them from behind, like a pro, or from the front."

Greater criminal involvement is also indicated by evidences of planning and preparation for the act. In the breaking and entering case described above, for example, the burglar's tools indicate not only professional technique but also fairly extensive preparation. Similarly, in handbag cases, evidence that the victim had been followed from a bank in order to increase the chance of getting a large sum of money indicates a criminal-like actor.

In contrast, delinquencies that give the impression of unplanned spontaneity and impulse suggest normal character. If the act appears as the product of a whim, of an inability to resist temptation, normal character is generally assessed. Shoplifting is particularly susceptible to this kind of interpretation, and is easily presented as an impulsive submission to immediate wishes and desires for something otherwise unattainable. There is also a strong sense of irresistible temptation in the concept of joyriding, both in the expectation that new, fast cars will be taken, and in the emphasis given control through prevention of temptation (e.g., "do not leave the keys in the ignition" campaigns). Again, typically hard-core handbag cases may be reconciled with normal character where it appears that the victim was a chance selection, and the attempt carried through in an inefficient, offhand, and haphazard manner.

This sense of spontaneity may also be heightened if the delinquency appears to be a product of group activity. For example, a spontaneous handbag snatch may be explained as resulting from the uncontrollable nature of a gang of kids loose on the streets. The presence of a group of youths in a stolen car strongly supports a "joyriding" interpretation of the act. Similarly, in the following case, an incident of fire setting (one of the main signs of a disturbed child) that occurred during an incident of school vandalism is not necessarily seen as indicative of disturbed character:

> Five young boys, ages 9 to 11, four Negro and one white, were charged with "wanton destruction" of public school property. Juvenile officer explained that the fire department had been called to the school one night and put out a fire in a second-floor closet, discovering considerable vandalism in a nearby classroom as well. Police had eventually got two boys to admit they had broken into the school, and these two had implicated the other three, all of whom still denied either going into the school or starting the fire. Judge devoted some time to questioning the boys trying to determine who had in fact been there (see pp. 160–61). He expressed very little interest in the fire, who had started it, or why. Rather he seemed to see the incident as involving a wild group of younger boys loose in the school.

In general, adolescents are assumed normally to engage in a certain amount of illegal activity. Preparation and planning become important signs of criminal-like character because they directly contradict this common-sense view of adolescent impulsivity and susceptibility to temptation. But in addition, careful planning and preparation indicate that the youth gave long and thorough thought to committing the offense. This tends to contradict any presumption that he "did not know what he was doing," that because of youthful innocence or ignorance he understood neither the meaning nor the consequences of the act. Depiction of acts as carefully planned and rationally executed events, therefore, helps establish the criminal character of the delinquent. Conversely, presentation of acts as spontaneous, spur-of-the-moment occurrences shapes assessment of character as normal.

Finally, several comments may be made on the qualities of delinquent acts that establish them as the product of a disturbed actor. Normal and criminal acts share a certain kind of *rationality*, both in that the purpose is acquisitive and the means employed, although illegal, are effective for realizing that end. Acts that can be made to appear without these qualities indicate disturbed character.

Thus, behavior tends to be considered "bizarre" if it does not materially benefit the actor. For example, "fire setting" by youths appears as a senseless and meaningless act to court personnel, since there can be no "rational" motive for a child to burn something down (e.g., he cannot collect insurance). Again, interpersonal violence that serves no rational purpose suggests disturbed character. Such violence seems unprovoked and gratuitous. For example, the judge described an assault case where he committed the assailant for psychiatric observation in the following terms: "This guy was just walking down the street and he hit him with a sidewalk brick and walked away." (He made no attempt to rob him.) Violence also becomes gratuitous where it seems more extreme than necessary to realize the purpose of the act:

> Two Negro boys, both 13, were charged with assault and armed robbery. Police stated the two had gone into a small chic store in an avant-garde shopping area and demanded money from the woman owner who had been there alone at the time. She had refused; the boys had grabbed her arms and hit her with a cast iron door stop. She fell to the floor, the boys took money from the cash register and left. Victim had identified the two boys at the hospital. Boys were initially held in high bail in detention, but the one judged the leader was sent to the Children's Mental Hospital for observation soon afterwards.

These conceptions of "bizarre" behavior reflect a general utilitarian bias underlying the court's ideas of wrongdoing. For one's basic rationality is not suspect as long as one's misdeeds clearly serve to produce some useful gain, particularly in material terms. Rationality appears suspect, however, if behavior that violates the law is undertaken to express emotion, feeling, or impulses, to demonstrate competence, or to show rebellion. This view assumes that the costs of violating the law are too high for any kind of behavior except that which is rational, utilitarian and materialistic in underlying purpose.

It may be added that while delinquencies committed without planning and on impulse suggest normal character, situations where the delinquent fails to carry through with a number of elementary precautions against detection and apprehension indicate disturbed character. For example, court personnel felt it to be a sign of mental disturbance that two boys made aggressive sexual advances to a woman teacher in the street before witnesses. For it is assumed that any rational actor, whether criminal or normal, will attempt to conceal delinquency where possible, and will either avoid detection or attempt to escape when detected. One factor confirming the essentially irrational and disturbed character of an attack on a schoolteacher by a retarded boy was the fact that he stayed at the scene of the crime, making no effort to run away (see pp. 92–93).

PRESENTATION TACTICS: BIOGRAPHY

Both denunciations and pitches must move beyond the presentation of the delinquent act, placing that act within a general framework that suggests the delinquent actor's place within the sequence of stages of a typical delinquent career. This is accomplished by constructing a biography that locates the delinquent and his offense within this developmental pattern.

A denunciation seeks to place the delinquent at or near the ultimate stage of this career, that where the case comes to be characterized as "hopeless." In a hopeless case commitment to delinquent and criminal activities is seen as irrevocable. There is no perceived likelihood or even possibility of change (reform) in the delinquent—he cannot be "saved." As a probation officer described one such case: "Springdale [the maximum security prison] is the only place."

In contrast, a pitch requires demonstration of some rehabilitative potential, of the inconsequentiality of the youth's delinquent involvement. To accomplish this, a pitch must construct a biography that shows that the youth is likely to grow out of or reject his misbehavior. In routinized form this involves showing that the youth is a "good kid," i.e., possesses normal character despite behavior suggesting otherwise.

There are two general processes employed in locating a delinquent in relation to an unfolding career. First, the current offense must be placed in relation to a *general pattern of behavior,* a pattern of consistently criminal-like conduct in the case of denunciation, of normal conduct in the case of a pitch. Second, the delinquent actor must be located in reference to wider social factors considered typical of the appropriate stage of career development. The most critical of such factors is the delinquent's family situation.

Finally, it should be emphasized that the need to establish the instant act as part of a wider pattern and the possibility of insulating character from the implications of even serious delinquent acts derive from cultural attitudes toward children. Cultural expectations about what is normal in the behavior of children show considerable latitude. The child is seen as an incomplete being who lacks inner control, discipline, and knowledge. Consequently he is easily tempted into misbehavior. A relatively high degree of deviation from appropriate behavior is tolerated with the expectation that the child will naturally "grow out of it." Thus, children are insulated from the implications of their misbehavior. For example, a certain amount of "adolescent conflict" with parents is seen as part of the normal process of growing up. So are problems in school, sexual curiosity and even experimentation, fighting, and other tests of masculinity. In general, youthful misbehavior can be accepted without implying anything out of the ordinary.

Establishing a Pattern

The most reliable way for a denouncer to connect a current offense with a general pattern of delinquent behavior is to present a history of prior delinquency. This process is highly routinized and may require no effort on the denouncer's part, since almost the first step the court takes in dealing with a case is to check into previous court record. Even before an accused delinquent is arraigned the probation officer calls the Board of Probation to determine whether the youth has had contact with courts anywhere in the state. Report of a prior record will fundamentally influence the court's subsequent assessment and handling of the case. Particularly where the youth has a lengthy record (even of minor offenses) or conviction for one or two serious offenses, movement toward serious criminal activity is inferred. Perhaps the most damaging of all possible items is prior commitment to the Youth Correction Authority, for this indicates to the court that some official has previously decided that this delinquent constitutes a "hopeless case."

In addition, court personnel are very much aware that lack of an official record does not necessarily mean that the youth has not been involved in recurring delinquent behavior. The court recognizes that enforcement agencies routinely exercise wide discretion, that juvenile officers, for example, frequently send kids home with only "a kick in the pants," taking no official action. The denouncer who can bring up instances of such unreported delinquent activities may therefore establish a general pattern of delinquency despite the lack of an official prior record.[9] These reports of unofficial delinquency constitute denouncers' primary weapon for shaping court assessments of moral character. Requiring some "inside" knowledge not part of any official record, these incidents can be brought forward to establish a general pattern at the discretion of the denouncer.

Reports of unrecorded "trouble" can be particularly telling where they indicate propensities toward violence and dangerousness. For example:

9. This produces a definite bias against lower class delinquents. The probation officer relies on his informal contacts with local officials, particularly with the police and the schools, in order to obtain reports of such unofficial delinquency. But these contacts are confined largely to the lower class, inner city districts where the probation officer regularly works. Therefore, he is cut off from such informal sources of information on delinquents from suburban areas, which provide almost all of the middle class cases received by the juvenile court.

The principal of the Harris School brought a complaint against a 15-year-old Negro boy, Jeremiah Taylor, for threatening him and several teachers with a knife during an incident in the schoolyard. No one had been injured, and the boy had surrendered the knife in return for his record player, which a teacher had been keeping in the schoolroom.

After the principal's description of the incident, the judge asked him how long the boy had been at the school (one year) and whether he had been a discipline problem (yes). Judge: "Has he assaulted any other boys during this time?" Principal: "Not to my knowledge." But he had been in constant trouble, and had been expelled from his former school for twice threatening to stab a teacher.

Following further inquiry the judge decided to hold Taylor at the detention center and have a psychiatrist from the court clinic examine him there.

In this case, reports of similar outbursts of hostile, threatening behavior in the past tended to accent the significance of the present incident, leading to decisions not to return the boy to the community and to seek a psychiatric diagnosis. Similarly, in the following case, moral character is established with presentation of a pattern of "dangerous" behavior:

A Methodist minister, who acted as Protestant court chaplain and who regularly appeared in court, approached several court officials on the case of a Negro boy. First he approached PO Manello and asked if he were going to give the boy a "good recommendation" in the disposition of his case scheduled for that morning. The PO avoided making a direct answer, pointing out that the boy was on parole from the YCA and the recommendation was to come from his parole officer. The minister then cornered this parole officer about the case, telling him: "Let him off. He's a good kid." PO: "I'm not going to. . . . He's got to go back. [Why?] He pulled a knife on a teacher." Minister: "So what? That was just a mistake. . . . You're not going to take him back, are you?" PO: "Yes, I am. He's giving everyone trouble. He's in everyone's hair." After further discussion, the parole agent added that he had it from a reliable source that the boy had a gun. Minister made no attempt to argue with this, and ended his efforts on behalf of the youth.

Here the court chaplain asks the parole agent to let the youth off, implying in his "good kid" comment that the current charge is merely an isolated and adventitious incident. The parole officer counters by emphasizing the seriousness of the incident (pulling a knife on the teacher) , by embedding the incident in a series of earlier and continuing "troubles" ("he's in everyone's hair"), and by demonstrating the real potential for even more dangerous criminality in the future (possession of a gun) . This denunciation, emphasizing past and future dangerous behavior and implying constant and disturbing trouble-making, discredits the youth's moral character, as a result cutting the ground out from any further attempt by the chaplain to "save" him from incarceration.

A pitchmaker in contrast will minimize the significance of prior "trouble." If possible he will point out that the youth has no prior record and has not done this kind of thing before. Where the delinquent does have a record, attempts will be made to reduce its impact by isolating it from the youth's general character and pattern of development. In presenting the delinquent as a "good kid," the pitchmaker tries to make misconduct seem an aberrant departure from an overall pattern of normalcy. Usually this involves depicting these acts as products of an earlier, temporary stage of development from which the delinquent has now begun to move. The transitory nature of such earlier delinquent conduct may be established by advancing an account that isolates it from the youth's dominant course of development: e.g., the death of a parent or suddenly learning of one's adoption led to psychological upset and hence misconduct. Similarly, in the following case, drinking was identified as the cause of an older boy's record for violent behavior:

> PO talked about a 16-year-old white boy [Irish] who had been involved in a drunken brawl and showed a record of similar episodes in the past. PO noted: "When he's not drinking, when he's in here, he's very passive—polite, pleasant, unassuming, mild." But he had a typical Irish drinking problem, becoming extremely violent and uncontrollable when he'd had a few.

Here excessive drinking is used to divorce and insulate violent behavior from the youth's moral character. For "drinking" represents an identifiable problem amenable to recognized forms of treatment; to depict the violence as a product of drinking rather than of character allows the violence to appear as atypical, as uncharacteristic of the youth's true nature and general behavior.

Another way of fixing a delinquent act as part of a more general behavioral trend is to document the existence of a "bad attitude" toward the legal order and its officials on the part of the delinquent (see Cicourel, 1968, pp. 222, 260). Reports of concerted resistance to legal authority, particularly to the police, suggests a "hard-core" delinquent youth to the court. To give the wrong name or a false age to the police, for example, suggests a criminally sophisticated delinquent trying to avoid being linked with a prior record. E.g., if he gives a false name, the police will find he has no record and hence be more inclined to release him as a "first offender" without taking court action. The same result is possible by giving an age over 17, for the police then check criminal instead of delinquent sources. But the delinquent also reveals his attitude toward the legal order in the apprehension process itself. Thus fighting with the police indicates desperation in wishing to avoid capture. Similarly, an obvious and concerted effort to escape the police is routinely reported in court in order to indicate a hard-core criminal mentality.

Similarly, reports of cooperation with the police may be introduced in such a way as to suggest that the delinquent's commitment to illegal activities is only occasional and partial. For example:

> Robert Hill, a 16-year-old Negro boy, was brought into court on a complaint of use without authority. In the courtroom the police officer reported that the boy had admitted stealing a 1965 Buick the previous evening. He had been caught and brought to the station this morning. He continued: "The boy cooperated and took us out and showed us where some other boys had hidden some of the stuff they took from the car. . . ." Everything had been recovered. On the basis of the probation officer's report that mother had been trying to get her son seen by a psychiatrist, the judge referred the case to the court clinic.

In this case, the officer's summary emphasized the youth's restrained and cooperative manner, providing evidence of a "good attitude" that supplemented other indications that this was not a hard-core delinquent.

Furthermore, a "bad attitude" may be demonstrated by the delinquent's conduct within the court system itself. For example, a denouncer may emphasize that a delinquent has a history of appealing juvenile court findings and dispositions, and perhaps even has a number of appeals pending. Law enforcement personnel view a record replete with appeals as a sign of criminal sophistication and outlook; to appeal regularly is regarded as a ploy for avoiding one's due. With the backlog of cases on the calenders of the higher courts, appeals are never heard in less than six months, and in several instances were pending as late as one year after the juvenile court hearing. By appealing a sentence to the Youth Correction Authority, therefore, a delinquent can effectively avoid incarceration, staying "on the street" until his appeal has been heard. Moreover, he may escape entirely, either by passing beyond the age jurisdiction of the Authority (17) during this time, or by winning reversal of his conviction and/or sentence. In sum, to show that a delinquent routinely appeals court decisions provides evidence of a criminal-like attitude toward the court process and hence of a general pattern of criminality. For it shows the youth too knowledgeable of the technicalities and loopholes of the legal system.[10]

A further expectation concerning a delinquent career is that it will manifest itself in "trouble" at school. Reports of misbehavior in school therefore may establish a particular delinquent offense as part of a wider pattern of illegal behavior. The significance attributed to behavior in school is apparent in the following comment:

> Probation officer noted that "severe cases" had to be dealt with severely, and I asked her how she decided whether a case was severe. PO: "Late hours, stubbornness, resentment to the parents, 'D' in conduct."

10. In a similar vein, delinquents who go to great lengths to obtain an aggressive private attorney instead of relying on the public defenders (i.e., delinquents from poor families who would normally be expected to use the public defenders) are regarded as overly sophisticated in the ways of the criminal law and hence criminal-like in character. In both instances, insistence on one's legal rights is seen by court personnel as a ploy for avoiding one's due and as a challenge to the court's considered judgment of what should be done with the case.

'C' in conduct was on the border: if the girl told her she got it for whispering, then it usually was not serious and could be passed over. Sometimes the parents had been called to the school, which was also a bad sign.

The court expects youths headed toward a career of serious delinquency to have "problems" in school and probes for reports of misbehavior in the classroom or on the school premises. Reports from school officials that a youth is a "troublemaker" or a "discipline problem" can be particularly discrediting.

Furthermore, truancy may provide evidence of a trend toward serious delinquency, particularly when the youth persists in this behavior. Truancy not only suggests that the youth is a "low achiever" and a behavior problem at school, but also indicates that a great deal of his time is being spent without control and supervision by adults. When youths stay away from school, the court anticipates that they will go around with a tough group of friends and get into trouble while wandering the streets. For example, it is felt that girls who truant are apt to become involved in further kinds of delinquency:

> Most say they go over to a friend's house during the day. "Some say they walk the streets all day. Then you ask them, did you come in town? Because this could lead to shoplifting or something like this."

Reported association with companions of bad reputation may also be used to establish a general pattern of delinquency which discredits moral character. Association with those possessing soiled reputations is a primary, court-recognized "cause" of delinquency. Inquiry into this subject is routinized on the probation face sheet where parents are asked about the youth's "associates." The police, particularly juvenile officers, may also inform probation officers about the membership and escapades of quasi-delinquent groups. Finally, judges routinely inquire into friendships, and frequently warn delinquents to "stay away from" friends regarded as bad influences:

associating with wrong crowd.

> Henrietta, a bulky Negro girl of 16, appeared in court on an incorrigible child complaint. The juvenile officer presenting the complaint

mentioned that the girl's mother had been "having trouble with her for some time," that she had been staying out late at nights, and that "she is palling around with a girl I sent to Mattonville [reformatory for girls] two years ago." Judge asked mother about her problems with the girl, then called Henrietta over and questioned her about her behavior. In the process he asked: "What about those friends you're going around with? Why pick those friends? . . . The officer tells me one of them is a former inmate of the girls' reformatory."

It should also be noted that the juvenile officer characterized the older girl as a "known lesbian," and added that she had been staying in a hotel in the "combat zone." To the court this clearly suggested the possibility that the incident involved prostitution and not merely an innocent runaway case.

Similarly, a probation officer noted that two boys in on a narcotics charge were not really bad kids, but were getting into trouble because:

> "they're always floating down to the Bolt Square area where there're a lot of undesirable and disreputable if not actually criminal companions. That's the major thing. . . . They're hanging out at one or two places with a pretty bad crowd—Georgie Porgie's or the poolroom."

Finally, a pitch may emphasize a delinquent's good (or even merely adequate) record in school to demonstrate an overall pattern of conforming behavior and hence normal character. If a youth has left school, a pitch may point out the delinquent's success in getting and holding a job, or even his intention to enlist in the armed services when old enough to do so. In each case, the pitch seeks to establish the viability of some conventional career path, in contrast to that into serious delinquency. In this the delinquent is pictured as having seen the error of his ways and as seeking to lead an upstanding life, despite the setback represented by the latest offense.

Family Background and Sponsorship

The construct of a delinquent career includes not only a general pattern of delinquent behavior, but also the presence of those family circumstances that are seen as causing serious delinquency. To establish moral character requires that one demonstrate the presence or absence of these circumstances.

Juvenile court personnel assume that "something wrong in the home" is a cause and a sign of a future delinquent career. This assumption appears in purest form in cases of parental neglect ("care and protection" cases, which if successful give custody over the children involved to the state), but also occurs in many strictly delinquency cases. For as the chief probation officer argued: "Delinquent kids are usually neglected anyway." In either case there exists a "bad home situation," that is, a home where the parent is felt to be unable or unwilling to provide the kind of attention, supervision, and/or affection a child needs to develop normally. If nothing is done in such a case, it is felt, the child will grow up uncared for, uncontrolled, and perhaps even warped in personality by the treatment received at the hands of his parents. Under such circumstances, the court feels obliged to intervene in order to correct the situation and prevent the probable drift of the youth into increasingly serious delinquent activities.[11]

However, a "bad home situation" may not only indicate a possible delinquent career, but also serve as an "excusing condition" for delinquency. That is, a pitch may point to a bad home in order to expand the framework within which the delinquent and his act are viewed. This obscures the individualistic moral standards generally imposed by the court, presenting the youth as not responsible or to blame for his behavior in general, and hence excusable at least in part for this particular wrong (see pp. 153–55). It should be noted that a bad home situation must appear beyond the level regarded by the court as normal if it is to

11. This finding, in conjunction with those reported earlier in this chapter, support the argument advanced by Matza (n.d.) that tables used to predict delinquency, particularly those developed by the Gluecks, reproduce the standards and indicators actually employed by juvenile courts and other officials to identify "real delinquents." Matza isolates parental neglect, behavior in school and with friends, and troublesome, predelinquent misconduct as the substantive items in the Gluecks' predictive tables. This analysis has shown that these are exactly the indicators attended to by the juvenile court as evidence of the general pattern of a delinquent career.

be acknowledged as an excusing condition. The more extreme and severe the youth's deprivation can be made to appear, the more likely it and its wider framework will be honored by the court, holding offense equal.

However, a pitch may also rely on the existence of a "good family." Such a family in fact constitutes the reliable and reputable *sponsor* desired by the court when it deals leniently with delinquents.[12] For this reason, denunciations may seek to discredit the moral character of a delinquent's parents, for this not only establishes that the youth's family situation as the kind that typically produces serious delinquents but it also undermines the acceptability of the family as sponsor.

Again, where a youth's family situation is bad, a pitch is often facilitated if the pitchmaker can advance a sponsor to serve in place of the discredited parents. Such a sponsor, generally a social worker or minister, commits himself to assuming personal responsibilty for the youth's behavior, both directly in terms of control and more indirectly in involving him in desirable programs or activities. The court, in fact, is extremely anxious to acquire reputable sponsors for delinquents under its control, and frequently takes the initiative in suggesting that the person making the pitch assume the role of sponsor. Acceptance of the proposal for leniency is often made contingent upon his so doing. In the following case, for example, a social worker managed to "save" a delinquent regarded as fundamentally criminal in character by making a firm commitment to the role of sponsor:

James Thornton, a 16-year-old Negro boy, was found delinquent for use without authority after a full trial. Private defense counsel then made a long statement on disposition, arguing that James had "real family problems," and lived under great tension, but "is not completely on the wrong track" and had been working regularly. He then introduced a social worker, Ellen Ruth, as someone firmly committed to working with the family and with James. Ruth, a woman in her early 30's, told the judge that James should be taken out of the local neighborhood where he was handicapped by his reputation as a trouble-

12. On the concept and role of sponsorship in juvenile courts, see Matza, 1964, pp. 125–28.

maker and be given "residential treatment." James did have great potential. Ruth suggested that he be sent to a camp during the summer while attempts were made to arrange this kind of treatment.

The judge reacted with great skepticism to this proposal: "I don't know why I should change my mind. I thought he should be committed six months ago, three months ago, and I think he should be now. . . . I see no other course for this boy." However, he then questioned Ruth about where she would find residential treatment for the youth. Ruth said she would try Family Service and Child Welfare. Judge responded: "You won't get it, but I'm willing to let you try," and continued the case for several weeks to see what arrangements Ruth could come up with.

In sessions over the next several months, Ruth reported on the progress of her placement efforts. Eventually, by getting her agency to agree to finance placement, she obtained tentative acceptance of the boy at a private residential school, to begin in the fall.

In sum, the court's assessment of the delinquent's moral character is fundamentally shaped by the reports made of his family situation. Reports of "good" behavior in the home from parents who favorably impress court staff make a crucial contribution to an assessment of normal character, while reports of "trouble in the home" and a "bad home" are considered reliable indicators of abnormal character.

Cicourel has argued that judgments made by probation officers and other court personnel about the quality and stability of a delinquent's family situation are fundamentally biased against the lower class. He contends that middle class families both provide the model for what home life should be and are better able to maintain the appearance of such a home than lower class families (1965, pp. 39*ff*; 1968, pp. 243*ff*). Juvenile court personnel, however, do not recognize only middle class values regarding family life. Dealing almost entirely with lower and lower-middle class families, they come to recognize important distinctions between family life within these classes. For the juvenile court the crucial difference lies not between middle and lower class families, but between the family life of the respectable and the "disreputable poor" (Matza, 1966). Court staff will readily acknowledge that a single Negro mother receiving welfare, for example, can provide a "good home" for her children. In assessing the worth of a family situation, therefore, the court does not look for middle class values and forms (e.g., a working father in the home, an intact marriage, etc.) so much as forms and values that distinguish the respectable from the disreputable poor. Hence, a mother who maintains control in her home, who disciplines her children properly, making sure they go to church and school regularly, and who tries to keep her children and apartment clean and neat will favorably impress court personnel despite being on welfare. In contrast, the mother who drinks, lives with a series of men, has too many children, and makes no effort to keep up appearances, will be condemned as someone producing a breed of criminal-like delinquents.

Finally, while Cicourel argues that middle class families have the financial resources that can be used to curtail contact with legal agencies by providing alternative solutions (1968, pp. 273–91), it should be noted that the juvenile court often relies on lower class kinship ties as an equivalent kind of resource. That is, while the middle class family can pay for psychiatric therapy or tuition at a private boarding school, lower and lower-middle class families possess a richer set of kinship relations upon which to draw in order to come up with some solution acceptable to the court. Thus, many delinquency cases are handled by having the youth go live with relatives in some other area. Negro youths, for example, are sometimes sent "down South" to stay with relatives as a solution to their delinquency.

THE PROBLEM OF ATYPICALITY

Act and biography, both understood in typical terms, are resources routinely used to establish moral character. At times, however, these routine procedures do not work: act or biography, or both, are ambiguous, and moral character remains obscure. This occurs when the act cannot be established as a member of any class of typical delinquencies and when biography does not reveal the typical patterns expected of a delinquent "of this kind." In these circumstances, other techniques are employed to establish moral character.

First, consider typical delinquencies. In most cases, the typical qualities of acts are readily apparent to all. But in others, the offense is not so clearcut; it is too ambiguous or confused to determine its typicality. Atypical qualities become noteworthy and lead the court to make further inquiry into moral character. Initially atypical qualities elicit more intensive study of the circumstances of the act in order to determine what is going on. Where this fails, the court seeks an alternative method for assessing moral character. One recourse is appeal to some outside knowledgeable source, as in the following case:

> Two Puerto Rican boys, ages 13 and 14, were brought into court for shooting a BB gun across a public way. They had been apprehended by chance; four policemen cruising by in a police car had noticed them on the roof of a project firing the gun. Probation officer then reported that both boys had been in court once before, both on larceny from parking meters; the complaints had been dismissed after successful probation. Judge then asked the priest accompanying the families and serving as interpreter (also well known at the court, as head of the local Spanish center) : *"Basically, what kind of boys do we have here?* I have not seen them before." Priest replied: "I think we have a *boyish bit of foolishness here*. These boys are not guilty of malice. . . . It's a case where they arrive home and there is not a great deal of supervision, at that time." [Emphasis added.]

Although the weight of evidence supported a "fooling around" interpretation, the fact that the boys had prior records (robbing meters suggested a certain experience in the ways of the street) at least implied that something more "serious" might be involved. Since the judge could not infer moral character from the act, he sought a direct assessment of character from a reliable outside source.

A second alternative when faced with an atypical or ambiguous act is to turn to expert psychiatric opinion in the court clinic in order to assess moral character. For example:

> A Negro boy reportedly tried to commit suicide while in confinement in the county jail. He was immediately returned to court and sent

down to the clinic for an interview with a psychiatrist. The psychiatrist reported to the judge later that morning, and it became clear that the major question for both was whether the suicide had been really intended or was just a "gesture." Psychiatrist reported that the boy had not really wanted to kill himself, but might have done so because he was so impulsive and anxiety-ridden. This analysis eventually led to a decision to detain the boy at the YCA Detention Center until the date of his trial.

Here confusion centers on which of several possible "motives" was actually operative. The facts of the case seemed to indicate that the boy's motive in his suicide attempt had "really" been to kill himself. But he was being held in an adult jail, which suggested a motive for wanting to get out. His act could thus be seen as "gesture" for attention and leniency. The clinic suggested that the suicide attempt was in fact "real."

Similarly, cases do not permit easy categorization in terms of moral character where biography does not show those features typical of a delinquent "of this kind." Moral character remains obscure where biography is not consistent with (able to account for) the kind of actor implied by the delinquent act understood in typical terms. In practice, such a discrepancy between the implications of act and biography usually occurs where the typical delinquency appears to be that of a criminally inclined actor, yet biographical material consistent with this expectation is lacking. Often there is a strong suspicion of disturbed character in cases of this kind. The solution, however, is to refer the case to the court clinic for psychiatric evaluation and assessment of character. For example:

A 16-year-old white boy was brought into court for stealing a number of bottles of perfume from a drugstore. His record revealed that within the last eight months he had been in court on a number of larceny and drug complaints. In fact, he was due in another court the next day on a charge of "possession of harmful drugs." PO also commented that he had been a good student in school, but had left when he turned 16. Since then had not been working.

Judge asked the boy's mother: "He got A's and B's in school and then quit?" Mother: "Yes, a year ago." Judge: "And he has not been working?" Had been helping an uncle repair his house. Judge: "How long has this drug business been going on?" Mother: "I don't know, your honor. I just found out about it."

After defense lawyer's argument, the judge found the boy delinquent and committed him for 35 days' observation to a local mental hospital.

In this case, then, moral character remains ambiguous because of the discrepancy between sudden but severe delinquent involvement and a prior good school record and apparently favorable home situation. The suddenness of the change seems to suggest mental disturbance to the judge. Again, the inconsistency of doing well in school while continually engaging in delinquent activity appears in the following case:

During the afternoon, the judge and a probation officer gossiped about the case of a boy who had been in court that morning and whose case was referred to the clinic.

PO: Did you see the record on that King kid?

Judge: There's something screwy there—getting A's and then starting to steal everything in sight. There's something wrong there.

PO: He's been into everything.

Judge: The father's got problems too. . . . As soon as I mentioned the words "psychiatric care" he got really upset. . . . He's got problems too.

In general, to turn to outside sources essentially involves soliciting assertions about moral character, relying on their surface reasonableness and the reputation of the asserter for their warrantability. Referral of cases to the clinic may both elicit new information and material for character assessments and introduce new (psychiatric) vocabularies and perspectives for describing character.

The problems posed by atypicality further reveal the reciprocal character of the relationship between act and biography on the one hand and moral character on the other. For not only do act and biography provide resources used to determine moral character, but also when moral character is established the act and biography become clarified as typical of that kind of actor.

For example, where the nature of an act is in question, this problematic quality can be dispelled by directly establishing the moral character of the actor. As in the above suicide case, a given quality of moral character may define the nature of the act (i.e., the clinic felt that because the youth was anxiety-ridden, he could have actually killed himself).

This process occurs in extreme form where moral character determines not the nature of the act, but the even more basic question of whether the accused actually committed it in the first place. For example, in a few cases where acts of very unusual nature were alleged, the judgment that the accused committed the act hinged on the clinic's determination that he was of such character that he *could have* committed it:

> A 16-year-old boy had been implicated in a brutal, homosexually tinged murder. The court referred him to the clinic for psychiatric evaluation, and he was seen several times by two psychiatrists. One fundamental focus in their interviews was whether this boy possessed the psychological make-up of one who could commit such an act, particularly if homosexuality and a "panic reaction" were involved.

In sum, moral character and its indicators exist in a fundamentally dialectical relationship: for act and general patterns of behavior that constitute a biography are ultimately "explained" as a product of a certain kind of moral character, but also provide important evidence as to the nature of this very moral character.[13]

---

13. In this respect, delinquent act and moral character are related in the same dialectic way as any "document" and the "pattern" it is felt to indicate. As Garfinkel argues:

> Not only is the underlying pattern derived from its individual documentary evidences, but the individual documentary evidences, in their turn, are interpreted on the basis of "what is known" about the underlying pattern. Each is used to elaborate the other (1967, p. 78).

In the juvenile court, once moral character has been established, not only are the delinquent's past acts reinterpreted in the light of this character and its typical motives, but also all present and future behavior will be attended to in these same terms. They will be seen as motivated by the typical motives of this kind of actor.

A NOTE ON TOTAL DENUNCIATION

Consideration of the structural features of total denunciation provides additional insight into the processes of establishing moral character in the juvenile court. For a successful total denunciation must transcend routine denunciation by *foreclosing* all possible defenses and by *neutralizing* all possible sources of support.

Foreclosure of defenses available to the delinquent (see Chapter 6) has two related elements. First, in order to discredit moral character totally, it must be clearly demonstrated that the denounced delinquent has been given a great many "breaks" or "chances" which he has, however, rejected and spoiled. Such a demonstration is necessary to prove that the case is "hopeless," that the delinquent youth's character is so ruined as to preclude any possibility of reform. The role of the disregarded "chance" is clearly seen in the following case, where a probation officer convinces both judge and public defender to go along with his punitive recommendation by proving that the youth has received chances not even officially reported:

> Two escapees from reform school were brought into court on a series of new complaints taken out by the police. Public defender argued that these complaints should be dismissed and the boys simply returned to the school. The probation officer, however, argued strongly that the boys should be found delinquent on the new complaints (this would require reconsideration of their cases by the Youth Correction Authority, perhaps leading to an extension of their commitment). The probation officer described how one of his colleagues had worked hard on one of these cases earlier, giving the boy a great many chances, none of which did any good. The judge accepted the probation officer's recommendation.
>
> After the hearing, the public defender admitted that he felt the probation officer had been right, acknowledging the validity of his picture of the character of this boy: "I did not realize he was such a bastard. . . . Apparently one of the probation officers had given him a lot of breaks. He had him on so many cases that he should be shot."

Second, it must be made to appear that the delinquent himself "messed up" the chances that he had been given. It should be established not only that the youth misbehaved on numerous occasions, but also that he did so in full knowledge of the possible consequences and with no valid excuse or extenuating circumstances. In this way, responsibility or "fault" for the imminent incarceration must fall completely on the denounced delinquent. Any official contribution to the youth's "messing up" (e.g., an official's intolerance) must be glossed over so that the delinquent bears total blame.

Court probation is in fact constructed so that responsibility for "messing up," should it occur, unavoidably falls on the delinquent (see pp. 237–38). Probationers are constantly warned that they will be committed if there is any further misconduct, and they are given a number of "breaks" on this condition. As one probation officer commented about a youth who had been "given a break" by the judge: "This way, if he gets committed, he knows he has it coming." Furthermore, the constant warnings and lectures against getting into trouble that occur throughout probation tend to undermine in advance the possibility of defending subsequent misbehavior. For example, it is difficult for a youth to excuse a new offense as the product of peer group influence when he has continually been warned to stay away from "bad friends."

A second key element in a successful total denunciation is the neutralization of all possible sources of support. There are several components in this neutralization. First, the assessment of discredited and "hopeless" character must be made to appear as a general consensus among all those concerned in the case. A delinquent without a spokesman—with no one to put in a good word for him—stands in a fundamentally discredited position.

Here the stance taken by the delinquent's lawyer, normally a public defender, becomes crucial. A vigorous defense and pitch by a lawyer often might dispel the appearance of consensus and weaken the denunciation. This occurs very rarely, however, because of court cooptation of the public defender. Working closely with the probation staff, the public defender comes to share their values and indexes of success and failure in delinquency cases. Consequently, he will generally concur with the court's highly negative assessments of delinquent moral character. As a public defender noted in response to a question about how he usually handled his cases in the juvenile court:

> Generally I would find the probation officer handling the case and ask him: "What do you have on this kid? How bad is he?" He'll say: "Oh, he's bad!" Then he opens the probation folder to me, and I'll see he's got quite a record. Then I'll ask him, "What are you going to recommend?" He'll say, "Give him another chance. Or probation. Or we've got to put him away."
>
> But probation officers don't make this last recommendation lightly. Generally they will try to find a parent in the home, "someone who can keep him under control, someone who can watch him." But if the probation officer has given the kid a number of chances, it is a different story: "He's giving the kid chances and he keeps screwing up. . . . [Commitment will then be recommended.] And I say the kid deserves it. Before a kid goes away he's really got to be obnoxious— he will deserve it."

Adoption of probation standards for assessing delinquent character becomes crucial in total denunciation. The public defender is then in the position of arguing on behalf of a youth whose moral character has been totally discredited in his eyes and who he feels should indeed be committed. His courtroom defense will generally reflect this assessment. He will make only the most perfunctory motions of arguing that the delinquent be let off, and he will do so in a way that communicates an utter lack of conviction that this is a desirable course of action. Or, as in the following case, he will not even go through the motions of making a defense but will explicitly concur with the recommended incarceration and the grounds on which it rests:

> A policeman told of finding an 11-year-old Negro boy in a laundry where a coin box had been looted. The officer reported that the boy had admitted committing the offense. Public defender waived cross-examination, and the judge found the youth delinquent.
>
> Probation officer then delivered a rather lengthy report on the case. The boy had been sent to the Boys' Training Program and, while no great trouble, did not attend regularly. He had also recently been transferred to the Harris School and had been in trouble there. Proba-

tion officer recommended that the prior suspended sentence be revoked and the boy committed to the Youth Correction Authority.

Judge then asked the public defender if he had anything he wanted
to say. Public defender: "The record more or less speaks for itself. He
does not seem to have taken advantage of the opportunities the court
has given him to straighten out." Then, after briefly reconferring with
the probation officer, the judge ordered the commitment. Public defender waived the right of appeal.

Second, the denouncer must establish that in "messing up" and
not taking advantage of the chances provided him, the denounced has created a situation in which there is *no other alternative open* but commitment to the Youth Correction Authority.
In some cases, this may involve showing that the youth is so dangerous that commitment to the Authority is the only effective way
he can be restrained; in others, demonstration that by his misbehavior the youth has completely destroyed all possible placements,
including the one he has been in. It is only by dramatically
showing in these ways that "there is nothing we can do with him"
that the proposed commitment can be made to appear as an inevitable and objective necessity.

The fact that many total denunciations concentrate on proving
that nothing else can be done with the case reflects the court's
basic resistance to unwarrantable agency attempts to "dump" undesirable cases onto them for incarceration. The court feels that
most of these institutions are too ready to give up on cases that
from the court's point of view are still salvageable. To overcome
this suspiciousness, the denouncer must not only present the
youth's character as essentially corrupt and "hopeless," but also
show that every effort has been made to work with him and every
possible opportunity afforded him. The denouncer, in other
words, must take pains to avoid appearing to be merely getting
rid of a difficult and troublesome case simply to make his own
work easier. This requires showing both that persistent efforts
have been made to work with the case and that at the present
time even extraordinary efforts cannot come up with anything as
an alternative to incarceration.

A final aspect of demonstrating that there is no viable alternative to incarceration involves isolating the denounced delinquent

from any kind of reputable sponsorship. In the usual case, where a parent acts as sponsor, successful total denunciation requires either that the parent be induced to denounce the youth and declare him fit only for incarceration or that the parent be discredited. In other cases, where the sponsor is a parental substitute, this sponsor must similarly be led to denounce the youth or be discredited. In this way, for example, sponsors who seek too aggressively to save delinquents considered overripe for commitment by other officials may encounter attacks on their motives, wisdom, or general moral character. This not only undermines the viability of any defense of character made by the sponsor, but also effectively isolates the delinquent by showing the unsuitability of his sponsorship as an alternative to commitment.

6
The Dynamics of Categorization:
Defensive Strategies

While denunciations are an essential feature of court hearings, their outcome does not depend solely on the content and technique of the denouncer's presentation. The success or failure of denunciation also hinges on the nature of the response made by the denounced. Thus, a delinquent in the court setting can employ a number of strategies to try to stave off possible discrediting. Appropriate use of such *protective* or *defensive strategies* can crucially affect the court's assessment of moral character and hence its ultimate disposition of the case.

Innocence, justification, and *excuse* represent the three basic defensive strategies available to the delinquent in the court setting. In different ways each functions to neutralize or dissolve the discrediting implications of wrongful behavior attributed to the delinquent—including but by no means limited to the current offense. Innocence directly refutes the accusation by denying any actual link between actor and discrediting act. Justification and excuse both seek to erase and redefine the presumed wrongfulness of the alleged act. A justification advances some higher or competing value against that violated by the act. An excuse mitigates the actor's responsibility for conduct, in this way attacking the moral connection between act and actor.[1] In addition, the fact

1. This conceptual distinction between justification and excuse departs slightly from that of Scott and Lyman (1968). According to their analysis, in making a justification "one accepts responsibility for the act in question, but

that character is discredited in an interactional situation opens up the possibility of undermining the credibility of the denouncer as a means of defense. This final defensive strategy can be termed *counter-denunciation*.

The defensive strategies to be described in the following pages represent a localized set of *accounts*, as Scott and Lyman have described that concept; i.e., "a statement made by a social actor to explain unanticipated or untoward behavior," hence where "action is subjected to valuative inquiry" (1968, p. 46). In the juvenile court, accounts serve primarily to protect character and self, and only incidentally to preserve "fractured sociation." Different defensive strategies provide different degrees of protection to moral character. Some strategies provide complete defenses that totally exonerate the denounced party, while others constitute partial defenses, merely mitigating the effects of the denunciation. The claim of innocence, for example, represents a complete defense, while an excuse is always partial, leaving unchallenged the basic connection between actor and wrongful act. Justifications may vary between either extreme; some seek to redefine completely the wrongful quality of the act, others merely to reduce it to a lesser degree. Here it is significant that the court discourages use of complete defenses, generally refusing to honor them. In contrast, it pressures delinquents toward the use of certain partial defenses.

As will readily become apparent, these protective strategies re-

---

denies the pejorative quality associated with it." With an excuse "one admits that the act in question is bad, wrong, or inappropriate but denies full responsibility" (p. 47) . While this distinction may be adequate on an abstract level, it fails to describe accurately the actual use of justifications and excuses observed in the juvenile court. Within the concrete situation of defending conduct, to deny responsibility represents a partial claim that the act was not "really" wrong. That is, in reference to an actual situation, an act's wrongfulness derives from the actor's responsibility (in terms of intent and foreknowledge) for it. To claim that an "offense" resulted from *accident,* for example, is not only to deny responsibility but also to depict the act as something other than wrong. The act becomes wrongful in some sense because the actor knowingly intended it to be wrong. Hence, since both justification and excuse are attempts to counter presumed wrongfulness, justification is better identified as an assertion of contrary values, a dimension of justification upon which Scott and Lyman do in fact place great emphasis (1968, p. 51) .

fer to the same phenomena Sykes and Matza have described as "techniques of neutralization." Techniques of neutralization are seen as "justifications of deviant behavior," which, once learned by youth, make delinquent behavior possible by protecting the youth's self-conception against the implications of his misconduct. Such techniques include denial of responsibility ("I didn't mean it"), denial of the injury ("I didn't really hurt anybody"), denial of the victim ("They had it coming to them"), condemnation of the condemners ("Everybody's picking on me"), and the appeal to higher loyalties ("I didn't do it for myself") (Sykes and Matza, 1957, p. 669). While most of these techniques are considered in this chapter, the focus therein is on their use by accused delinquents as means of defending moral character before an official audience sitting in judgment over their fate. The assumption here is that no matter how a delinquent interprets or "rationalizes" his offense to himself, it is in his interest to present and justify it (and the self it can be taken to imply) in the most favorable terms possible to the court. To establish such defenses successfully before an often hostile and supicious audience requires the skillful use of various techniques of presentation—in short, requires a competent performance of the part of the delinquent actor involved. This analysis, then, considers some features of the successful staging, as well as the more formal content and characteristics, of such defenses against denunciation.

INNOCENCE

One defensive strategy, when denounced for delinquent behavior, is assertion of one's innocence, either technically or in fact. Assertions of factual innocence often confront the juvenile court with one of those rare occasions where it must determine the "truth." Such a situation arises when there are two conflicting factual versions of "what happened" presented to the court, with no confirming or refuting evidence available beyond the reports themselves. Here the court makes a choice between these "proposed competing facts by deciding that the (possible) fact is present for which there is an adequate explanation, and the (possible) fact is not present for which there is not an adequate explanation" (Sacks, 1967, p. 213). Consider, for example, the following case:

> A 16-year-old white boy, Joe Kennedy, was charged with car theft. Juvenile officer called as a witness the owner of the car, a 25-year-old man named Alvin Beaumont. Beaumont told of meeting the defendant and a friend outside a bar in the early AM on Saturday. They had driven around for a while, Kennedy driving the car. "We talked and agreed to entertain one another." Beaumont had been sitting between the two boys. He had suddenly been grabbed by Kennedy's buddy, had a knife put to his throat, and been forced to give up what money he had. The boys searched him, took all his papers, and decided to let him go home but to keep the car. They had dropped him off at a railroad station, but when he had been unable to get a train home, he had reported the car stolen to the police.
>
> Juvenile officer then told of apprehending the boy the next day, noting: "He said he did not steal the car; he was allowed to take the car." Kennedy himself then testified that he had been given the car, and that neither he nor his friend had carried a knife. The judge questioned this, concluding: "What were you doing at the Midnight [a well-known homosexual bar]?" Kennedy: "I went down to the Midnight." Judge: "Playing homosexuals, you mean." Kennedy repeated that he had been loaned the car for several weeks by Beaumont, and had his permission. Judge: "You want me to believe that a man you never met before just gave you an automobile?" Kennedy: "Yes, sir." Finally, Kennedy's father spoke up and defended the boy, saying the boy had told him that the car had been loaned to him, and talking at some length about how the boy was no trouble at home. But the judge found him delinquent, and gave him a one-year suspended sentence.

Here the judge determined the "truth" behind the incident by probing for an explanation or account of the fact alleged by the youth—that Beaumont had voluntarily lent him the car. The lack of any reasonable account for this undermined the youth's claim of innocence and hence led the court to accept as true the facts alleged by the complainant.

A delinquent defending himself on the grounds that he "did not do it" must be able to provide an adequate account for the facts alleged in support of this innocence. However, to establish innocence successfully often requires that the competing account seem at least comparatively unreasonable. Consequently, a defense of innocence has a greater chance of success if the accused can cast doubt on the reasonableness or adequacy of any explanation for the competing facts alleged by the accuser. In this respect the defense of innocence may come to involve a form of counter-denunciation, a strategy to be considered later in this chapter.

Under certain circumstances the explanations advanced for competing facts may appear equally probable (or equally improbable). One court response to this impasse is to seek a wider framework of explanation for the competing versions of "what happened," extending inquiry beyond the facts as presented into the moral character of those involved. That is, where the "truth" cannot be determined from the established facts or from the adequacy of the respective accounts for the disputed incident, it may be judged by the consistency between the moral character of each party and his behavior and motives as depicted in each version of the facts. For example:

A teenaged boy, with frequent contact with the court and regarded as somewhat "mixed up," charged that a couple had induced him to come up to an apartment and to perform a variety of sexual acts with the woman while the man watched. The unmarried couple, an elderly businessman and his younger secretary, were brought into juvenile court on charges of contributing to the delinquency of a minor. Their lawyer, in what he later contended was an attempt to avoid publicity, agreed to admit to the facts as alleged by the boy. The judge referred both adults for psychiatric evaluation, reserving his verdict.

Subsequently, both of the accused insisted that they were innocent of the charge against them. The psychiatrist eventually returned his evaluations of the couple to the court. Noting the lack of any psychotic or depressive symptoms in the man, he concluded: "This defendant does not represent the typical type of sexual offender that is found in this age group." He also described the woman as showing extreme guilt over an early sexual experience with another man that had led to an illegitimate child. This suggested that she was not likely to engage in the kind of behavior she had been charged with. Complaints against both defendants were dismissed.

In this case, the explanations for the competing versions of "what happened" offered no firm grounds for deciding between them. (I.e., there was no apparent reason why the youth should simply make up such an accusation, yet the charges involved actions totally out of line with the apparent respectability of the couple.) As a result, the court sought psychiatric assessment of the moral character of those involved, in this way determining that the accused couple's version was the "true" one. For the assessments made of their moral character destroyed the reasonableness of the youth's explanation of his alleged facts: particularly given the psychiatric conclusion that the woman was strongly repressed sexually, the only reasonable explanation for the "offense" (sexual promiscuity and exhibitionism) could hardly be maintained.[2]

In general, assertions of factual innocence are evaluated against what is known about the moral character of the accused. In the following case, for example, the undoubted criminal-like character of the delinquent involved led the court to reject his defense without hesitation:

> A 16-year-old Negro boy with a long and serious record was implicated in a stolen car. The police testified that they had captured the boy after a long foot chase, but could not say that they had seen him either in the car or jumping out of it when it stopped. The boy claimed he had been walking home when the stolen car stopped and three boys jumped out and ran. When the police had started shooting to stop them, he ran too. All the male probation officers had assumed, as soon as the boy was brought into court, that he he had committed the act charged, and felt his version was an outright lie. And after the testimony, the judge immediately found him delinquent.

Again, the youth's established criminal-like character undermined all warrant for his claim of *coincidence* (i.e., by chance he

2. Furthermore, in this case the accused had to provide an account not only for what they claimed was the false charge against them, but also for their initial behavior in court which seemed to acknowledge their guilt. By way of providing this second account they claimed that they had not wished to contest the charge, seeking to avoid publicity in order to get the case disposed of as quickly and quietly as possible.

was near the spot where the stolen car was deserted) as an account for his innocence.[3]

Finally, the defense of innocence must be exercised within the limits imposed by court norms of what constitutes reasonable evidence of guilt. Hence, while many delinquents do persistently claim that they "did not do it," it can be very damaging to do so in the face of what the court regards as overwhelming evidence to the contrary. In such cases the delinquent will be subject to considerable pressure to change his stance in the face of an apparently "open-and-shut" case. The public defender, for example, may insist that a client not rely on a story that he and the court consider "ridiculous":

A 16-year-old white boy was identified by two people as having left an accident involving a stolen car. Represented by Public Defender Scott, he insisted on basing his defense on an alibi, supported by a friend, that he had been fishing at the time. The judge rejected this alibi and found the boy delinquent on the complaint of use without authority. Afterward the lawyer characterized the whole hearing as "ridiculous" because the boy had tried to defend himself with such a trite and unbelievable alibi. He had tried to talk the boy out of relying on his fishing story, but to no avail. Similarly, when the boy had been interviewed at the public defender's office (to prepare the defense), Scott had really torn into the story, asking the boy, "Who do you expect to believe a story like that?" But the boy would not change it.

In sum, the assertion of innocence represents an effective stance only so long as the evidence of the case remains inconclusive

3. The reverse of this process may also occur, however. In the following case, for example, the fact that the police felt a youth to be of normal character led them to believe him incapable of committing a criminal-like delinquency:

A tall, 16-year-old Negro boy was accused of having stolen the handbag of a 79-year-old white woman while she had been coming out of the subway. The police felt that the woman had wrongly identified the boy, informing the judge that she had changed her identification of the clothing worn by the culprit when confronted with this boy. They also noted that they had received reports of three other suspicious Negro men in the area at just that time. The judge dismissed the complaint.

After the hearing I talked to the juvenile officer who had handled the case. He repeated several times that this kid just was not the type to steal a handbag and knock over a woman: "He wouldn't take a handbag."

enough not to contradict it. To maintain one's innocence under other circumstances, particularly where there has been an official validation of guilt, appears to court personnel as an unrepentent rejection of culpability and serves only to discredit moral character.[4]

JUSTIFICATIONS

If a delinquent has conceded committing the alleged act, he may turn to the strategy of justification, seeking to challenge the presumed wrongfulness of the condemned behavior in the name of other values. Actions initially defined as wrongful may be justified in two general styles. On the one hand, the denounced person can advance what can be called *principled justification*. Here one depicts the act as an attempt to realize some absolute moral or social value that has precedence over the value violated by the act. The emphasis falls on the universal relevance of this value or principle. Sabotage may be justified on principle, for example, as a necessary means to overthrow an immoral and unjust social system. Obviously principled justification directly challenges the validity of the violated norm and hence involves clear-cut opposition to the legal and moral order supporting this norm.

The fact that no such principled justifications were observed in the juvenile court probably reflects the high degree of consensus governing delinquent and criminal acts. At the time of the study there was no expressed disagreement about the wrongful nature of most delinquent acts and no articulated set of higher values to which to appeal in order to offset this assumed wrongfulness. However, the recent rise of militant black power groups in the

4. The *Yale Law Journal* study of the guilty plea found that some judges were particularly antagonized by what they considered to be "frivolous defenses" in connection with the not guilty plea. As it noted: "The view was expressed that a defendant faced with overwhelming evidence of guilt who presented a frivolous defense in a desperate gamble to sway a jury deserved additional punishment." As one of the judges responded: "No person should ever be given a longer sentence because he insists upon a trial unless it is apparent that he is guilty and is just attempting to win an acquittal at any cost" (Comment, *Yale Law Journal*, 1956, pp. 217–18).

ghetto may change both conditions. The future may well hold more frequent resort to principled justification as a defense for many delinquency charges brought against black youth.[5]

Delinquents may also seek to justify their conduct in a much more muted and indirect way, employing what might be called *situational justifications*. Here the delinquent seeks to reverse or dilute the imputation of wrongdoing by showing that the act was proper, or at least permissible, *given the contingencies of his actual situation*. A recent analysis has highlighted this basic dimension of justification by noting:

> Justifications recognize a general sense in which the act in question is impermissible, but claim that the particular occasion permits or requires the very act (Scott and Lyman, 1968; p. 51).

The techniques of "denial of injury," "denial of the victim," and "appeal to higher loyalties" (Sykes and Matza, 1957) are almost always used as justifications in this situational sense. Thus, a youth who steals a car may implicitly justify his action by suggesting that although it was against the law, in the particular circumstances no one was injured by it. Again, a youth charged with stealing a car from a homosexual attempted to reduce the wrongfulness of the offense by highlighting its concrete circumstances, particularly the homosexual activities of the victim. Finally, certain offenses may be justified by invoking other values as relevant in the concrete situation, for example, the right of self-defense or perhaps retaliation in charges of assault growing out of fight situations.

Again, many justifications are advanced implicitly with the assertion of values tied to the immediate contingencies of the delinquency situation. For example, a delinquent's accounting for car theft with "we wanted to go to the game" justifies this conduct in

5. Reichstein and Pipkin (n.d.) report only one justification out of 203 appeals by college students facing suspension because of low grades. They attribute this to consensus on the validity of the grading system and to a strategic interest in not prejudicing the outcome by attacking a major premise of the current academic system. These authors also suggest that justifications may become more frequent in this situation as radical students increasingly challenge traditional college practices.

terms of convenience and immediate need, clearly expressing a judgment that the act itself was not particularly wrong. Values of peer group solidarity or of spontaneous self-expression may similarly justify other delinquencies as permissible in that particular situation. However, such situational contingencies, advanced in implicit justification of the behavior, are only rarely honored in the juvenile court. Such justifications are almost uniformly denied legitimate status and systematically opposed by the reassertion of absolute standards. Hence, in response to the delinquent's claim that his act was permissible in the particular circumstances of the offense situation, the court tends to reassert the absolute relevance of the value violated by the offense. In this way it is difficult to get even this muted kind of justification honored in the juvenile court.

It should be emphasized, however, that delinquents seeking to justify their behavior in these situational terms are generally trying only to mitigate and not to dissolve totally the wrongness of their conduct. For example, justification by the claim of self-defense or retaliation against prior wrong does not completely exculpate the delinquent, but merely shifts part of the blame onto the other party. Moreover, the court routinely counters assertions of complete justification and total denials of wrongdoing by reestablishing the delinquent's culpability, denying his plea of complete blamelessness.

Finally, situational justification has the greatest chance of success where strictly limited and supported by a technical legal defense. For example:

> A 16-year-old Negro girl was charged with loitering in a subway station, assault and battery, and profanity. Three subway policemen testified about the incident, which occurred in a bus and subway station in the heart of the Negro ghetto just after the public school had let out. As the first officer explained: "It's our job to tell school kids there's no loitering and to get on a bus. I told her to move and to go home. . . . Most of them move, but this girl seemed just too arrogant and did not move." He had told her to move on several times, and had arrested her for loitering when she had made no effort to do so. Girl had then "started kicking and screaming," and two more policemen had had to come over and restrain her, finally putting her in the paddy wagon.

The two other officers testified in support of this story. Lawyer cross-examined, trying to bring out that the girl had not been in the station particularly long (15–20 minutes) and implying that the cops had been unnecessarily quick and rough in dealing with her.

The girl herself then testified that after school she rode the bus to a job at a hospital, and had to hurry to get there. She had just missed one bus when she had arrived and was moving to get on the next one when arrested. Finally, the police had only told her curtly to "move" or "move along," and then grabbed her and hit her, so that she began struggling and yelling.

Lawyer then made his final argument, beginning: "I think the evidence has shown that this incident resulted from sheer pique on the part of a subway official because someone did not move along as fast as he wanted her to." Then argued that the girl would not loiter because she had to get to work on time, and had no time to spare. Moreover, she had a legal right to remain on the premises for a reasonable amount of time. Finally, the subway police did not possess the power to arrest someone for loitering: at most they could escort them from the premises.

Judge recessed the hearing and consulted state statute on this point. He then returned and questioned the lawyer about his interpretation of the statute. Another recess and more study. Then back in court the judge announced: "I'm satisfied that the police had no right to arrest the girl. . . . She was only in the station for 15 minutes. Even though the police have terrific problem in that station. Especially school children who should get in and out as fast as possible. But you might want to meet someone there and it would take a lot longer than 15 minutes. . . . Under the facts of the case I don't think there were reasonable grounds to make an arrest." Girl was found not delinquent on all counts.

In this case, the technical argument that the police lacked reasonable grounds for making the arrest limited the issue before the court to the propriety and justification of the girl's conduct prior to the arrest. Here she could present convincing evidence that she had acted properly and reasonably prior to being accosted by the subway police. Once the police's initial efforts had been judged wrong, the girl's subsequent "kicking and screaming" become justifiable under these particular circumstances. Without the technical defense, this justification would be considered illegitimate as a violation of the injunction against violent and abusive resistance to duly constituted authority.

EXCUSES

Delinquents more regularly employ excuses than claims of innocence or justification as a defensive strategy in the juvenile court. Excuses deny responsibility for an offense, in this way seeking to mitigate its wrongful quality. Excuses, combined with the proper repentant demeanor to be analyzed in the following chapter, isolate character from the contaminating qualities of delinquent behavior. For although excuses ordinarily do not directly determine the outcome of cases (see also Reichstein and Pipkin, n.d., pp. 7ff.), reasonable excuses allow the court to form and maintain an acceptable evaluation of moral character, and in this way further favorable dispositions.

Some commonly employed excuses focus directly on the delinquent's guilt, countering his implied intent or knowledge for the offense. For example, the excuses of *duress* most completely diminishes this guilt:

> A 12-year-old white boy was charged with runaway, during which he had been living with two older men and had performed "unnatural acts" with them on a number of occasions. The police reported: "The boy claims he had been kidnapped and held prisoner all that time but we found no ground for this." But the boy later claimed that a friend had seen the handcuffs owned by one of these men, and with which he said he had been secured.

> A 12-year-old Negro boy, defended by several volunteer law students, was charged with breaking and entering a bicycle shop. Police told of answering an alarm and finding the boy inside the building standing by the safe, complaining of an injured ankle. He told them he had dropped through the skylight on the roof. The boy then testified, saying that on his way home from the store a big boy had threatened him and made him go up on the roof. This boy had then kicked a hole in the skylight, and made him go through. He had hung by his hands until the older boy had stepped on them and forced him to drop to the floor. The boy had patted his pocket as if he had a gun or knife.

Second, the delinquent may claim that his involvement in an offense was the product of accident or ignorance. To take an example of the former:

> Three young Negro boys were accused of trying to grab a handbag from a woman in a subway station. There was evidence that they had been running up and down in a tunnel connecting two subway lines, and they claimed the incident was an accident: they had merely run against the woman and her shopping bag in passing. The woman, however, claimed they had grabbed her purse out of the shopping bag and ran. When questioned by the judge, the older boy (11) defended himself and his two friends by saying they had just been playing in the tunnel. At this time the judge responded angrily: "What do you think, the lady's lying? Is that what you want me to believe?" The boy stood with head bowed before the judge's glare.

And in the following case the attempt is made to excuse a delinquency by pleading ignorance of the illegal nature of the act:

> A 15-year-old white boy, Vic Fusco, was in court on a charge of use without authority. He had been caught in a stolen car driven by another boy whose case was continued. Police reported on what Fusco had told them at the station: His friend had pulled up after school and asked if he wanted a ride. He had gotten in and been driving around some time before being picked up. Police continued: "I asked him whether D [driver] had told him the car was stolen. He said he told him it was his brother's car."
> Fusco then testified, telling essentially the same story the police had reported. He had been picked up and driven around, believing the car belonged to the driver's brother. They had been picked up by the cops. After ordered to go to the station, the driver told him: "The car's stolen and it ain't my brother's and we're going to take off." Fusco had tried to stop him but had not been able to. Judge probed into this story, asking how long he had been in the car and where they had gone. Judge: "Was anything said about the car in that time [while driving around]?" Fusco: "Yes, he told me it was his brother's." Judge: "Do you know his brother? [No.] Do you know whether he had a brother?" Fusco: "Yes, I heard he had a brother, Billy." Older, in the service.
> Finally, public defender made his closing argument, beginning with

the statement: "I don't think this boy had any knowledge that this was a stolen car until the chase started." The judge agreed and found the boy not delinquent.

Both of these cases reveal the difficulties involved in successfully establishing an excuse, and the efforts at verification the attempt elicits from the court.

A final kind of excuse employed to mitigate responsibility for a delinquent act is to picture the act as initiated by someone other than oneself. In this way the delinquent can try to represent the offense as the "idea" of another youth, reducing his own role to that of a mere "follower." This tactic works most effectively where the youth blamed is older and has established a reputation as a severe delinquent.

In addition to excuses for a specific delinquent act, excuses may focus on the delinquent's general condition and circumstances, in this way implying a blanket reduction of responsibility for misbehavior. Such *excusing conditions* coincide with the kinds of causal explanations for "trouble" and delinquency analyzed earlier (Chapter 4). The most commonly encountered excusing conditions include: a "bad home," including parental neglect and lack of supervision; recurring intrafamilial tension and conflict, particularly as a reflection of adolescence; temporary emotional upset (as from the death of a parent, or as in one case, from learning that one is an adopted child); a "bad neighborhood"; and undesirable friends and associates. The delinquent generally cannot present these excusing conditions himself, but rather must rely on their presentation in the pitch made by a sponsor on his behalf. Finally, while act-specific excuses tend to mitigate directly the actor's criminal intent, excusing conditions serve to expand the framework within which the offense is viewed, bringing into relevance nonindividualistic factors concerned with family and social conditions.

COUNTER-DENUNCIATION

As noted earlier, the courtroom proceeding routinely comes to involve a denunciation of the accused delinquent in the course of a confrontation between him and his accusers. This fact creates the conditions for the use of _counter-denunciation_ as a defensive strategy. This strategy seeks to undermine the discrediting implications of the accusation by attacking the actions, motives and/or character of one's accusers.

The underlying phenomenon in counter-denunciation has been noted in a number of other contexts. McCorkle and Korn, for example, have analyzed the concept of the "rejection of the rejectors" as a defensive reaction to imprisonment (1964, p. 520). Similarly, Sykes and Matza explain the "condemnation of the condemners" in the process of neutralization in the following terms: "The delinquent shifts the focus of attention from his own deviant acts to the motives and behaviors of those who disapprove of his violations" (1957, p. 668). The concept of counter-denunciation, in contrast, focuses on the communicative work which accomplishes this shift of attention. Furthermore, it gains relevance as a defense against attempted character discrediting. Use of this strategy, however, is extremely risky in the court setting. While counter-denunciation may appear to the delinquent as a "natural" defense as he perceives the circumstances of his case, it tends to challenge fundamental court commitments and hence, even when handled with extreme care, often only confirms the denunciation.

It is striking that counter-denunciation has the greatest likelihood of success in cases where the complainant or denouncer lacks official stature or where the initiative rests predominantly with private parties who have clearly forced official action. Under these circumstances the wrongful quality of the offense can be greatly reduced if not wholly eliminated by showing that the initiator of the complaint was at least partially to blame for the illegal act. For example:

A 16-year-old Negro boy, Johnny Haskin, was charged with assault and battery on two teenaged girls who lived near his family in a public housing project. Although a juvenile officer brought the case into court, he was clearly acting on the initiative of the two girls and their mother, for he had had no direct contact with the incident and did not testify about it. He simply put the two girls on the stand and let them tell about what happened. This was fairly confused, but eventually it appeared that Johnny Haskin had been slapping the younger sister in the hall of the project when the older girl had pulled him off. He had then threatened her with a knife. The girls admitted that there had been fighting in the hall for some time, and that they had been involved, but put the blame on Johnny for starting it. Mrs. Haskin, however, spoke up from the back of the room, and told about a gang of boys coming around to get her son (apparently justifying Johnny's carrying a knife). And Johnny himself denied that he had started the fighting, claiming that the younger girl had hit him with a bat and threatened him first.

Judge then lectured both families for fighting, and placed Johnny on probation for nine months, despite a rather long prior record.

In this case, by establishing that the girls had also been fighting, the boy was at least partially exonerated. The success of this strategy is seen in the fact that the judge lectured both families, and then gave the boy what was a mild sentence in light of his prior court record.

Similarly, the possibility of discrediting the victim, thereby invalidating the complaint, becomes apparent in the following "rape" case:

Two Negro boys, ages 12 and 13, had admitted forcing "relations" on a 12-year-old girl in a schoolyard, the police reported. After a full report on the incidents surrounding the offense, the judge asked the policemen: "What kind of girl is she?" Officer: "I checked with Reverend Frost [the girl's minister and the person instrumental in reporting this incident] and he said she was a good girl."

As the judge's query implies, the reprehensibility of this act can only be determined in relation to the assessed character of the girl victim. Had the police or the accused brought up evidence of a bad reputation or incidents suggesting "loose" or "promiscuous" behavior, the force of the complaint would have been undermined.

In the above cases, successful counter-denunciation of the complainants would undermine the moral basis of their involvement in the incident, thereby discrediting their grounds for initiating the complaint. But this merely shifts part of the responsibility for an offense onto the complaining party and does not affect the wrongful nature of the act per se. Thus, by denouncing the general character of the complainant and the nature of his involvement in the offense, the accused does not so much clear himself as diminish his guilt. If the offense involved is serious enough and the culpability of the complainant not directly related to the offense, therefore, this strategy may have little impact.

For example, in the homosexuality-tinged case of car theft described earlier (see p. 145), both the accused and his father tried to support their contention that the car owner was lying by pointing to his discredited character. But the "victim's" homosexuality had no real connection with the act of stealing the car nor with the threatened physical violence it entailed, and hence did not affect the judge's evaluation of the act and of the delinquent's character. Under these circumstances, the soiled nature of the victim simply was not considered sufficiently extenuating to dissolve the reprehensibility of the act.[6]

In general, then, a successful counter-denunciation must discredit not only the general character of the denouncer but also his immediate purpose or motive in making the complaint. Only in this way can the counter-denunciation cut the ground out from under the wrongfulness of the alleged offense. For example:

> An 11-year-old Negro boy was charged with wantonly damaging the car of an older Negro man, Frankie Williams, with a BB gun. With the boy was his mother, a respectably dressed woman, a white lawyer, and a white couple who served as character witnesses.
>
> A juvenile officer brought the case in and then called Mr. Williams up to testify. The witness told of going outside to shovel his car out of the snow several weeks previously and finding his windshield damaged in several places. He had noticed the boy at this time leaning out of the window of his house with a BB gun. Lawyer then cross-examined,

6. Note, however, that even though this denunciation succeeded, the denouncer suffered both discrediting and penalty. Immediately after the delinquency case had been decided the police took out a complaint for "contributing to the delinquency of a minor" against him, based on his admitted homosexual activities with the youth. This "contributing" case was brought before the juvenile court later that same morning, complainant and accused changed places, and the first denouncer was found guilty, primarily from what he had revealed about his behavior earlier in establishing the delinquency complaint.

getting Williams to admit that he had been bickering with the family for some time, and that a year before the mother had accused him of swearing at her son and had tried to get a court complaint against him. (Judge ruled this irrelevant after Williams had acknowledged it.) Williams seemed flustered, and grew angry under the questioning, claiming that because of the boy's shooting he would not be able to get an inspection sticker for his car.

Juvenile officer then told judge that although he had not investigated the case, his partner reported that the marks on the windshield were not consistent with a BB gun. Williams had also admitted that he had not looked for any BB pellets. On the basis of this evidence, the judge found the boy not delinquent. He then severely warned all parties in the case: "I'm going to tell you I do not want any more contests between these two families. Do you understand?"

Here, by showing that the complainant had both a selfish motive for complaining about his damaged windshield (to help get it repaired) and a grudge against the defendant and his family, as well as bringing out the lack of concrete evidence to substantiate the charge, the lawyer was able to get the complaint totally dismissed.

Similarly, the circumstances of the following case were such as to suggest initially that complaints had been taken out to intimidate or at least get even with boys against whom there was some resentment:

Two teenaged Negro boys were brought to court for breaking windows. Case was continued, and policeman gave the following account of what had happened. Several weeks previously there had been a disturbance and some windows broken in a middle class section of the city. There were six boys apparently involved, including these two. One of the occupants of the home had come out and begun shooting at the boys, who were on the other side of the street, "allegedly to protect his property." One of these two boys had been hit in the leg, and another man (apparently a passerby) had also been hit. The shooter, named Barr, "is now up before the grand jury" for this, but meanwhile had taken out complaints against these two boys. A private attorney representing the two accused then took over, explaining how his clients had just been summonsed to testify against Barr. Lawyer next questioned the cop about why complaints had been brought only against these two of the six boys, including the one who had been shot, and the other who had been a witness to the shooting. Cop replied that the other boys had been investigated, but there was nothing against them.

Here the boys' lawyer successfully established that the complaints against his clients had been initiated by the defendant in a related criminal action, suggesting an attempt to discredit in advance their testimony against him. The judge responded by continuing the case, releasing both boys to the custody of their parents, even though one had a long record.

Finally, successful counter-denunciation requires that the denounced provide a convincing account for what he claims is an illegitimate accusation. The court will reject any implication that one person will gratuitously accuse another of something he has not done. The youth in the following case can provide this kind of account:

Five young boys were charged with vandalism and with starting a fire in a public school. Juvenile officer explained that he had investigated the incident with the school principal, getting two of the boys to admit their part in the vandalism. These two boys had implicated the other three, all of whom denied the charge.

The judge then took over the questioning, trying to determine whether the three accused had in fact been in the school. In this he leaned heavily on finding out why the first two boys should lie. One of the accused, Ralph Kent, defended himself by saying he had not been at the school and did not know the boy who had named him. Judge asked how this boy had then been able to identify him. Kent replied that he had been a monitor at school, and one of his accusers might have seen him there. And he used to take the other accuser to the basement [lavatory] because the teacher would not trust him alone for fear he would leave the school.

The two other boys continued to deny any involvement in the incident, but could provide no reason why they should be accused unjustly. The judge told them he felt they were lying, and asked several times: "Can you give me a good reason why these boys would put you in it?" Finally he pointed toward Kent and commented: "He's the only one I'm convinced wasn't there." He then asked Kent several questions about what he did as a monitor. When it came to disposi-

tions, Kent was continued without a finding while the four other boys
were found delinquent.

In this situation an accused delinquent was able to establish his
own reputable character in school (later confirmed by the probation report on his school record), the discredited character of one
of his accusers, and a probable motive for their denunciation of
him (resentment toward his privileges and position in school) in
a few brief sentences. It should be noted, however, that this successful counter-denunciation was undoubtedly facilitated by the
fact that denouncers and denounced were peers. It is incompara-
bly more difficult for a youth to establish any acceptable reason
why an adult should want to accuse and discredit him wrongfully.

Counter-denunciation occurs most routinely with offenses arising out of the family situation and involving complaints initiated
by parents against their own children. Here again it is possible
for the child to cast doubt on the parents' motives in taking court
action, and on the parents' general character:

> A Negro woman with a strong West Indian accent had brought an
> incorrigible child complaint against her 16-year-old daughter. The
> mother reported: "She never says anything to me, only to ask, 'Gimme
> car fare, gimme lunch money.' . . . As for the respect she gave me I
> don't think I have to tolerate her!" The daughter countered that her
> mother never let her do anything, and simply made things unbearable
> for her around the house. She went out nights, as her mother claimed,
> but only to go over to a girl friend's house to sleep.
>
> This case was continued for several months, during which time a
> probation officer worked with the girl and the court clinic saw mother
> and daughter. The psychiatrist there felt that the mother was "very
> angry and cold." Eventually an arrangement was made to let the girl
> move in with an older sister.

In this case the daughter was effectively able to blame her
mother and her intolerance for the troubled situation in the
home. But in addition, counter-denunciation may also shift the
focus of the court inquiry from the misconduct charged to the
youth onto incidents involving the parents. This shift of attention facilitated the successful counter-denunciation in the following case:

A 16-year-old white girl from a town some distance from the city was charged with shoplifting. But as the incident was described by the police, it became clear that this offense had occurred because the girl had run away from home and needed clean clothes. Police related what the girl had said about running away: She had been babysitting at home and was visited by her boyfriend, who had been forbidden in the house. Her father had come home, discovered this, and beaten her with a strap. (The girl's face still appeared somewhat battered with a large black-and-blue mark on one cheek, although the court session occurred at least three days after the beating.) She had run away that night.

The rest of the hearing centered not on the theft but on the running away and the incident which precipitated it. After the police evidence, the judge asked the girl: "How did you get that mark on your face?" Girl: "My father hit me." Judge: "With his fist?" Girl (hesitating) : "Yes, it must have been his fist." Later in the proceeding, the judge asked the girl specifically why she had run away. She emphasized that she had not tried to hide anything; the kids had been up until eleven and the boy had left his bike out front. "I didn't try to hide it. I told them he'd been there."

With this her father rose to defend himself, arguing with some agitation: ". . . His clothes were loose. Her clothes were loose. Her bra was on the floor. . . . She was not punished for the boy being in the house, but for what she did." Girl (turning toward her father): "What about my eye?" Father: "She got that when she fell out of the bed (angrily, but directed toward the judge) ." Girl (just as angrily) : "What about the black and blue marks?" Father: "Those must have been from the strap."

The relatively high probability of successful counter-denunciation in cases arising from family situations points up the most critical contingency in the use of this protective strategy, the choice of an appropriate object. Denouncers with close and permanent relations with the denounced are particularly vulnerable to counter-denunciation, as the accusation is apt to rest solely on their word and illegitimate motives for the denunciation may be readily apparent. But again, where relations between the two parties are more distant, counter-denunciation has more chance of success where the denouncer is of more or less equivalent status with the denounced. Thus, the judge can be easily convinced that a schoolmate might unjustly accuse one from jealousy, but will reject any contention that an adult woman would lie about an attempted purse-snatching incident.

While a denounced youth has a fair chance of successfully discrediting a complainant of his own age, and some chance where the complainant is a family member, counter-denunciations directed against officials, particularly against the most frequent complainants in the juvenile court, the police, almost inevitably fail. In fact, to attempt to counterattack the police, and to a lesser extent, other officials, is to risk fundamentally discrediting moral character, for the court recoils against all attacks on the moral authority of any part of the official legal system.

One reflection of this is the court's routine refusal to acknowledge complaints of *unfair* treatment at the hands of the police. On occasion, for example, parents complain that their children were arrested and brought to court while others involved in the incident were not. Judges regularly refuse to inquire into such practices:

> Two young Puerto Rican boys were charged with shooting a BB gun. After police testimony, their mother said something in Spanish, and their priest-translator explained to the judge: "What they've been asking all morning is why they did not bring the other two boys." The judge replied: "I can only deal with those cases that are before me. I can't go beyond that and ask about these other boys that are not here."

Similarly, in this same case the judge refused to inquire into a complaint of police brutality when the mother complained that one boy had been hit on the head, saying: "The question of whether he was injured is not the question for me right now."

But beyond this, the court will often go to great lengths to protect and defend the public character of the police when it is attacked during a formal proceeding. To accuse a policeman of acting for personal motives, or of dishonesty in the course of his duties, not only brings immediate sanctions from the court but also tends to discredit basically the character of the delinquent accuser. Accusations of this nature threaten the basic ceremonial order of the court proceeding and hence the legitimacy of the legal order itself. The most extreme and blatant challenge to the legitimacy of police operations and the moral character of the arresting officer occurred in the case of Frank Riccio:

Riccio and another boy were charged with being present where narcotics were found. The police claimed that they saw the narcotics on the floor of the car while standing outside, while the public defender objected that even this constituted an illegal search. Probation officer defended Riccio, but the judge put on a "tough," hard show, continually emphasizing that commitment to reform school seemed indicated.

Then Riccio spoke up: "Your honor, I'd like to say something." Judge: "You can say anything you want, because right now there's very little between you and reform school." Riccio hesitated, then: "I'd just like to say that I'm not guilty. I did not do it. I think these officers would do anything to get promoted. They lied about what happened. . . . I didn't have anything to do with the narcotics." Judge looked disturbed and asked the boy what he was saying. His lawyer interrupted that he had said enough but was ignored. Riccio: "I think they dropped them there to make us look guilty." He continued: "Look, no one would be so dumb as to leave narcotics out in plain sight when stopped by the police. No one could be that stupid." You would not simply drop narcotics on the floor, out in the open, but would put them out of sight.

Judge looked angry and almost incredulous during this, but responded that he had seen many stupid things during his years of law practice, and this did not surprise him at all. Policeman commented that addicts did stupid things. He then defended himself, noting his years of work in narcotics, and added, "I've gone as far as I can for promotion without an examination." Judge reassured him: "Don't worry about that, officer. . . . Anyone who comes around here saying they were framed by the police does not impress me at all." Riccio protested again, fairly loudly and with evident feeling: "All I'm saying is I'm not guilty. That's it. I'm not guilty!" Judge replied that he did not like anyone who came in defending himself by blaming the police, and that he would commit such a person.

Things then calmed down. The judge, apparently not wanting to commit the youth even after his outbreak, asked the probation officer if he thought he could work with Riccio. Probation officer said he could. Judge then said he would be willing to put the boy on the street under a suspended sentence, if he apologized to the police. Lawyer refused the suspended sentence, suggesting that the case be continued without a finding for a long period. Judge would not accept this. Riccio ended the exchange, however, by announcing that he wanted to appeal. Judge found both Riccio and his friend delinquent, and set low bail at the YCA Detention Center.

In this case Riccio committed a fundamental breach of court etiquette by attacking the personal motives of the police officer who arrested him. The judge, however, consistently defended the character of the police, and simply would not entertain the possibility that they had behaved as charged by Riccio. The youth's outburst, moreover, apparently had an important effect on the judge's eventual decision in the case. In not making a finding of delinquent immediately after the facts had been heard, he was leaving open the possibility of the continued-without-a-finding disposition later requested by the lawyer. It is unclear to what extent the boy's prior record led the judge to reject this option, but it is obvious that Riccio's attack on the police reflected adversely on his character and contributed to the ultimate severe sentence.

In conclusion, there is no faster way to discredit character than to direct a counter-denunciation against the police. These disastrous consequences result from the care shown by the court staff to protect the personal and moral character of the police from symbolic attack and damage within the ceremonial event constituted by the court hearing. This reflects not only the closeness of the court's working ties with the police, but also the fact that both police and court are part of the same legal structure. Both are concerned with the exercise of legal authority. An attack on the police, therefore, symbolically attacks the legal order which the court both represents and feels obligated to protect. An attack on the police represents a denial of the normative or moral order on which the court's activities are based.[7]

7. The fundamental importance of this ceremonial integrity of the legal order also appears in Sudnow's description of the public defender's working relations with the district attorney's office. In general, continued cooperation from the district attorney requires that the public defender not "make an issue of the moral character of the administrative machinery of the local courts, the community, or the police" (1965, p. 273). The police in particular receive this kind of ceremonial protection, as the public defender faces great pressure not to "morally degrade police officers in cross examination" (p. 273).

In addition, the fact that the court will go to such lengths to protect the moral character and legitimacy of the police has great consequences for the delinquent's view of the proceeding. Not only may this tend to increase his sense of receiving unjust and unfair treatment from the court, but it may also make self-defeating any attempt to defend character from the accusations of the police (and other officials). To present such a defense only serves to increase the court's acceptance of his discreditation. The delinquent who feels he has been unjustly accused by a police officer is thus in a bind between being discredited on the basis of the officer's accusation and version of the delinquency, or being even more fundamentally discredited by trying to defend himself through counter-denunciation of the policeman.

CONCLUSION

I would like to discuss some of the implications of denunciation and counter-denunciation for deviance theory, as suggested by their occurrence in the juvenile court.

To begin with, it should be emphasized that denunciation is inherently "dirty work," for strong cultural values exist in our society against telling tales and making derogatory statements about other people. This attitude is particularly strong against attacking or defaming the character of another. In general, then, it would appear that there is something intrinsically dirty and suspect about the role of the denouncer.

One consequence of this is works of denunciation are hedged with a kind of procedural safeguard. Since denunciation is looked upon as a basically dubious enterprise, it cannot be lightly attempted. Thus, in any attempted denunciation the denouncer must establish a right to undertake such action. This has two related aspects. First, the denouncer has to establish his legitimate interest and concern in the denounced party and his behavior. This requires showing that he has some recognized relationship or involvement with this person, or some recognized right to survey and judge his conduct. If this in not established the denouncer will appear as a "busybody" or a "meddler" in affairs that do not concern him.

Second, the denouncer must take active steps to establish his own rectitude and upright character. This is particularly relevant where the denouncer is somehow involved or associated with the alleged misconduct (as injured party or victim, for example). In this situation, successful denunciation depends on presenting these misdeeds and their author as indefensibly wrong. If the denouncer's character and involvement in the situation are not impeccable, misconduct cannot be presented as unmitigatedly wrong. The denouncer who is a "victim" of the person he denounces must be seen as totally innocent, for otherwise the offense can be represented as the product of the actions of two individuals, each partially wrong and, hence, each partially right.

From this it is clear that denunciation can become not only a suspect but also an extremely hazardous undertaking. In the first place, to make a denunciation is to claim that one is entitled to do so. Yet this right has to be established and defended as the denunciation unfolds. Consequently, the denouncer has no guarantee that his credentials will be accepted by those witnessing the denunciation or that his character will survive questions and attacks that may arise during the course of the denunciation. Moreover, the situation is complicated by the fact that the right to denounce hinges on the success of the denunciation. If for any reason the denunciation fails, the denouncer is left in the vulnerable position of having acted as if he had a right to do something he has no legitimate business doing.

But irrespective of its success or failure, a denouncer exposes himself in an even more fundamental way in making the denunciation. For as noted, a person can establish the total depravity of another only by proving his own complete rectitude. In making a denunciation a person therefore automatically opens up his own motives and moral character to examination and evaluation, with the distinct possibility that they will be found wanting. In order to discredit another person completely, one must establish not simply one's worthiness relative to that person, but rather one's *absolute rectitude*. But to justify and maintain a stance of absolute rectitude is a difficult and hazardous task. This is particularly relevant given the fact that one reaction to denunciation, as was seen in the juvenile court, is to counterattack the denouncer's immediate motives, his ultimate moral character, or both. In all cases, the risk to the denouncer of being shown to be other than what he claimed is greatly increased.

The situation of the rape "victim" dramatically illustrates the risks of denunciation for the victim-complainant. As suggested by the charge of indecent assault discussed previously (see p. 157), successful denunciation requires evidence of the girl's own morality and purity. As a result, she risks inquiry into her moral worth and perhaps exposure from the court's efforts to assess the nature of the offense. But in addition, she risks counter-denunciation from the boys, who could well have defended themselves by claiming that she made the first advances and consented to the acts. A girl denouncing others for rape, therefore, may ultimately suffer greater discrediting than those she accuses.

The risks of denouncing, however, are greatly reduced where the denunciation can be presented as an occupational responsibility of an official or expert who has some preestablished right to concern himself with other people's misbehavior. These official and expert roles are defined exactly by this capacity to denounce and hence lower the status of others. This applies to the policeman operating within the juvenile court, as well as to the psychiatrist dealing with the mentally ill and to the social worker handling the poor. In the first place, such figures possess exactly the legitimate right, if not obligation, to respond to troublesome acts, and hence by implication, to denounce their authors. This right constitutes part of the license granted the occupation or profession. Second, inherent in this legitimated capacity is the assumption that the occupant of the status is acting on behalf of important professional and public values, for this is the very meaning of legitimate. His motives are then by definition not personally selfish.[8] Consequently, the licensed denouncer has to establish

8. Bittner's findings on police apprehension of the mentally ill suggest that the capacity to demonstrate nonpersonal motives for denunciation, independently of professional competence, can lead to successful denunciation. Thus the police tended to remove to mental hospitals patients complained of by those standing in an *instrumental relationship* to them, e.g., "physicians, lawyers, teachers, employers, landlords." However, "similar requests, in quite similar circumstances, made by family members, friends, roommates, or neighbors are usually not honored" (Bittner, 1967a, p. 284).

neither immediate motive for the denunciation (it is assumed to derive from the objective nature of his duties and responsibilities) nor his own personal rectitude, for it is built into the very professional or official status as a representative of which he is assumed to be acting. Garfinkel in fact defines successful denunciation as established identity with public values and motives:

> The denouncer must so identify himself to the witnesses that during the denunciation they regard him not as a private but as a publicly known person. He must not portray himself as acting according to his personal, unique experiences. He must rather be regarded as acting in his capacity as a public figure, drawing upon communally entertained and verified experience (1956; p. 423).

As suggested by the nature of denunciation in the juvenile court, however, the motives for even an official or professional denunciation may be suspect, although not on personal terms. That is, while it is assumed that a licenced denouncer would not do so for purely personal reasons (e.g., to "get even" with the denounced), it is held possible that a denunciation is undertaken for some *occupationally* selfish reason. It is recognized, for example, that an agency worker might denounce a delinquent in order to lighten his caseload of a difficult and time-consuming case. For this reason, such denunciations require demonstration that the delinquent has received extraordinary attention and frequent "breaks" (see pp. 137–40). This prevents negative evaluation of the reasons for the denunciation. But even where the denouncer fails in this demonstration, he is not completely discredited in this exposure in the way a nonofficial denouncer would be. He is discredited only in his claim to be a competent and conscientious worker and not as a total moral being.

This fundamental difference between licensed and unlicensed denouncers determines the point at which denunciation is most vulnerable to counterattack. Where denounced by someone without general license to do so, one may respond most successfully by attacking his reasons for the denunciation, i.e., by showing that he was motivated by any of a number of personal, selfish, or vindictive considerations. Or, less successfully, one may attack his general character in such a way as to imply: "Who is he to accuse me?" But where the denouncer is a party licensed to make such accusations, either of these courses may prove disastrous. For example, in a study of the legal commitment of the insane, those who resisted their own commitment successfully did so by turning on the private party who bore the brunt of the denunciation, and not by challenging the professional legitimacy of the psychiatrist who examined them:

> Resisters who were not committed differed from those who were committed in that they were able to question the validity of the complainants' case, rather than just the doctors' testimony. All those who attacked the decision or recommendations of the professionals were committed, often with some abrupt terminal remark by the judge. However, the defendant who turned on his complainants had the best of it and, in such cases, the tables were turned (Miller and Schwartz, 1966; p. 29).

Similarly, in the juvenile court, it is generally disastrous to attack the personal motives of the police or other officials. Rather, other strategies must be employed to counter licensed denunciation successfully.

In conclusion, it should be emphasized that the socially necessary work of denunciation is facilitated by delegating it to those occupying social roles that possess recognized license to denounce. This institutionalization of responsibility for denunciation in officially or professionally qualified roles not only creates a supply of denouncers otherwise largely unattainable, it also protects these denouncers from contamination by the inherent dirtiness of their work. Denunciation becomes objectified: it is seen as arising out of the contingencies of a job, not out of personal commitment; it can be presented as objectively necessary and justifiable, not as the product of subjective choice or prejudice. Finally, this institutionalization is protected by processes whereby those who witness and eventually legitimate the denunciation condemn and harshly sanction those who defend themselves by attacking these licensed denouncers. To question their motives or character is to threaten the basic presumption of competence and objectivity that justifies the performance of such intrinsically dirty work as denunciation. It threatens to strip away the elaborate system of legitimation that clothes and rationalizes processes of denunciation, and hence elicits strong preventive and punitive reactions from those overseeing such processes.

7
Courtroom Ceremony and Interaction

Just as one may look at the ways in which individuals present and defend desired images of self, so one may look at what have been called "presentational strategies" employed by institutions to create and maintain desired impressions of their ongoing activity (Ball, 1967). In this sense, "staging" constitutes a basic aspect of institutional functioning. Accenting the luxury, cost, and antiseptic medical features of an abortion clinic, for example, fosters a conventional and legitimate rather than a deviant definition of the situation. Such a presentational strategy "allows the clinic to minimize problems inherent in typically anxious and fearful patrons" (Ball, 1967, p. 301). And in looking at any ongoing institution, one should consider what presentational strategies are employed with various sorts of clients and toward what ends they are directed.

While the juvenile court hearing serves a variety of purely instrumental ends, court staff invest it with much more than mere administrative character. The courtroom proceeding is perceived and constructed as a ceremonial confrontation between the legal order and one who has violated that order, a confrontation consciously shaped to induce a certain kind of impact on the violator. In the first place, this ceremony is structured so as both to intimidate the delinquent and to accentuate the authoritativeness of court pronouncements and decisions. Second, the ceremony seeks to impose upon the delinquent the role of wrongdoer and systematically to deny him power or opportunity to express less than

172

full commitment to this discredited role. This chapter analyzes this ceremonial structure of the courtroom hearing, focusing on the nature of the interaction processes that take place during it. These processes assume fundamental significance for two closely related phenomena—the assessment of moral character and the degradation of the delinquent.

In the first place, it should be emphasized that moral character is judged and established in the course of encounters and interactions between accused delinquents and the officialdom of delinquent control (Cicourel, 1968; Piliavin and Briar, 1964). In this sense, the ritual parameters imposed by the courtroom hearing may fundamentally shape court assessment of a delinquent's moral character. In general, the manner in which the delinquent handles himself during this ceremonially framed confrontation, particularly the ways in which he presents and defends himself within the limits imposed by the ritual demands of the occasion, critically affect the court's understanding of his moral character, and hence its response to his case.

Paradoxically, while the courtroom ceremony provides the court with important materials for its assessments of moral character, the staging of the hearing also rests on assumptions about this very character. The hearing is staged in accord with the assessed character of the delinquent involved. More concretely, the court employs a routine presentational strategy of enhancing intimidating authority and individual culpability with exactly those children considered *most normal in character* (or at least, not totally discredited and identified as of criminal or disturbed character). This presentational strategy assumes children who are not quite mature enough to appreciate the wrongness and potentially serious consequences of their delinquent acts or to comprehend fully the severity of the sanctions to which they make themselves liable by so acting. Youths of this kind—those who are (or may be) normal in character—can be expected to be intimidated by such a proceeding. Threatening tone and moralistic lecturing, in other words, become the routine methods for deterring further offenses by normal delinquents. But finally, in presuming the deterability of the normal delinquent, these techniques come to provide an additional test of this normality.

Second, this courtroom ceremony is characteristically organized to degrade and humiliate the delinquent involved. Such personal degradation is not some accidental or peripheral quality of the courtroom scene but often an inevitable consequence of the staging of the court event. Moreover, these humiliating conditions often possess great significance for the court's assessment of moral character.

While this analysis will center on the structure of the courtroom hearing, it should be noted that many of the patterns of interaction relevant to character assessments and the conditions for degradation found there are also characteristic of less formal court scenes. Thus, the issues and dilemmas faced by the delinquent in handling himself in the courtroom setting continually recur in his relatively informal encounters with his probation officer, or with a psychiatrist in the court clinic. The formal and ceremonial features of the courtroom setting merely introduce some additional problems without essential modification of the underlying processes.

AUTHORITATIVE AND INTIMIDATING FEATURES OF THE COURTROOM HEARING

The juvenile court's routine presentational strategy seeks to subordinate the delinquent and highlight the authority of its own actions in order to produce an intimidating impact on delinquents. This strategy finds formal expression in a commitment to maintaining a formal and solemn atmosphere in court proceedings. In contrast to philosophies of juvenile court procedure which emphasize informality, avoidance of legal technicality, and rapport with delinquents and their families, that held by the juvenile court insists on dramatizing the legal quality of the hearing and the formal authority of the court. This basic approach was set down by the founding judge of the court and has prevailed with minor modification in all subsequent judicial regimes. As the founder argued:

> morals enter . . . largely and directly into the work of the court . . . and therefore it seems desirable to create deliberately to some extent

an atmosphere of seriousness and solemnity in the proceedings. . . .
Then again it is probably in the interest of efficiency that the fact of
the court being a department of public authority and having power to
compel compliance should be indicated distinctly . . . and for that
reason children and parents are usually kept standing while talking to
the judge. The platform contributes to this purpose also. [Emphasis
added.]

The proceedings of the contemporary court create and maintain this "atmosphere of seriousness and solemnity" in a variety
of ways. The setting clearly indicates a tribunal conducting hearings of a legal nature. Physically the main courtroom is closely
modeled on the traditional criminal courtroom (Hazard, 1962).
The judge's bench rests on a raised platform, his place marked by
a high-backed leather chair, placed before a blue wall drape and
flanked by flags. Moreover, the spatial arrangement of the rest of
the courtroom is such as to focus attention on the judge. All other
parties in the proceeding are so seated that they necessarily face
the judge. Officials (police, lawyers, probation officers) sit at floor
level at a long low desk in front of and resting against the judicial
bench. Accused delinquents sit on a row of small movable chairs
(usually three) immediately to the judge's right. Parents sit on
the front bench about ten feet behind the official desk, while witnesses and observers sit on the two long benches immediately behind them. In general, spatial arrangements clearly indicate the
roles of all those officially involved in the case and particularly set
off the place of the judge presiding over the occasion.

A number of ceremonial rules also emphasize the preeminent
position and authority of the judge and hence contribute to the
solemnity of the proceeding. His dress, the traditional black judicial robe, highlights the semisacred character of his position
(Kessler, 1962). A court officer or probation officer leads him
through the often crowded hall to the courtroom door, and ushers
him in and out of the hearing. More importantly, various forms
of deferential behavior are due the judge. When he enters or
leaves, those present in the courtroom should stand in conform-
ance with the court officer's cry, "Court rise!" During the course
of the proceeding, anyone, whether delinquent, family, witness,

or official, making a statement or comment is expected to stand. Statements by juveniles to the judge should be accompanied by such deferential terms of address as "your honor" or "sir." Finally, the judge directs the hearing in ways that reflect both his authority and the extraordinary nature of the occasion. Not only are all statements and testimony directed at him, but he can also interrupt anyone, take over questioning from police and lawyers, and generally guide and control the course of the inquiry.

Furthermore, court personnel take great care to safeguard the sanctity of the occasion from profaning incidents. Personal appearance as well as speech is subject to scrutiny in this regard. In the following case, for example, the probation officer acts to protect the deferential tone of the proceeding (as well as the girl's moral character):

> A 16-year-old white girl, who had been involved in several runaway incidents, appeared in court for disposition after visiting the court clinic. She wore a blue-and-white striped sweater and a tight skirt that exposed three or four inches of flesh above her knees. She carried a coat over one arm. Just before she entered the courtroom a probation officer directed her: "Pull it [skirt] down and put your coat over your knees [when sitting in the courtroom]." When she sat down before the judge the girl followed these instructions.

In addition to these structural features the hearing itself is conducted on terms that promote a solemn and serious definition of the occasion. In order to impress the court experience indelibly on the delinquent involved, the court staff tries to structure the courtroom proceeding so as to both highlight the youth's *wrongness* in having committed the delinquent act and accentuate his *powerlessness* before the legal sanctions he consequently faces. These constitute the basic dimensions of courtroom staging. On the one hand, delinquent conduct is made to stand out as illegal, immoral, and indefensible—as a threat to the moral and legal order—and not as minor and dismissible. On the other hand, the delinquent must be impressed with the severe penalties that lie within the discretion of the court to invoke and that may well be leveled against this and any future delinquency. These two features complement one another: a youth made to appear essentially guilty and sinful will feel more vulnerable, while this very vulnerability will deepen his sense of wrongdoing. In this way, the hearing assumes an intimidating character and the youth is made to feel and acknowledge the full significance of his misconduct.[1]

Earlier analysis of denunciation has described the way in which complainants present delinquent activity so as to focus attention on the qualities of wrongness and criminality. It must be added, however, that the court may also conduct its proceedings in order to transcend the "natural" depiction of delinquent misconduct and guilt. The court may go beyond the matter-of-fact description of the act and seek to dissolve any sense of normalcy and inevitability, isolating the act in all its blameworthiness. These processes whereby delinquent behavior is recast as something apart from and in opposition to the normal moral order are an integral part of the courtroom ceremony. However, since these processes are fundamentally related to another structural feature of the courtroom ceremony, namely, denying the delinquent access to face-saving techniques, detailed analysis will be postponed until a later part of this chapter.

A delinquent's subordination to court authority is highlighted in a variety of subtle ways during the courtroom hearing. To begin with, if a youth has been held in detention prior to his court appearance, he is usually led into the courtroom by a court officer in ways that dramatize his captivity. One such officer, for example, commonly conducted a delinquent to and from the court's detention cell with one arm around his neck and shoulder, a violation of body space clearly demonstrating the youth's lack of personal autonomy in the court scene. Furthermore, ceremonial rules prescribing deferential behavior in the courtroom serve to emphasize and affirm the delinquent's subordinate position, as well as accenting the authority of the judge as previously mentioned (Goffman, 1967, pp. 47–95). In showing appreciation of the legitimacy and authority of judge and court, the youth also

---

1. Claude Brown's autobiographical account of a delinquent boyhood in Harlem (1966) includes several very sensitive and penetrating comments on these qualities of juvenile court proceedings. Some of these will be reported in subsequent footnotes.

acknowledges his own subordination within this setting. More-over, the court may dramatically reaffirm the delinquent's sub-ordinate position by sanctioning any breach of these ceremonial rules. And in general, the judge's right to lecture and rebuke the delinquent publicly underlines the latter's essential powerlessness in the court setting.[2]

In addition, courtroom deliberations often make the delin-quent highly aware of his own irrelevance and inability to affect the course of the proceeding. Many decisions are reached, for ex-ample, without consulting the youth and in ways that suggest his complete impotence to determine his own future:

> Children's Mental Hospital returned a report on a 14-year-old Negro boy charged with robbery and assault. In court the judge read the report over, noted that it found the boy not psychotic, and asked the public defender whether he had seen it. Yes. Judge then turned to the boy's mother and explained the report to her: the hospital had found him "a problem with regard to containment," as he had been very uncooperative and hostile, and felt that "commitment is in order." Judge then asked public defender if he wanted to say anything about this. Defender replied: "Your honor, I have no argument" and waived right of appeal. Boy was then committed to the Youth Correction Authority. Judge again turned to the mother, and asked if she under-stood what he was doing. No. A very brief explanation: "I think your son needs a lot more help than we can give him on the street." For this reason he was being committed. Case then left the courtroom.

In this case the delinquent youth is not really present on the

2. Imposing deferential behavior in acknowledgement of official power and authority may involve very subtle interaction processes. In the following inci-dent, for example, Brown describes a scene where a juvenile court judge exacts deference from a group of delinquent boys appearing before her by forcing them to tolerate her disregard of a norm of ordinary interaction:

> Whenever she wanted to show the people there how bad she was, instead of hitting somebody or yelling at them she just looked at them or talked even softer. When she started talking softer, she was bullying everybody in the queen's courtroom. I thought, It's like she's sayin', "Goddamit, you peasants better shut up and listen to me, 'cause I'm gonna ask you what I said, and everybody who don't know is gonna git his head chopped off!" So the softer she talked, the quieter everybody was and the harder they listened, because their heads depended on it (1966, p. 60).

occasion of his own commitment. Similarly, officials frequently discuss details of a delinquent's life and behavior as if he were not there, making no acknowledgment of his presence either by word or by glancing in his direction.

Less subtly, the delinquent's powerlessness is signaled by highlighting his vulnerability to major legal sanctions at the hands of the court. To this end, the youth's confrontation with the judge routinely accents the authority and discretion of the court, particularly the delinquent's liability to important court sanctions. For example:

> A 14-year-old white boy, Joseph Richardson, was in for violation of probation. He was supposed to attend the Boys' Training Program, but had begun skipping both it and school. After Probation Officer Ackerly explained about this, the judge called the boy over and lectured him: "You're going to learn something right now, that we give the orders around here and you had better obey them. . . . Personally I think you should be committed right now. I thought so last Saturday, and I still think so. [Saturday was when the boy had been apprehended and arraigned.] . . . You're testing me, that's all. . . . You can't get away with it. . . . Mr. Ackerly seems to think you deserve another chance. Why I don't know." PO then went into more detail about the boy's truanting from school. Judge commented: "Maybe three years at County Training School is what he needs."

Similarly, in cases involving more than one youth, the fact that one is to be committed to the Youth Correction Authority is frequently pounded home to those who have been kept on the streets:

> Four Negro boys, ages 13 and 14, had broken into a five-and-ten store at night and been caught by the police. Two of these with long records were committed to the Youth Correction Authority by the judge and were taken out of the courtroom and locked in the cage before being transported out there. Judge then called the remaining two boys over to the bench and lectured them: "See what happened to the other two?" Both boys nodded and answered yes. Judge: "What?" Boy: "They got shipped away." Judge: "That's what's going to happen to you the way you're going."

Again, the court uses detention not as a threat but as an actual demonstration of its power to determine a delinquent's fate. This can be seen in the case of Joseph Richardson introduced previously:

> PO Ackerly described how Richardson had started skipping both school and the sessions of the Boys' Training Program. He had apprehended the boy on Saturday and had the case continued almost a week until this Friday so that he would be held in detention during that time. PO added that then "at least he'd lose vacation" (i.e., the boy was held in detention for all of that week the schools had been on vacation). PO had talked to him during the week at the detention center and found the boy "somewhat chastened—he realizes he can't do what he wants to do now." Judge then began to question Joseph about his experience at the detention center. Judge: "How did you like it out there?" Joseph: "No (inaudible)." Judge: "Did the boys talk about reform school?" (Joseph nods yes.) "How would you like to go there?" Joseph: "No (again almost inaudible)."

The delinquent's powerlessness in the face of court power to sanction and incarcerate may also be dramatized in the announcing of dispositions. In municipal court juvenile sessions, for example, suspended sentences were routinely announced in the following form: either judge or clerk would proclaim that the youth was committed to the Youth Correction Authority, pause, and then add that this sentence was suspended and the delinquent placed on probation. The intended effect was that of having been "sent away," then suddenly getting a reprieve.

A more elaborated version of this strategy occurs when judge and probation officer team together to first stage a denunciation of the delinquent, leading to an apparent decision to incarcerate, then reverse this sentence and "save" the youth. As the judge described this staged "saving":

> Sometimes the probation officer would arrange for him to just about commit a kid so that he [PO] could intervene and save him. "I sometimes play the bad guy role so they can plea for the kid and get him off."

While the probation officer often uses this "saving" performance to establish and increase rapport with a probationer, the procedure again highlights the power and authority of the court as against the liability of the child. A concrete example of this procedure, but one not worked out in advance, occurred in the case of Joseph Richardson, described above. This hearing ended with the following exchange:

> After the judge had lectured the boy and threatened him with commitment to the County Training School, PO Ackerly spoke up: "I would like to get the chance to work with him." The judge accepted this recommendation, and ordered that the boy's probation be continued. He then turned to the boy again: "Mr. Ackerly has saved you this time, but he is not going to save you the next time. You understand that?" Joseph: "Yes, sir."

Beyond highlighting its power to sanction and the vulnerability of the delinquent to these sanctions, the court also tries to impose a definition on the courtroom event as "fateful" in such a way as to give the youth the impression that his future hangs perilously in the balance of the proceedings.[3] Sanctions become all the more intimidating if it appears that the court is still seriously weighing the possibility of invoking them. If the offender feels that the outcome of his case is predetermined and that no matter what he says or does he will be released or committed, the desired impact of the ceremony will be severely diminished. To counteract this possibility, the court tends to carry on until the very last moment as if the disposition of the case and the fate of the offender were undecided or open to change. Thus the judge often will not announce his disposition until very late in the hearing, occasionally because he actually has not made up his mind, but generally so as to keep the delinquent up in the air concerning his ultimate fate.

There are several tendencies, however, that make it more difficult to present legal sanctions as a realistic and intimidating

3. For an analysis of the social qualities which make events and occasions "fateful," see Goffman's article, "Where the Action Is" (1967, pp. 149–270).

threat. In the first place, dispositions in the court are made in fairly routinized terms. Thus it may be difficult to convince delinquents familiar with the standard operating and commitment procedures of the court that they are on the verge of commitment.[4] But in addition, it often happens that the real purpose of the hearing is to work out an acceptable disposition. In the process of ironing out administrative details in the presence of the child, the possibility of impressing him with his vulnerability is often lost. On several occasions, however, the judge tried to recoup the situation by acting as if he had yet to make a decision that in fact he had clearly made previously:

> A white boy from a nearby suburb, about 13 years old, was surrendered by his probation officer for violating his probation. PO noted that "the boy seems to react badly at home," reported late for all his probation appointments and so missed them, and "cannot adhere to authority whatever." PO recommended either sending him to the Boys' Training Program or committing him. Judge looked over the record. He then turned to the probation officer who ran one unit of the BTP and asked him whether he would take this boy in his program. This PO looked at the boy's record briefly and then agreed to take him for "at least one chance." Judge then called the boy over to the bench and began lecturing him very severely. Here he had promised to behave and do well the last time he had been in court, so that he would not be held in detention, and here he was, not doing anything his PO told him to. Judge continued very harshly, arguing that he had not yet decided between the Boys' Training Program and commitment to the Youth Correction Authority: "I have not made up my mind." But he finally concluded: "You're going to get one more shot, Mister, and that's it. Now get this through your head. . . ."

In this case, then, the judge made the practical arrangements with one of the heads of the Boys' Training Program, arrange-

4. Brown provides an excellent example of how knowledge circulating among delinquents about the operation of the legal system may dissolve the fateful quality of the court proceeding:

> The judge kept talking to us about how we had risked our lives and how we were lucky not to get hurt. He said he was going to give us another chance. We'd expected this; we'd heard that every place they could have sent us was all filled-up—Warwick and Wiltwyck and Lincoln Hall (1966, p. 123).

ments required because of shortage of space in the program. But while lecturing the boy, he steadfastly maintained the fiction that his decision had not been made, only at the end appearing to relent and give the boy "one more shot."

CULPABILITY AND REPENTANCE

The courtroom ceremony is characteristically structured to thrust the delinquent into the status of wrongdoer: the delinquent is pressured to conduct himself in a repentant, contrite manner and hence to acknowledge his own guilt and blameworthiness. But beyond this, the delinquent is not only thrust into this discredited and soiled role, but he is also subjected to systematic pressure to show full commitment to it. He is prevented from withdrawing or showing distance from the role of wrongdoer in any way that might stave off its discrediting implications for both character and self. In this sense, the courtroom proceeding is one of those "barbarous ceremonies . . . expressly designed to prevent the mark from saving his face" (Goffman, 1952, p. 462). Rather than "cooling out" the delinquent, smoothing disengagement from his involvement with wrongdoing (Goffman, 1952, p. 453), the structure of the court ceremony seeks to inescapably impose on him a discrediting self-conception and status.

This section analyzes these complementary processes whereby the delinquent is pushed into the role of wrongdoer and prevented from saving face before its discrediting implications. In so doing it demonstrates how the courtroom ceremony creates conditions for profound personal degradation and how this in turn may set in motion processes that fundamentally change subsequent evaluation of moral character.

By pressuring delinquents to express contrition and remorse for their behavior, court officials structure the courtroom proceeding in a way that places delinquents in the role of wrongdoer. In general, it is made clear to the delinquent that he must show that he is "sorry" for what he did.[5] By indicating remorse in this way,

5. Claude Brown was made acutely aware of this expectation in an early encounter with the juvenile court, making an effort to conduct himself accordingly:

he admits that in some ultimate sense his act was wrong and neither denies nor depreciates his essential culpability. This often culminates in a protestation of intent (often only implicit) conscientiously to avoid offending in the future, as in "I won't do it again."

But in addition, the court presents the delinquent act in ways that reaffirm the delinquent actor's reprehensibility. This reaffirmation is often achieved through use of a rhetorical style premised upon individual responsibility and guilt. This rhetorical style is routinely employed in questioning delinquents about the act and *why* they did it. This "why" question is regularly posed by the court in attending to any delinquency case and serves to elicit the subjective view of and justification for the offense held by the youth. However, this and subsequent questioning *is conducted on such terms that no legitimate reason or justification for the act can be maintained and defended.* Whatever the reasons the delinquent advances, the response is framed in terms of this rhetoric of individual responsibility and morality, in this way taking the act out of the realm of the extenuating and excusable and depicting it as the willful product of the delinquent actor:

> Two boys, both about 12 and both felt to be retarded by court staff, were brought into court in the middle of winter for stealing several pairs of gloves from a downtown department store. After the store detectives had presented the evidence, the judge called the boys over and asked the lawyer: "What's the idea, George?"
> George: My hands were freezing. My hands were freezing. My gloves has all holes in them.
> Judge: Peter?
> Peter: My hands were freezing.
> Judge (sarcastically) : Your hands were freezing. . . . What makes

---

Mrs. Jones, Toto's mother, was standing right next to Toto and me. And Toto was watching her and trying to look pitiful, just like I was. Mama and Mrs. Jones sure did look crazy with their heads going up and down faster and faster as they peeped up at the mean queen from the bottom of their eyes and tried to look as if they knew what she was saying to them. All I knew was that I was supposed to look sorry for what I had done. Toto knew this too, so we were both looking real sorry while our mothers nodded their heads (1966, p. 66) .

you think you can take property that belongs to someone else?
(Neither boy answered.)

Here the judge responds to the boys' excuse that their hands
were cold with open sarcasm in such a way as to dismiss it as
totally inadequate. His subsequent question shifts the blame for
the act right back on to the boys, placing the act within a framework of individual will ("what makes you think you can . . .")
and hence of simple right and wrong.

Even where the delinquent tries to avoid taking a stance toward his offense in order to minimize his exposure as a wrongdoer, the judge will reject this attitude and seek to affirm the
framework of individual responsibility and guilt. To cite two
cases from the Municipal Court:

Judge: What do you have to say for yourself?
Boy: I don't have anything to say.
Judge: What?
Boy: I don't have anything to say.
Judge: Do you think it's right to stick your hand in a man's pocket and
take his wallet?
Boy: No.
Judge: Is it any different to steal somebody's car than his wallet?
Boy: No.

Judge: Well, what's your excuse for this?
Dan: I don't have any.
Judge: That's as good as any I suppose. (Pause.) What can you say
when you go about getting into somebody's car, stealing it, wrecking it?

Recasting the incident in terms of individual responsibility
and guilt also involves the rejection of the delinquent's framework and rationale for accounting for the behavior. Thus, when
asked why they committed the delinquency, youths frequently
reply in naturalistic, cause-and-effect terms. Thus in the glove
theft above, the offense is explained with the words: "My hands
were freezing. My gloves has all holes in them." Similarly, in the
following case, the delinquent provides a simple cause and effect
account for his conduct:

A 14-year-old Negro boy, already on probation for purse-snatching, was returned to district court on two counts of use without authority. The judge lectured him about being back in court less than a month after his previous appearance. Then: "Do you think it gives you a license to steal when you're on probation?"
Boy: No
Judge: Then why did you do it?
Boy (hesitates, then answers) : We wanted to go some place and got in a car.
Judge: It doesn't make any difference to you whether it's a wallet or a car. (a statement, not a question)
Boy: No, sir.
Judge: You're just a thief.
Boy: Yes, sir.

Here again the judge counters this naturalistic account by shifting the framework, specifying the act as "theft," and compelling the youth to acknowledge this redefinition.

Again, such accounts for delinquent activity characteristically make implicit reference to the contingencies of the concrete social situation in which the activity arose. In the car theft case described above, for example, reference is clearly made to the situation of company and to contingencies growing out of peer group involvement in a Negro ghetto. However, the court's recasting of these accounts into an individualistic, moral framework denies legitimacy to these situational contingencies. This denial of legitimacy assumes great importance in light of the fact that delinquents tend to perceive and evaluate their behavior exactly in reference to such situational factors, perhaps even "drifting" into delinquent conduct on the basis of this kind of situationally narrowed definition of events (Cicourel, 1968; Matza, 1964) . Accentuation of the wrongness of delinquent conduct is thus a dual process: on the one hand, it involves an across-the-board rejection of the situational framework within which the act was originally formulated according to relative, situationally specific standards; on the other, it entails imposition of a framework of individual responsibility and universal, absolute morality. As Cicourel has emphasized, this process involves subjecting the act to evaluation in terms of consequences that may become apparent only after the event:

> The juvenile is always asked to express "what happened" in his own words, then the officer provides a more explicit interpretation spelling out the consequences of the acts involved. The "right" course of action is then provided abstractly as if the "right" course was always available to the juvenile. The contingencies of collective behavior—peer group pressures, taunts, or provocations, and the like, or simply viewing the situation as a "lark" or "kicks"— are not seen as admissible excuses by the officer (1968, p. 141).

Court preoccupation with forcing the delinquent to acknowledge ritually his status as wrongdoer often assumes an extreme form when the decision that imprisonment is necessary is reached. Thus a successful denunciation generally culminates in an interrogation where the delinquent is compelled to acknowledge ceremonially his own responsibility for this dire fate and to accept the legitimacy of the court's action. This ritual process wherein the delinquent is made to express involvement in his own incarceration is dramatically illustrated in the case of Ralph Robinson:

> The probation officer had surrendered Robinson for running away from the Roberts School, a private residential school with a large population of lower class boys, where he had been placed, and strongly recommended commitment to the Youth Correction Authority. Judge turned to the boy and asked him if he had anything to say. No. Judge, however, did not let this pass, but commented: "You ran off fully knowing what would happen to you." (A statement of fact, not a question; boy made no response, sitting on chair, eyes downcast.) Judge continued that commitment to the Youth Correction Authority was now unavoidable. "It has to be. You knew when you went off [from the school] you were going, didn't you?" (No answer.) "Huh?" Robinson: "No, sir." Judge: "You figured you wouldn't get caught? You expected a miracle?" Boy shook his head no, eyes downcast, still making no response.
>
> Judge then turned to the probation officer and asked him if Ralph had offered any explanation for why he would not stay. The probation officer answered that the boy thought his only obligation to the

court had been to go to camp that summer, and that come fall he would be through with the court and allowed to go to public school. "He felt he should have been left at home and allowed to live with a friend." Judge then asked the boy whether it had not been clear that he would either go to the Roberts School or be committed to the Youth Correction Authority—that he had no other choice. Robinson stood up, approached the judge, and nervously began his defense, noting: "I didn't want either of them." Judge: "Don't you know you can't do what you want?" Boy continued that he had gone to the camp but felt that it was up to him to decide whether or not he went to the Roberts School in the fall; "You did not make it clear." Judge, however, replied that this was not the point; just before he had been sent to the school he had told him it was either that or the Youth Correction Authority; "You had your choice." But Robinson denied this, saying it had not been clear that he had to go to Roberts, and he did not want to. But the judge again repeated that just that Wednesday he had been told it was either one or the other, and that was his only choice. The boy shook his head no, but said nothing, eyes downcast. He was then told to sit down. Shortly afterward the judge formally committed him.

This kind of ceremony serves a crucial function in the court's handling of delinquency cases. In those cases where normal measures have failed, it shifts all blame for this failure away from the court and its programs. By defining the situation in terms of "chances" given the delinquent, the adequacy of the court's efforts to "help" the delinquent is not brought into question. The delinquent's failure to avail himself of these "chances" can only be attributed to his own action and character. In this way, in such cases where probation "fails" and the court comes to feel that the youth must be incarcerated, failure can be attributed to the delinquent's own shortcomings of moral character—at best his lack of discipline and self-control, at worst to his inherent criminality. The kind of ceremonial confrontation illustrated by the above case thus ritually affirms both the legitimacy and competency of the court's efforts and the personal responsibility and discredited character of the youth involved.

The court's concern with accenting delinquent culpability and with making the delinquent acknowledge his condition of wrongdoer frequently creates crucial presentation problems for the court when a spokesman for a delinquent defends or excuses his misbehavior. For example, a lawyer's pitch on behalf of his delinquent client will generally bring out the strong points in the delinquent's life and character, note any features of his general situation that tend to diminish responsibility for and excuse his misconduct, and minimize the seriousness of the delinquency or the youth's intent in committing it. The lawyer thereby defends the delinquent by trying to present him in the best possible light, advancing excuses for the delinquent behavior, and absolving the actor of as much responsibility as possible. But this approach directly conflicts with the definition of the courtroom proceeding fashioned by the court: it obscures and glosses over the wrongness of the act; it defends and vindicates the delinquent rather than accenting the error of his ways; and it mitigates his responsibility for the commission of a serious delinquent act by appealing to psychological and social frameworks. Under these circumstances, then, the court must counter the lawyer's plea, reasserting its desired definition of the proceeding and of the delinquent's place within it. In this way, the judge will belittle all arguments advanced by the lawyer, not because he disagrees with them, but because they tend to undermine the desired impact of the court proceeding on the child. For example:

Two white boys, both 16, were charged with breaking and entering into a factory. They were defended by private counsel, a lawyer politically active in a neighboring city. The police officer briefly told of apprehending the boys, and probation officer gave his report on the first boy, Jim Michaels. Lawyer then said he had interviewed Jim for an hour, learning that he wanted to go into the service when old enough. He was currently holding a job. "He appears to have something on the ball, and could be salvaged." Boy recognized the seriousness of this offense, and "he is fairly intelligent." Requested that the case be continued without a finding. Probation officer agreed with this recommendation.

But the judge reacted: "I'm afraid I cannot agree with either of you." The boy had run from a policeman who had told him to stop and had fired warning shots. "I wonder what you would think if he had been hit and could not come in here." The fact that the boy had run and might have been shot disturbed him greatly. He then asked Michaels directly: "Why didn't you stop when he fired?" The boy replied that he had not known he was a policeman. Digression on whether police officer had announced himself as such. Then judge: "When are you 17?" Boy replied in about seven months. Judge: "Well, you're lucky you're alive. There's another case in here today where the boy [slightest hesitation] is dead." Boy then put on probation until he was 17, with the comment: "I don't like what you did. And I don't believe it was any accident you were up on that roof, either!"

Here the defense lawyer, in not contesting the charge, minimized the seriousness of the delinquent act. And although he was very careful to choose language acknowledging the fact that the boy had done wrong, he also tried to present the boy's character as basically good. The judge, however, countered by reemphasizing the centrality of the offense and of the attempted escape, thereby reasserting the intimidating definition of the occasion.

Similar problems arise whenever a probation officer puts in a good word for a youth. The judge often feels called upon to reassert the desired definition of the court event and the delinquent's discredited and precarious position within it. The following case suggests one possible consequence of this development:

Frank Riccio and another 16-year-old boy were brought to court on the charge of being present where narcotics were found. Evidence presented by police alleged that narcotics had been on the floor near the front seat when the car had been stopped for going through a red light. Public defender objected strenuously that an illegal search had been made to obtain the narcotics, but after long argument and deliberation the judge noted: "I am satisfied the state has satisfied the statute." But he made no finding of delinquent; instead he called the probation officer for a report on the boys' backgrounds.

Probation officer reported that both boys had extensive records, and summarized them. Riccio was still on probation from the YCA, where he had been committed for truancy. Probation officer, who had worked with the boy while a parole agent for the YCA, said he had felt he was getting somewhere with the family after a year and a half: "His adjustment had an irregular pattern—up and down, that kind of thing. . . . His mother and I worked together on it, and he was making some kind of adjustment." He was encouraged, and the mother had been very cooperative. "The main problems seemed to be that there was no male figure in the home to exercise some control over the boy at this stage of his life."

After this generally favorable report, the judge looked over the face sheet, commenting that Riccio had been into a local court for drunkenness just three days after being picked up on his narcotics violation. Probation officer replied the boy had not really done anything serious there, just going to drink with some friends. . . . Judge sat back in his chair and commented: "I can't make up my mind whether to commit these boys or not." Their records certainly seem to demand it. Probation officer again spoke up, saying that from his experience in their neighborhood they were not really bad kids, but got into trouble because they were always hanging around with undesirable and disreputable companions.

Judge then turned to Riccio, and asked: "I suppose you don't know anything about this [i.e., about the drugs]?" Riccio replied he knew nothing; he had just been in the car, and had just called his mother and had been ready to go home before they had been picked up. Judge: "Well, in that case why did you go to the North side?" Riccio (very softly) : "To find some girls." Riccio continued that he had not done anything. . . . Judge again commented on what a bad record he had, creating the impression that commitment was required.

Here, the probation officer, drawing on prior contact with Riccio and his family, gave a generally favorable report in light of the boy's long record and earlier commitment to the Youth Correction Authority. But even more important, the complaint against the two boys was rather flimsy. One reflection of this was the strong objection made to the arrest and introduction of the narcotics as evidence by the usually docile public defender. Under such circumstances, the judge usually continues the case without a finding. While he undoubtedly intended to do so here, he nevertheless reacted strongly against the probation officer's plea, both emphasizing Riccio's prior record and raising the possibility of committing him, in this way reestablishing the desired definition of the proceeding.

Finally, this reassertion of the delinquent's soiled character may provoke the youth to expose his character to further discrediting. The subsequent course of the Riccio case provides an excellent example.[6] Here the youth did not grasp the fundamentally ritual nature of the judge's behavior. He failed to appreciate that the probation officer's plea had prevailed, that he would not be "sent away." As a result, Riccio took a firm stand on his innocence, attacking the police for framing him. Failure to understand the ritual nature of the proceeding, then, led him into a course of action that totally discredited his moral character in the eyes of the court.

ISSUES OF DEMEANOR

In general, mere verbal expressions of remorse and contrition do not adequately communicate the commitment to the role of wrongdoer expected by court officials. A totally consistent performance is required, and this demands that the repentant delinquent convey a properly deferential and remorseful attitude by his demeanor.[7] Deferential demeanor, expressing appreciation and respect toward both the court and the violated norm, constitutes a basic expectation in the courtroom ceremony. In this way, posture and expression should conform to the solemn and serious definition of the occasion. It is expected that the child maintain a formal, rigid, and controlled posture, both in entering the courtroom and in sitting through the course of the hearing. Facial expression must be carefully controlled in order to show worry and concern or at least serious interest in the unfolding scene. Similarly, any talking or comment must be addressed to the whole court and show respect for the officials involved. Thus the delinquent is expected to stand, use honorary terms of address, speak politely and in complete sentences:

> The family of a teenaged Negro girl had initiated a complaint against a 16-year-old Negro boy for assault in an incident growing out of continual bickering in a public housing project. Judge lectured all

6. See Chapter 6 (pp. 164–65) for the detailed report and analysis of this incident of aborted counter-denunciation.

7. The following analysis draws heavily on Goffman's seminal articles, "The Nature of Deference and Demeanor" (1967, pp. 47–95) and "Role Distance" (1961b).

parties involved about such fighting, and placed the boy on probation for nine months, warning: "If there's another incident and you're involved in any way and you'll go. Do you understand?"

Boy: Yes (muttered somewhat resentfully, looking at floor).

Judge: What?! (less a question than a command, judge staring at boy).

Boy: Yes (somewhat louder, looking up this time).

Judge: What?! (louder still, harsher).

Boy: Yes—sir (making his reluctance clear).

Judge paused, glared at the boy, then commented: "If you think I'm kidding, just test me!" Continued to stare, repeated this statement, then turned away from the boy.

As this case illustrates, violations of the proper forms of demeanor routinely draw court sanctions.[8] Moreover, less obvious violations of expected demeanor than neglect of honorary titles, such as laughter, grinning, whispering, etc., also regularly elicit strong official reaction. For example:

Three young Negro boys in court for trying to steal a woman's purse. Judge had heard the testimony in the case, and had questioned the boys at length about what they had done. He then motioned them to sit down and began lecturing them, warning not to come downtown on their own. One of the boys (10) showed a slight smirk during this

8. Court failure to sanction such violations of deference and demeanor may offend those others on the court scene committed the legal and moral order supported by these rules. Just such dissatisfaction with a judge's perceived failure to uphold the symbolic order apparently provided the spark leading to the crystallization of the right-wing Law Enforcement Group in the New York City Police Department. This group grew out of a protest against the manner in which a Criminal Court judge handled a group of Black Panthers in his courtroom. As the petition circulated by police officers from Brooklyn claimed: "On the night of Aug. 1, 1968, [the judge] did permit members of a racist group in his courtroom, to smoke, permitted them to wear their hats while the court was in session and permitted them to shout threats at the members of the Police Department and at the bench in a successful effort to have two defendants before him paroled and walk out of the courtroom. . . . The [judge] paroled the defendants, although the prisoners' addresses were not properly verified, disregarding the pleas of the arresting officers, one of whom was kicked in the groin by one defendant" (*New York Times*, Aug. 5, 1968).

Here it seems clear that the police felt a lack of deference in and to the court hearing constituted a challenge to their own authority, a challenge all the more menacing because of court failure to follow police recommendations seeking to protect this authority.

lecture. The judge broke off in the middle and warned the boy: "If I see you crack another smile in here—you had better crack it on the other side of your face! . . ." Then he summoned the boy up to the platform by his bench, staring at him, then stating: "You think you're a big shot, don't you?" Boy bowed head, looked at floor. Judge made it clear he was not and told him: "You go over there and sit down and don't crack another smile."

Probation reports were being given on a group of young boys. One Negro boy, Jimmy Irwin, aged 9, grinned slightly when a parent reported that her son was always getting into things at home. He turned his head partially toward the wall, raising his hand to his face, apparently trying to repress the grin. But the judge noticed it, abruptly wheeled around in the boy's direction and growled: "You think it's funny, Irwin? You had just better mind your own business!" The grin disappeared, and the boy shifted his glance away from the judge's stare.

As the above cases illustrate, these expectations reflect a basic requirement of the court ceremony, namely, that one show undivided and total attention to the courtroom scene. Any kind of side involvement tends to undermine the serious definition of the occasion by indicating that participation is not totally consuming and demanding. For this reason, court staff directly sanction such denials of the overriding importance of the proceeding, including laughing, grinning, and even guarded smiling, as well as exaggerated gum chewing and whispering. By sanctioning such expressions of alienation from or limited commitment to the proceeding, the court exerts systematic pressure on the delinquent to show total involvement in the ceremony and in the determination of his own guilt. Hence a youth is not allowed to express distance from the soiled role of sinner and culprit in which he finds himself as the court ceremony unfolds.

While contrition and remorse, expressed through acknowledgment of wrongdoing and exhibition of deference, allow the court to accept a favorable definition of moral character, such a stance may well be experienced by the delinquent as personally humiliating. By showing contrition and deference in general behavior and demeanor, the delinquent both condemns his own past be-

havior as "wrongdoing" and conducts himself in his present encounter in a manner he may feel is demeaning. Hence, pressured
into showing remorse and deference, he may simultaneously experience considerable inclination to show distance from the role
of repentant wrong-doer. Demeanor is often the most convenient
means of expressing such distance.

It is clear, for example, that the ceremonial import of verbal
apology and repentance can be totally destroyed by undeferential
demeanor that contradicts the explicit message of the performance. One reflection of this possibility is the requirement that
deferential demeanor of an extremely exacting and consistent
kind accompany any *defense* presented by a delinquent, if it is to
be accepted. While the presentation of defenses by spokesmen
tends to contradict the delinquent's culpability—a basic ceremonial feature of the courtroom staging—defense attempts made by
the delinquent himself do so to an even greater degree. Failure to
maintain exemplary demeanor, for example, may transform an
excuse into a plea for vindication, into a basic denial of the seriousness and wrongness of the offense itself.

The delinquent who advances an excuse for his offense without
making it very clear that he is not trying to deny completely his
responsibility for doing wrong is apt to be sharply rebuked by the
court. The judge's reaction to the accident excuse of the three
young boys charged with attempting to steal a handbag (see
p. 154) is typical of what can occur if excuses are put forward
with too great an assertion of personal worth and autonomy. In
general, then, only a combination of valid defense and exemplary
demeanor allows a delinquent to isolate wrongdoing from character without challenging the court's ceremonial structure and,
ultimately, the moral and legal order it defends. The following
case provides a clear example of the successful presentation of an
excuse:

A 16-year-old white girl from a rural town in another part of the
state had been discovered living in the city with an older married
man. She was brought to court by the police and charged with runaway. Her father and mother told about the girl's getting into a car
during a dance and not returning again. This had occurred two

months previously and she had been living with the man all this time. Parents both appeared to be solidly lower-middle class, respectable, well dressed, polite, and obviously very upset by the whole incident. Father concluded his statement: "All I know is if we can get her home we can take care of her."

Judge next turned to the girl, asking if she had anything to say. She began, almost in a sob: "I just wanted to say I didn't want to run away. I was afraid of what would happen if I tried to get out of the car." She continued in this vein, showing great emotion and pleading that she had not meant to do it and to worry her parents. Police officer tended to support her story, saying of the man she had run away with: "This fellow could talk a dog off a meat train." Judge accepted this version of the delinquency, later noting: "This child has been listening to the wrong people." He then ordered the probation officer to make arrangements to have the whole family seen at a local psychiatric outpatient clinic, and dismissed the complaint.

Here, the girl apologizes and expresses deep remorse for having run away, offering no defense of the offense itself, no claim that running away from home was defensible and perhaps justified. With the apparent sincerity of her remorse she is then able to successfully advance her excuse: that she did not mean to do it, that she could not help herself but had been led on by the older man. The police support this shift of responsibility by noting what a persuasive sort he is. The judge accepts this version of the incident, blaming the man. He also holds the parents partially responsible (they had admitted that they had been spying on the girl at the dance just before she had run off, and this the judge interpreted as a sign of family problems and perhaps parental restrictiveness) and consequently orders the whole family to visit a psychiatric clinic. In sum, with the sincere and deep-felt expression of remorse, the judge is led to make a lenient disposition despite the rather obvious superficiality of the girl's substantive excuse (i.e., even if she could not get out of the car as her boyfriend drove away, why did she stay with him for several months after that?).

Since a delinquent may have a strong inclination to flaunt proper demeanor in order to show distance from the discrediting role and situation in which he finds himself, breaches of proper demeanor and rules of deference occur with some regularity in the court setting. The delinquent can try to save face in this way, however, only at considerable risk, for such breaches of the ceremonial order draw the immediate negative attention of court officials. This official sanctioning of violations of proper demeanor may well initiate processes that lead to negative assessments of moral character. In particular, since the proper expression of deference through contrition and demeanor indicates a delinquent of normal character to the court, consistent violation of these rules of deference—and consistent resistance to efforts to sanction such violations—frequently discredits character.

Under these circumstances, a youth who has any reservations about the role of contrite wrongdoer in which he finds himself encounters a basic dilemma. In adopting the penitent stance in order to protect character and save face from the full implications of his misconduct, he must become personally involved in his own discrediting; but if he tries to maintain a sense of personal dignity by showing distance from this role he is apt to face severe sanctioning and perhaps more fundamental discrediting at the hands of the court. It is to some of the latter possibilities that I now turn.

Certain forms of courtroom demeanor on the part of delinquents lead the court staff to make interpretations of the youth's character as "defiant," "fresh," "wise," etc. To begin with, both posture and facial expression can be employed to indicate disdain for the court and legal order. This also involves that tacit assertion of an autonomous and unrepentant self at odds with the expectation that a normal offender will express deference and contrition in his public presentation of self. For example:

> A 16-year-old girl, Irish name, dark hair worn piled high on head. Juvenile officer noted that the girl was a runaway who had been found in the apartment of an 18-year-old boy, adding: "The girl did tell me she had relations with the boy." Judge talked with mother, who said she had forbidden her daughter from marrying this boy until she went back to school. The runaway had followed this.
> Judge then indicated to the girl that he wanted to talk to her. She stood up, but did not move from her chair toward the platform by the judge's bench. Her posture was rigid, both hands stuffed low into the

pockets of her green sweater, arms locked stiffly. She looked directly at the judge, cocking her head first to one side and then to the other. Throughout her confrontation with the judge her face showed an only slightly disguised sneer.

Similarly, the manner in which questions posed by the judge are answered can be used as a means of asserting one's autonomy and sense of worth in a situation and proceeding that explicitly deny them. This can be achieved not only by avoiding deferential titles of address and polite tone of voice, but also by answering in brief, curt phrases. To continue with the above case:

The girl answered all the questions the judge asked her, but only after pausing slightly, and always restricted herself to monosyllables. These answers were delivered with her more or less openly sneering expression, the words slightly overemphasized. For example:

Judge: How are you doing in school?
Girl: Same as before (i.e., as before she met her boyfriend, who had been blamed for her decline in school) .
Judge: How was that?
Girl: Badly (head tilted, grinning sneer) .[9] (Probation officer commented that she had done very well in grade school, but had a terrible record now and did not attend regularly.)
Judge: Why don't you go to school?
Girl (long pause) : I *don't* care for school, and just don't want to go! (Every word spoken with great care, very distinctly and clearly accented.)

Probation officer then suggested having the girl seen at the clinic, and recommended allowing her to go home during the continuance. The judge was skeptical: "What makes you think she'll stay at home?" PO: "Just from talking to the mother and the girl. The mother says she will . . ." After arrangements had been made, the judge explained to the girl that he was releasing her, and asked if she understood. The girl answered, "Yes," a delayed response delivered with

9. Here the girl attacks the moral order by revelling in the fact that she is doing badly. The meaning of her answer, "badly," is determined by her assertive and unrepentant demeanor and tone, which clearly communicate that she is *not ashamed* of doing badly in school and moreover that it is not something that one *should* be ashamed of. The impact of the answer "badly" would have been completely different (and acceptable to the court) if delivered with bowed head and in subdued voice.

one of her typical sneers. Judge: "You get too smart with me, young lady, and you'll—" (breaking off, staring at girl who looks at him without making much effort to change her expression). Judge dismissed the case, commenting to the PO: "I don't know why you think she'll be around, but I'll take the chance."

Here, the girl's delay in answering direct questions asserts control over and autonomy in the situation. Moreover, it may initially appear to represent a major rejection of the ceremonial authority of the court, a refusal to answer at all. Answering in short phrases, without subjects or articles, not only avoids polite and deferential forms of address, but also reduces one's involvement with the court and its inquiry, in this way minimizing exposure of self. Finally, emphasizing and overemphasizing each word or phrase, by departing from normal conversational styles, indicates that one's commitment to the situation is minimal and coerced at that.

Demeanor of this nature is considered to be openly "insolent"; it involves a direct challenge to the projected definition of the situation, an implicit denial of wrongdoing through refusal to conduct oneself as a wrongdoer. But while this kind of "defiant" or "insolent" behavior may in itself suggest criminal-like character, such an assessment becomes almost inevitable if the delinquent persists in such conduct in the face of court sanctions against it. Thus, a criminal-like assessment becomes almost inevitable when the delinquent consistently maintains a defiant stance throughout the proceeding (and likewise, throughout other encounters with court staff) despite strong counter-measures. Court personnel interpret such behavior as a conscious challenge to their authority and a conscious denial of the validity of the rule that was contravened. For example:

Nicholas Despisa, a 13-year-old Italian boy, was charged with taking a 1966 Oldsmobile. He stated that he had been taking the car somewhere to sleep because he was afraid to go home. Several master keys to cars were found on the boy, who claimed he found them (see p. 116). The judge called the boy over to his bench to question him about the incident. Youth was dark complexioned, long black hair, slender, very lively eyes. He wore a blue parka and tight black pants. Judge asked: "Is there anything you want to tell me about this? Anything about what happened?" Boy: "No." Judge: "No?" Judge paused, eye brows raised, then turned to PO for a report on his contact with the boy. Boy had answered judge's question in a curt, toneless voice; his facial expression was somewhat contorted, somewhere between a grimace and a sneer. This was characteristic of his behavior throughout the rest of the questioning.

After the probation report, judge turned back to the boy (who had stayed standing by the bench) and asked: "Where did you get the keys?" Boy: "Found them" (muttered in a low tone, but eye contact maintained directly with judge). Judge: "What?" (combining harshness with sense of not having heard correctly; stern look). Boy: "Found them" (a little louder, but still looking judge in the eye). Judge, who had been in the middle of his desk, about five feet from the boy, pulled his chair towards the boy, cutting the distance to several feet, now glaring at the boy. Judge: "Found them? You expect me to believe that?" Boy made no answer, but continued to meet the judge's stern glare.

Judge then asked the boy how he had learned to drive. Boy answered that it was his first time. How could it be if he had not damaged the car? Youth insisted he had never driven before, and had driven very slowly so he would not have an accident. Judge: "You expect me to believe that?" (sternly, as if reprimanding a liar, not incredulously). Boy: "It's the truth" (very assertively, again looking the judge in the eye). Judge stared at boy for several seconds, then turned away and considered disposition. Probation officer recommended clinical study, and judge agreed, commenting: "All right, I'll hold up on this until the recommendation [from the court clinic]. I'll give you time for your study. But I tell you right now. He had better be psychotic because if he's not he's going" [i.e., will be committed to the Youth Correction Authority].

In this case, the youth throughout his questioning maintained an expression bordering on defiance on his face. When pressed on his story, he became assertive and almost aggressive in tone. At no time did he conform to the amenities of address expected in the courtroom setting. Not only did he avoid such terms as "sir" or "your honor," but he also did not answer in complete sentences, even when rebuked by the judge. This abbreviated, curt address pointedly refuses to pay deference to the court and to the official position of the judge. The boy also failed to acknowledge symbolically the authority of the court proceeding in his eye movement; when confronted with a condemning accusation from the judge he refused to lower his gaze, but continued to meet the judge's eye directly. Maintaining eye contact under such an accusation denies guilt and wrongness by tacitly asserting autonomy and rectitude. The judge's final statement reveals his evaluation of defiance and criminality in the behavior of this boy, an evaluation he will reverse only if a severe mental problem is found: "He had better be a psychotic, because if he's not, he's going!"

In conclusion, it is clear that demeanor is a crucial factor in the courtroom proceeding and the character evaluations made therein, as it is in most encounters between delinquents (and other wrongdoers) and those official agents controlling them. The very subtlety with which disrespect and distance can be expressed through demeanor may make such behavior particularly attractive to a delinquent in court. It may effectively allow him to contradict both his own explicit performance and the court ceremony of which it is part. The delinquent can tacitly show his disdain for the court event by showing limited or irreverent commitment to the court situation through his demeanor. He can implicitly justify his delinquent conduct by refusing to comport himself in the totally contrite and repentant way the court expects. But the court is itself extremely aware of the significance of demeanor, and will actively sanction violations of the rules of deference maintained in the courtroom. "Defiance" thus tends to take on a tentative and episodic quality, and becomes a very difficult and costly stance to maintain throughout the proceeding. Persistently improper demeanor will be interpreted in criminal terms, for it will be perceived as a direct and intended denial of the authority and legitimacy of the court.[10]

10. The perceived intentionality of improper demeanor seems to be the critical factor in assessments of criminal character. Hence inappropriate comportment that does not appear intentional will have very different consequences. Two general patterns emerge here. In the first place, there are breeches of rules relating to the court's projected definition of the solemn nature of the proceeding, such as relaxed facial expression, grins, laughter, whispering, etc. While such expressions are regularly rebuked by court staff, they are not perceived as open and direct challenges to court authority and are generally interpreted as but momentary and incidental lapses of basically normal children.

"TRANSFORMED" INTERACTION
IN THE COURT SETTING

The previous analysis has emphasized how, in compelling commitment to the discredited role of wrongdoer, the court seeks to prevent delinquents from routinely using a number of techniques and devices to save face. But in addition, the delinquent may be prevented from saving face more or less incidentally as a consequence of the nature of the rules governing interaction in the courtroom setting.

Interaction in "natural" settings, between relative equals, proceeds according to norms that by and large protect the interactants from embarrassment, humiliation, and discrediting. The parties cooperate to protect both the encounter and the claims advanced by the other (Goffman, 1959). In contrast, interaction in the court setting proceeds according to a set of norms characteristic of authority-permeated relationships. Thus, during the courtroom hearing, court officials may disregard many of the conventional norms of face-to-face interaction. The hearing is conducted on the basis of "transformation rules" (Goffman, 1961b, p. 33), which enable officials to act in ways that in normal interaction would constitute clear violations of appropriate rules of behavior.

In the first place, normal rules of eye movement and engage-

Second, where this less directly challenging but still improper demeanor appears to be beyond the control of the delinquent, it tends to lead to assessments of disturbed character (Goffman, 1963a, p. 218). For example, "psychological problems" are routinely attributed to delinquents who fail to attend to the proceedings in an appropriate way. If the youth looks around the courtroom but not at the focus of the hearing, he is apt to be seen as "disoriented" and probably mentally disturbed. A psychiatrist commented to the judge about a girl she felt was on the verge of a psychotic break: "She looked odd . . . vague, staring into space." Again, the judge characterized as "strange" a boy who sat through his hearing staring blankly straight ahead, showing absolutely no involvement in the proceeding. Similarly, unusual body movements and gestures may suggest a mental problem to the court. Finally, if a youth shows proper involvement and attention span and yet gives no indication that he comprehends what is happening, the court will generally conclude that he is retarded.

ment are transformed in the court setting. In this way, the judge may fixedly study and openly stare at delinquents, as well as at their parents, and need not turn his glance away when met by these others.

Second, the judge and other court officials may openly express disapproval of the appearance, behavior, and comments of delinquents. Thus judge and probation officer may glower at juveniles misbehaving in the court setting. Similarly, the judge may comment on and ridicule the youth's personal appearance. Youths of either sex may receive comments about disheveled and "slobby" clothes, hair, and other aspects of physical appearance. An extreme instance of this occurred in the Municipal Court during the course of a probation interview:

> A tall, well-dressed Negro boy reported to the probation office at the district court. Although his probation officer was out, the white office secretary helped out with several questions concerning restitution. The secretary then asked him a number of questions about his job, how he was doing at school. During the course of this interview, she asked him why he wore so many rings and commented about his "do." Then, referring to the absent PO, she commented: "He's gonna see no restitution and your hair done. You'd better take those rings off too." After a series of questions about when he could make his restitution payments, she asked sternly: "How much are you paying to have your hair done?" Richard (turning, grinning slightly in an embarrassed way) : "Six-fifty every two weeks." Secretary: "I don't know, but Mr. Lewis will probably say that you can't get your hair done until you've paid the restitution." Then, as the boy began to leave the office, Secretary: "Let me ask you one question: Why do you want to do that [i.e., have his hair done] for? Answer me!" Richard (mumbling, looking at his feet) : "I don't know." Secretary: "Do you think it makes you look handsome or sharp or something?" No answer.

Again, as this "interview" suggests, court officials may go beyond mere negative comment and actually force the youth to correct his court-identified blemish. Boys with long hair, for example, are frequently ordered to have it cut.[11]

11. As an extreme example of this, it is reported that an earlier judge at the juvenile court often required boy delinquents to wear girls' clothes to school as a form of probation punishment.

The most frequent and telling breaches of normal rules of interaction, however, derive from the court's power of interrogation. Information control is a critical power in the effort to present and maintain a favorable image of self (Goffman, 1959, p. 141). Normal interaction protects against the revelation of discrediting information, prescribing circumspection and avoidance in clearly dangerous areas and valuing tact in moving away from dangerous areas into which one has blundered unawares. In the court setting, however, the judge and probation officer need not avoid such areas or show any tact or circumspection in approaching them. Thus, in inquiring into the facts and circumstances of a case, the judge may publicly probe into intimate, embarrassing and humiliating areas. For example:

Alvin Beaumont had been charged with contributing to the delinquency of a minor for a homosexual incident and pleaded guilty (see (p. 158fn). The judge questioned him at length about his readily admitted homosexual proclivities and about his general background. Beaumont had a very noticeable scar on one cheek, and at one point the judge asked him: "How did you get those scars on your face?" Beaumont explained that he had cut himself on his grandfather's straight razor when he was 3 years old.

A complaint was brought against a 16-year-old Negro boy to obtain support for the unborn child of a 14-year-old girl. Somewhat incoherently, the girl told of going up to the boy's apartment where she was forced to submit to intercourse. She was clearly embarrassed and ill at ease, both about the incident and in being before the court. This persisted when the judge began to cross-examine her about what had happened, brushing aside her attempts to gloss over all details. She eventually described the act which took place in the bedroom. Judge: "When this act took place, what did you do? [Girl makes no response, keeping her gaze on the floor.] Something happened on the bed? [with mild exasperation]. (Yes.) Did he use any force? You were willing? (No.) . . . Is this the first time you've had intercourse with this boy? Have you done it before? Or since?" Girl: "No, only that time."

And as the latter case indicates, the youth may be denied any right to answer evasively. For the judge can reject and sanction efforts to avoid answering even the most personal and humiliating questions.

Similarly, normal expectations about the use made of discrediting information do not apply in the courtroom. Court officials, for example, are free to introduce any information they possess about delinquents, whether gleaned from prior contact, gossip, or direct knowledge. Hence they do not confine themselves to acknowledging information obtained only from the other party himself (here the delinquent).

Finally, the standards in terms of which the juvenile's courtroom conduct are evaluated differ from, and may explicitly contradict, those relevant to normal interaction. The most important instance of this concerns the value usually placed on *poise* in our society. A competent person is expected to retain composure even under the most trying circumstances; to become flustered and lose poise usually reflects adversely on one's character (Goffman, 1967, pp. 97–98). But in the courtroom hearing, where the delinquent is expected to conduct himself as a contrite wrongdoer, to maintain composure can be basically discrediting. To appear too "cool" and in control under these circumstances suggests to the court that the delinquent remains both unimpressed by the court confrontation and committed to his wrongdoing. In fact, the dual emphasis on the delinquent's vulnerability and wrongness, characteristic of the court's ceremonial structure, involves an attempt to fluster and disconcert the delinquent. To remain composed in the face of this staging is considered inappropriate, as it controverts the expectation that the juvenile is intimidated, contrite, and resigned to the role of impotent wrongdoer. More concretely, to remain cool and unaffected during the court confrontation signals an inner "hardness" and sophistication, reflecting an overexposure to criminal ways, and hence indicates criminal character to court personnel.

In summary, courtroom interaction proceeds according to rules transformed from those applicable to ordinary face-to-face interaction. The effect of this transformation is to deny the delinquent access to many routinely employed face-saving devices. In this way a delinquent cannot count on court officials to disregard discrediting information they may obtain about him. In fact, he faces probings into exactly those subjects and areas apt to be most humiliating and discrediting to him. Moreover, he may not be allowed to evade or avoid these probings. Not only is the delinquent subject to inquiry into personal and intimate subjects ordinarily beyond the bounds of legitimate comment, but he may also become subject to court authority to change his conduct or appearance in exactly these areas. Finally, it is not only as a witness that the delinquent is "not allowed to use procedures for withdrawal and role distancing" (Linton, 1965, p. 10). Rather, the delinquent is always "on stage"—his conduct and demeanor is always subject to scrutiny by court personnel—such that it becomes difficult and hazardous to express disdain or alienation from the courtroom proceeding at almost any point.

ALTERNATIVE COURT STYLES

As noted previously, the routine staging of the courtroom ceremony presumes a delinquent of probable normal character and in fact comes to constitute a kind of testing of this normalcy. In line with the logic of this kind of staging, there are two separate occasions when the hearing is conducted on terms devoid of devices aimed at heightening the intimidating authority of the court and the blameworthiness of the offender.

In the first place, where it is felt that children are clearly not responsible for their delinquent behavior, this misconduct is dealt with in a very matter-of-fact way. There is no emphasis given to the wrongness of the act. Rather attention centers on getting the child under the care of some qualified specialist. If lectured at all, the tone is very mild and sympathetic, a simple cautionary note. In the following case, for example, the child is sympathetically lectured to convince him to go along with the court "plan":

An 8-year-old Negro boy had been evaluated at the Children's Mental Hospital and then held in detention. Finally the court decided to try to get the boy to live with his father, who had separated and remarried, as his mother was under outpatient psychiatric care. In the courtroom, after arranging this with the faher, his new wife, and the boy's mother, judge called the boy over to his bench:

Judge (very mildly and gently) : "I'm going to send you to your father's house. Okay?" Boy shakes his head up and down. "Do you want to go with your father?" Boy responds again in the same way. "Can you say yes or no?" (Again very softly.)
Boy: "Yes."
Judge (conversational tone) : "No more stealing, no more running away. Do you understand that?"
Boy: "Yes." Judge then asked if he had liked it out at detention, and boy replied no. "Then obey your aunt so you don't have to go out there again." As the boy was leaving, the judge added in the same mild tone: "Don't have people go bringing you back in before me, okay?" Boy nodded yes.

Here, although the boy is warned against future misbehavior, the warning is delivered in a very mild tone, with the court's intention being simply to prevent the boy from causing trouble and hence getting thrown out of his new home.

Similarly, in other cases where the child is not considered responsible for his misconduct, the court consciously tries to decrease distance and to minimize authority in order to extract information from the child, often on his feelings and attitudes:

A mother brought an incorrigible child complaint against her 9-year-old daughter, claiming that she stole things all the time. PO suggested the possibility of sending her to the clinic. In the courtroom, the judge called the girl over to his bench, moved his chair very close to her, and began to ask her questions in a very soft and mild tone. Judge: "What have you been doing, huh? [Girl shakes her head, yes, once.] Why did you steal? Why do you disobey your mother? Why do you get her all upset? [Another pause, judge looking at girl, girl looking back at him, saying nothing.] Don't you like your younger brothers and sisters? [Nods yes.] Which one do like best? [All.] All of them? Do you like Barbara? [A slight pause before his last question, as the judge picked up the face sheet to look up the names of the other children. Girl replies yes.] Don't you fight with her? [No.] What about Martha? Don't you fight with her? [No.] Don't you fight with any of them? [Kenneth.] Why do you fight with him? [He hurts me.] And what about your baby brother? [He doesn't do it.] . . . Aren't you going to tell me why you're doing all this stealing? [No answer.] What makes you think you can steal from other people? Doesn't your mother keep tellin' you it's wrong?" [All said in the same gentle tone.]

In this case, the judge employs a very mild and friendly tone to question a young girl about her behavior at home in order to form his own opinion about the possibility and severity of mental disturbance.

In general, when the judge wishes to impress a delinquent with his understanding and helpful attitude, he adopts a conversational instead of inquisitorial or lecturing tone, moves his chair closer to the child, expresses his sympathy and concern. But in addition, he may try to reduce personal distance by letting fall standard rules of deference, permitting a child to remain seated while talking, and not requiring the usual "your honor" or "sir." For example:

> A 16-year-old white girl was surrendered for violating her probation by running away from her home for a weekend. Probation officer recommended giving the girl another chance because she had turned herself in. Judge clearly blamed the girl's mother and general home situation for the trouble, at one point commenting: "Sending this girl back home is flying in the face of reality—" and inquired about the possibility of getting the Child Welfare Department to place her in a foster or group home.
>
> Judge then turned his chair toward the girl and began questioning her about why she had run away. As he began, the probation officer whispered loudly from her seat: "Debbie, stand up!" Girl started to rise, but the judge briefly interrupted himself and said: "No, that's okay," motioning with his hand that the girl could remain seated. He then continued his questioning, in a very gentle voice, trying to get Debbie to talk about why she had gone.

But note that even here it is only the style and tone of the proceeding that has been changed; the basic inquisitional format, premised on the superordinate position of the judge, remains unchanged.

A second deviation from the typical solemn court style often occurs in cases where the court had given up and decided that the youth is "hopeless." The hearing is then generally brief and unemotional, limited often to the routine technicalities needed to bring about a commitment:

An 11-year-old Negro boy had been brought in as an "incorrigible" child and seen at the clinic. The psychiatrist there felt that the boy needed more than "simple probationary supervision." Judge talked briefly to the mother, who complained that there had been no improvement in the boy's behavior. After a few questions to the boy, asked in a very mild tone, the judge told the PO: "For his own sake I'm going to commit him to Westfield" (Youth Correction Authority school for delinquent boys under 12). He then explained to the mother in a very earnest tone why he was going to do this and what Westfield was like.

In this and similar cases the judge delivers no lecture or warning, and is apparently totally unconcerned with the impression made on the youth. The court must simply work through certain procedural details, and perhaps make some effort to gain the acquiescence of the parent to the impending commitment.

Finally, rules of deference are generally relaxed in cases where the court faces purely administrative decisions. For example, in a case of a girl from out of state, concerned solely with the formalities of extradition, the courtroom atmosphere turned very informal and relaxed, the girl participating more or less as an equal in the deliberations and even making a well-received joke. Similarly, in another extradition case, a girl was able to make an extremely defiant entrance into the courtroom without drawing comment and without ruining the court's subsequent evaluation of her character and handling of the hearing:

Grace, a 14-year-old white girl, was brought into the courtroom by a probation officer. She walked to her seat with a cocky, bouncing swagger and sat down. She then began to laugh, not making any noise, but making the body motions of laughing while her mouth was wide open. She leaned back in the chair and grinned broadly, looking over the courtroom. Caught the eye of a woman who had come with her and grinned widely again. Started to laugh, but as the judge lifted his eyes to look at her she lowered her head and covered her face with her hands, as if making a great effort to control herself. Judge stared at her, almost glowering. Grace lifted her head and met his gaze, uncovering her face, still grinning slightly.

Policeman testified then that Grace had been picked up over the weekend at a late party and had turned out to be an escapee from a reform school in a neighboring state. She had been charged with runa-way. PO then explained that the school had been contacted, and had sent a social worker (the woman in the back) to return the girl. Judge commented: "I guess we've got enough problems without interfering in yours," and agreed to return her. But he then asked Grace if she wanted to go back. No. What did she want to do? Grace: "I want a home." She wanted to go to a foster home and not back to the school. Judge questioned both the girl and the school social worker about this, finally commenting: "Well, I hope you do everything there is to get her out into a foster home."

Judge then explained to Grace that she could either sign a volun-tary return form, or wait for a formal hearing on the question. If the latter she would be held at the detention center until the hearing date. Grace (grimly) : "I'll sign." General laughter from court staff. Girl left the courtroom, and judge commented to PO and myself about what a "nice" girl she was.

This analysis suggests that the juvenile court's presentation strategies may heighten a delinquent's sense of blatant inconsist-ency and injustice in his encounters with the court (Matza, 1964, pp. 110–36). The court presents its most intimidating front to those delinquents it regards most favorably and treats most leni-ently, and hands out its severest penalties in a neutral, matter-of-fact style to those delinquents it considers "hopeless." Thus, this sense of inconsistency and injustice results not only from the ideology of individualized justice that obscures the bases of judg-ment and cloaks punishment in the phrases of therapy. It is also created through the use of a harshly punitive style as a technique for maximizing the drama and impact of the court ceremony in situations where no penalties or sanctions are imminent.

"COOLING OUT" DELINQUENTS

Up until this point, the court proceeding and the courtroom en-counter have been depicted as an occasion on which delinquents are embarrassed, humiliated, and degraded. The court ceremony generally attempts to "shake up" delinquents, denying them ac-cess to face-saving and role-distancing devices with which to stave off degradation. However, these processes often create situations in which it is expedient or necessary to cool delinquents out (Goffman, 1952). This occurs most frequently after a court proceeding in which a delinquent has been incarcerated, whether permanently or provisionally. (Note that this distinction may not be apparent to the delinquent at the time of his incarceration.) Prior to his actual commitment the delinquent has undoubtedly been threatened with the specter of detention center and reform school. Court lecturing relies heavily on this threat, picturing such an eventuality as the worst imaginable fate. With commitment the delinquent suddenly finds himself a member of what has been described to him as a despicable population of a defiling institution. Routine court procedures, therefore, endow commitment with extremely destructive and mortifying meanings for self.

Problems of simple physical control often make "cooling out" an expedient measure at this point. Incarceration tends to loosen many controls and restraints on the delinquent's conduct. On an institutional level, the court's major sanction has actually been invoked; there is thus a moment stretching from the formal sentence until the actual transfer of custody to the detention center when the delinquent is between control structures. More personally, incarceration may well lead the delinquent to feel that he has fallen as low as possible and increase the likelihood of his "flooding out" (Goffman, 1961b, pp. 55–61). Under these circumstances he may see nothing to lose by becoming hostile, abusive, or assaultive:

> A 15-year-old white boy, Patrick Quinn, was found delinquent for use without authority. The probation officer presented his rather lengthy record, and added that his mother felt he was becoming more and more difficult. Here the judge cut him off, noting, "I've heard enough." The judge then revoked Quinn's prior suspended sentence and committed him to the Youth Correction Authority. But with this sentence, Quinn rose and muttered angrily, "Why, you fucking asshole!" At this the court officer, standing near the door into the hall, rushed over, grabbed the boy by the arm, and pulled him out of the courtroom, while commanding: "All right! That's enough! Come on!"

Thus, as the case illustrates, a potentially anomic situation is created with regard to the immediate control of the just-incarcerated delinquent.

This problem of interim control falls to the court personnel responsible for managing and transporting the committed delinquent, generally court officers but also probation officers. These officers seek to effect transfer smoothly and without violent outburst. The process of getting delinquents out of the cell and into a car for transportation to detention, and of controlling them during the trip itself, can be handled with less exertion and unseemliness if the youths "cooperate" and "go quietly." Not only must court officials forcibly restrain the youth who becomes violent, an unpleasant eventuality for most staff, but resistance also ties up more court personnel in the transfer process. In general, then, court officials have a definite interest in inducing delinquents who have been committed to "cooperate" and not to "make trouble" on the way to the detention center.

"Cooling out" the incarcerated delinquent facilitates this process. In communicating to the delinquent that he is not at the end of the world and that his fate is not so desperate as previously pictured, it is also indicated that he has something to gain by compliance to ordinary social restraints. "Cooling out" begins with the delinquent's exit from the courtroom following his sentence. In leading the youth back to the temporary cell, the court or probation officer generally expresses sympathy, indicating that despite his incarceration the youth still shares some human quality. While waiting in the cell, the delinquent may receive considerate treatment from court officials—an offer of a cigarette or food. Sometimes a probation officer will express his sympathy while using the language of "rehabilitation" to attempt to redefine the delinquent's situation:

> A probation officer from the Boys' Training Program had been attempting to work with a 13-year-old white boy for some time, but finally decided he could not control him and gave up on the case, arranging for a truancy complaint to be filed. The boy was committed to the County Training School on this complaint. In the cell after the hearing, the youth was very upset and the probation officer talked with him for some time, presenting the institution as a school and not a prison, a place where he would receive care and treatment. After spending some time trying to get the boy to accept the disposition, the probation officer left him. In passing another probation officer, he

complained: "He doesn't understand. He thinks he's going to a correctional institution."

But perhaps more important, cooling out involves redefining the commitment in neutral, matter-of-fact terms. The court official presents incarceration as something that can be accepted and lived with. The delinquent is told that things are not really that bad in the reform school: it is out in the country, he will learn a trade, the staff will give him a fair shake, he can get along if he behaves himself. He is shown that his future is not completely hopeless, for with good behavior he will be out in a matter of months. In this way the prior definition of incarceration as a totally degrading and despairing event is denied, as the delinquent is offered a conception of self other than the anticipated complete social outcast.

Basic to the neutralization of the immediately destructive effects of incarceration on the delinquent's self is the presentation of the institution involved in favorable terms. This is reflected in the findings of an interview study of delinquents in detention awaiting transfer to reform school:

> Before being actually committed by a court, the bulk of what the youths hear is unfavorable. But from the time of the court appearance that leads to their commitment until their arrival at the institution, the bulk of what they hear is positive. Those in contact with the youths present the coming events in their most favorable light (Wheeler and Blum, 1968, p. 163).

In this way, the incarcerated youth is reincorporated into the normal social order following an event previously presented as social death. While this reincorporation may only be temporary and may collapse before the realities of institutional life, it effectively secures the delinquent's cooperation in the initial process of his own incarceration.

CONCLUSION

This analysis has emphasized how degrading and humiliating the courtroom ceremony may become for the youth involved. This emphasis would appear to contradict Blumberg's description of the "cop-out" ceremony characteristic of the adult criminal court (1967a, pp. 32–38; 1967b, pp. 88–94). Blumberg argues that the "cop-out" ceremony is so superficial and transparent that it produces no significant effect on the defendant who is its object:

> The "cop-out" is in fact a charade, during which an accused must project an appropriate and acceptable degree of guilt, penitence, and remorse. If he adequately feigns the role of the "guilty person," his hearers will engage in the fantasy that he is contrite and thereby merits a lesser plea. . . . What is actually involved, therefore, is not a "degradation" or "reinforcing" process at all, but rather a highly structured system of exchange cloaked in the rituals of legalism and public professions of guilt and repentance. Everyone present is aware of the staging, including the defendant.
>
> For the accused, his conception of self as a guilty person is largely temporary. In private he will quickly reassert his innocence . . . (1967b, p. 89).

The contrast this description provides with the juvenile court can be partially attributed to differences in the proceedings in the two courts. The juvenile court is less formal and legalistic, gives much less of a role to lawyers, and routinely inquires into the facts of the offense rather than merely accepting a plea of guilty. These factors not only increase the amount and intensity of interaction between accused and court officials, but also compel greater participation in role of the "guilty" and limit the possibility of using face-saving techniques of role-distancing and withdrawal.

In addition, youthful wrongdoers are culturally defined as more malleable than adult offenders, reflecting conceptions of the different nature of children and adults. Delinquents are generally felt to be less committed to their misconduct and more susceptible to the impact of the immediate situation. Consequently, it becomes appropriate to structure the delinquency hearing so as to intimidate the delinquent as a means of deterrence. For this reason, the juvenile court hearing may acquire greater emotional and dramatic overtones than the criminal trial, where the culprits are adults and where more purely instrumental problems surrounding the negotiation of pleas occupy court attention.

But despite these differences, it cannot be denied that in general criminal trials are intrinsically structured to isolate and degrade accused criminals, however much "mass, bureaucratized justice" may routinize these processes. Moreover, Blumberg's finding that the criminal convicted on a guilty plea quickly reasserts his innocence does not, as the author argues (1967b, p. 89), unequivocally indicate that the courtroom ceremony is without profoundly degrading effects. Indeed, it is a plausible suggestion that the post-guilt proclamation of innocence reflects exactly a need to reassert and reestablish self on favorable terms after a deeply humiliating experience. In this light, the claim of innocence represents a defense against the contamination of self and character that occurs during the court proceeding.[12]

And in general, it is important for the sociologist to attend to the distinctly ceremonial and ritual qualities of institutional processes, irrespective of any degrading effect. For as this analysis has tried to suggest, the ceremonial structure of the occasion takes on significance in itself, becoming a virtual trial of moral character, distinct from but growing out of any degradation of self.

12. To the extent that the stance of innocence is a self-protective strategy, the finding that a high percentage (51.6%) of those who plead guilty and later assert their innocence in presentence probation interviews (Blumberg, 1967b, p. 91) reflects less discredit on the legal system than Blumberg contends. For this hypothesis suggests that this figure may not accurately reflect "actual guilt," and hence may distort the extent to which this system of bargain justice produces guilty pleas from those "actually innocent." This percentage may also be inflated because probation officers uncritically accept such reassertions of innocence as part of a cooling out procedure allowing the now-convicted criminal to save face.

III

The Dilemmas of Authority

Thus far, analysis of the juvenile court's processing of cases has focused on the courtroom hearing as the locus for judgments of moral character. In the next two chapters, attention shifts to the nature of the delinquent's continuing contacts with court personnel and their effect on assessments made of his character. Such contacts with probation and clinic staffs are considered in Chapters 8 and 9 respectively. Briefly, in encounters with these personnel, the delinquent directly confronts the dilemmas posed by the court's dual treatment-control orientation. He must somehow deal with the inherent inconsistencies and confusion posed by relations with officials who simultaneously claim to "help" him and yet exercise a fundamental coercive authority over his conduct. As will be seen, the delinquent's success in handling these inconsistencies may determine both the assessments made of his character and his fate at the hands of the court.

8
Character and Probationary Control

Probation represents the routine court response to delinquency cases. For the delinquent probation becomes a period of trial during which his activities and character are under constant scrutiny and evaluation by court personnel. Most delinquents pass unscathed through this probationary trial and lose contact with the court. A few do not escape so easily, finding their moral character discredited and facing the prospect of incarceration as a consequence of this encounter. These respective outcomes are determined within the framework set by the nature and contingencies of probationary supervision.

THE NATURE OF PROBATION

The formal goal of probation is to improve the delinquent's behavior, in short, to "rehabilitate" him. This goal is short-circuited, however, by a pervading preoccupation with *control*. Reflecting insistent demands that the court "do something" about recurrent misconduct, probation is organized to keep the delinquent "in line," to prevent any further disturbing and inconveniencing "trouble." The ultimate goal of permanently "reforming" the delinquent's personality and conduct becomes subordinated to the exigencies of maintaining immediate control. Probationary supervision consequently takes on a decidedly short-term and negative character; probation becomes an essentially disciplinarian regime directed toward deterring and inhibiting troublesome conduct.

This regime relies fundamentally on the authoritative enforcement of rules. Control initially involves subjecting a probationer's conduct to a variety of stereotypical rules: report regularly and on time to the probation officer; attend school if under 16; find and hold a job if over 16 and out of school; observe the curfew, stay off the streets late in the evening, and be home when ordered by parents. These rules are generally supplemented by a less concrete set of requirements regarding conduct. The youth may be warned to behave himself around the home and to obey his parents. He may be cautioned to stay out of trouble in school and encouraged to complete his school work. Association with undesirable friends may be prohibited. Parts of the city may be placed off-limits; shoplifters, for example, are frequently warned to stay out of the downtown area and the department stores. Finally, participation in some after-school program, generally of a recreational nature, may be encouraged and even arranged.

Probation officers, however, apply these rules and their more general control efforts differentially to different kinds of delinquents. Probationers who appear normal in character require no special action and are perhaps not even seen again after the courtroom hearing. Probation involvement in such cases is at a minimum. In contrast, troublesome delinquents demand special attention and become the objects of more active rule enforcement and control measures. Generally, as problems of control come to be regarded as more acute, the probation officer progressively increases his involvement with the case and strengthens his legal power over the delinquent. This power, however, derives from his capacity to impose burdens and liabilities on the delinquent and, ultimately, from his right to "surrender" a delinquent for violating the terms of his probation.

To surrender a probationer may well bring about his incarceration and is often undertaken with this end in mind.[1] But in

1. Surrender power is a tool for incarcerating delinquents that can be used when other means are not available. In one instance, a probationer characterized as "a real troublemaker" was found not delinquent on a new complaint for drunkenness. But using evidence presented during this hearing—the fact that he had been in the city at 3 A.M.—his probation officer immediately afterwards surrendered him for violation of probation, leading to his commitment to the Youth Correction Authority.

general it is the *threat* of incarceration that provides the probation officer with his main weapon for affecting the behavior of his
probationers. Hence the probation officer routinely invokes this
surrender power in order to reassert his authority and that of the
court.[2] The following cases illustrate this use of surrender to revi-
talize the threat of court sanctions and to confirm probation authority:

> A probation officer from the Boys' Training Program surrendered a 15-
> year-old Negro boy for not attending the program. He noted that the
> boy had been brought to court for not attending school, although he
> was no behavior problem and was capable of doing the work. The
> probation officer then turned to the current problem: "As far as not
> attending the Boys' Training Program, I don't think it was due to
> defiance. I think the boy just did not realize the seriousness of attend-
> ing the program and fulfilling his court obligations." He gave the
> judge a psychiatric evaluation of the boy completed by the court clinic.
> Then: "I think the boy could be worked with while he's on proba-
> tion and in the home." Judge agreed, and together they worked out
> details of a program for the summer. Judge then lectured the boy
> about the need to cooperate.

> The probation officer surrendered a young white boy from a nearby
> upper-middle class suburb. He noted that "the boy seems to react
> badly at home," and had also consistently resisted probationary super-
> vision: "He cannot adhere to [any] authority whatever." He consist-
> ently comes in for his probation appointments after four o'clock
> "when I'm not here." Finally: "I set down the rules, and he just vio-
> lated them one after another, and could give no reasons for that. . . .
> [He has] a foul mouth and is a real trouble-maker."

> Judge made arrangements with the probation officer from the Boys'
> Training Program to have the boy enrolled there. He then gave the
> boy an extremely harsh lecture, emphasizing: "You're going to get one
> more shot, mister, and that's it. Now get this through your head.
> You've pressed one of our men too far. If you get out of line one
> iota—that's it."

2. Public school teachers similarly rely on this kind of appeal to higher
authority to support their classroom regime. As Becker has noted:
> The teacher's authority, then, is subject to attack by pupils and may be
> strengthened or weakened depending on which way the principal throws
> the weight of his authority. Teachers expect the principal to throw it
> their way, and provide them with a needed defense (1953, pp. 136–37).

It should be noted that this use of the surrender sanction by the probation officer provides the basis for the staged saving from commitment previously analyzed. Even where this kind of staging does not explicitly occur, the youth may be kept in ignorance of the probable course of the courtroom proceeding and of the probation officer's intended recommendation. In this way, the threat of pending sanctions achieves maximum impact.

The importance of the threat of surrender (and the possibility of incarceration) for maintaining probation authority produces a concern with maximizing the ability to invoke this sanction reliably. On the one hand, the probation officer tries, wherever "trouble" appears likely, to have a delinquent placed on a suspended sentence instead of ordinary probation. If surrendered for violation of probation while on a suspended sentence, the probationer can be committed with no right of appeal (appeal being possible only when the probationer is first placed on a suspended sentence).

Furthermore, the probation officer strenuously resists getting into situations where he must deal with delinquents without the power he feels necessary to control and sanction their conduct. This possibility arises most often when a youth is placed on probation without being found delinquent, a situation that occurs when a case is "continued without a finding." If the probation officer tries to control the delinquent by routinely setting down rules for him to obey, he leaves himself without effective sanction or penalty to invoke in case of violation. One alternative open to the probation officer here is to take the case back into court and try to get a finding made.

Finally, probation officers employ a kind of moralizing exhortation as a standard way of relating to delinquents in enforcing rules and controlling behavior. Such "lecturing" or "preaching" [3] emphasizes avoiding trouble as a general policy applicable to the delinquent's actions. Initial probation interviews routinely

3. Cicourel (1968) provides a detailed analysis of a tape-recorded probation interview which highlights this kind of persistent lecturing and moralizing. See the case of Audrey, pp. 130–66.

Matza uses the term "preaching" to describe this form of interaction, emphasizing the presumption of superiority and rectitude that this stance implies (1964, pp. 145*ff.*).

employ this kind of lecturing, while later "incidents" reported to or observed by the probation officer frequently trigger new lectures. For example:

A probation officer had by chance encountered a probationer, a 14-year-old white boy, walking the streets at around midnight. The next morning he had the boy come into court and proceeded to lecture him for twenty minutes. The boy lived alone with his mother, who sang in night clubs for her living. The boy had been in constant trouble previously and the mother and probation officer had been working on getting him admitted to a private military school to forestall the otherwise probable commitment to the Youth Correction Authority.

The probation officer began by first bawling the boy out for "prancing the streets last night." Asked him why, and the boy answered he had been returning some pants to a friend. Probation officer: "At a quarter to 12?" (incredulous, depicting this excuse as totally inadequate). Then talked with mother, who pointed out that the problem was that she worked nights and had to leave the boy alone. Probation officer warned the boy again about being out on the streets so late. Then switched his tactics, threatening the boy with what would happen to him if he did not behave: "I have the power here. . . . I can send you up until you're 21! You can spend seven years at a place where you have to get up when they say—no fancy boarding school." Probation officer continued in this vein, saying that, if the boy did it again, he would be held in detention: "I can set the bail at $25,000. If she can raise that, I'll get it raised to $30,000—whatever it takes so she can't make it. I can do that too!"

Finally the probation officer appealed to the boy's feelings for his mother, noting all the pain and anxiety he caused her by making her come down to the court all the time. And again: "You have no reason to be on the streets at that hour."

In addition, probation rules themselves may provide a kind of artificial issue for "preaching" and hence for stronger control efforts. The probation officer may use infractions of the very rules he has established as occasions for underlining his power over the delinquent:

A girl probationer called in to say she could not report in person because she lacked car fare. The probation officer responded: "What do you mean you could not earn the money to get down here? You've known that you'd have to come down here for some time. . . . You should have earned it before." After discussing several other incidents, the probation officer concluded the conversation: "This isn't the first time you haven't kept an appointment with me. And you know it's not the first time you told me you could not earn the money to come down here. You have to obey your probation officer. These disobediences have got to stop!"

In general, probation preaching pictures avoiding trouble not as problematic but as a decision completely within the delinquent's grasp. Situational contingencies, such as the pressure of peer group contacts, are ignored, as are the obstacles to staying out of trouble routinely encountered by youths who necessarily spend a good deal of time on the street. Furthermore, it is assumed that this kind of verbal exhortation will change the delinquent's attitude, motivating him to control his behavior at all times and in all places. In this respect, "preaching" is central not only to direct control and rule enforcement, but also to probation strategies for more indirect control.

Although probation officers may prefer to exercise direct control over delinquents, their ability to do so is severely restricted. In the first place, it is inherently impossible to provide any immediate supervision of all or even most of the activities of those under control.[4] Second, a relatively high caseload and time-consuming administrative chores in the court itself limit the probation officer's contacts with his delinquents, even with those to whom he allocates most of his time and effort. As a result, probation officers must develop techniques enabling them to exercise *indirect* control over delinquents. To do so, probation officers gear their efforts to those of primary control institutions. Probation is in fact explicitly oriented toward firmly integrating the delinquent into those institutions that normally function to keep children out of trouble.

Thus, probation officers shift responsibility for direct and regular control of delinquents to other agents as a routine part of their enforcement strategy. The family and the schools are con-

4. The parallel with the situation of the policeman, who only rarely and by chance observes a crime being committed, is particularly striking here.

sidered critical in this respect. As a probation officer at the Municipal Court commented on his handling of his high caseload:

> We keep a close look at the most serious. But with the rest, we probably don't see them all year—we rely on the family and the schools to back us up. Though often the family just doesn't, and if the school reports them—then we surrender them.

In so doing, the probation officer see!;s to reaffirm the authority and legitimacy of these primary control institutions, relying primarily on the preaching techniques previously described in warning delinquents to obey their parents or their teachers.

Similarly, an effort may be made to reaffirm religious ties. In the Municipal Court, probation officers routinely inquired into church attendance and made it clear that they expected delinquents to participate regularly in church programs. The juvenile court recorded information on church affiliation and attendance on the face sheet, but probation officers were less vociferous in requiring church participation. However, Protestant and Catholic court chaplains were encouraged to become involved in delinquency cases. These chaplains "covered" new cases on a daily basis, talking to the delinquent and his family about church participation and later contacting the local minister or parish priest to insure renewed efforts to involve the youth in church activities.

Underlying these reintegrative efforts is the belief that much delinquency results from loss of contact with supervision from these primary control institutions. Thus, a second focus in indirect probationary control is simply to subject the delinquent to as continuous adult supervision and control as possible. The court makes an effort to involve delinquents in YMCA recreation programs, settlement house activities, summer camps, etc., simply as means of occupying and organizing their free time, keeping them "off the streets" and out of trouble. The juvenile-court-operated Boys' Training Program, with both school year and summer programs, serves exactly this function and receives many probationers who would not be accepted in more conventional settings. Similarly, out-of-school delinquents are required to work, since jobs occupy their time and place them in an adult-supervised setting.

Development of a system of *surveillance* as a means of enforcing probation rules complements reliance on the primary control efforts of other institutions. Those institutions and agents with primary control responsibility for and regular contact with the delinquent keep him under surveillance for the court staff. To cite several instances of the operation of this system of indirect surveillance:

> A 14-year-old Negro boy appeared in court on the day his probation was scheduled to terminate. His probation officer, however, told the judge that he had bad reports from school on the boy: he had been using "foul and abusive language," and had been "defiant" to his teacher. He recommended extending probation, and the judge did so.

Similarly, in the following case, a girl probationer is surrendered following reports from the police on her activities:

> A woman probation officer came into court to surrender a 15-year-old white girl with whom she had been working for some time. The probation officer told the judge that the girl had been out on the streets. Twice policemen had seen her in one of the main vice districts of the city, "approaching colored males." One time this had occurred at 2:30 in the morning. Finally, the girl had been hanging around with a lesbian friend; the two of them had been in trouble together before and had been brought into court.

In general, the probation officer assumes that a delinquent is keeping out of trouble unless or until reports of misconduct reach him from these sources. Such reports then provide the incidents that become the subject of most probation interviews and the focus of discussions of disobeying the rules.

In effect, the probation officer "deputizes," as best he can, parents, teachers, school officials, and other adult agents to extend surveillance over the youth's activities. Here his concern lies not merely in current delinquency, but also in behavior felt to be symptomatic of future delinquency and trouble. In this respect, the probation officer extends surveillance into areas far from outright delinquency, particularly seeking out troublesome conduct in home and school. In turn this creates a situation where the probationer is easily discredited. Activities and incidents only peripherally related to delinquency, and apparently far beyond the purview of the probation officer, are regularly brought up during the course of probation interviews. For example:

During the afternoon, a woman probation officer received a telephone call from a probationer who was due to report that day but who reported she did not have the carfare necessary to get down to the court. During the course of the phone conversation with the girl, Marcia Reynolds, the probation officer brought up the subject of the girl's school attendance: "Mr. D [the assistant principal] tells me you've been tardy for school the last [few] weeks. He says you're an hour late. Your mother tells me you leave on time. What do you do in that hour? [Pause while Marcia replies.] Other children can ride the bus and get there on time."

The need to account for one's time can become part of the routine of probation, and where one was and with whom can assume great importance in the assessment of moral character. Under these circumstances, the probationer may tend to see his world in paranoid terms; all adults begin to appear as possible informers and hence as possible discrediters. Moreover, the probation officer often cultivates this impression, confronting the delinquent with reports of his misbehavior in such a way as to present himself as all knowing and all powerful. In so doing the probation officer highlights his power in an effort to deter the delinquent from further misconduct.

These circumstances necessarily affect the nature of the youth's relations with his probation officer. The delinquent will generally feel that the probation officer is constantly "checking up" on his daily round of activities and associations. He is apt to feel that he is being watched at all times and that the probation officer sees him as the kind of youth who has to be watched. It is thus natural that a degree of distrust comes to pervade the relationship.

In an overview of the nature of probation, the consequences of the negative focus on immediate control and on preventing trouble become apparent. Routine probation becomes passive and noninterventionist in character, changing neither the personality nor the everyday life circumstances of the delinquent.

In the first place, the probation officer functions in largely negative and reactive ways, devoting very little time and effort to "helping" delinquents. Probation officers generally eschew any clinical role, do not conceive of their work as encouraging youths to talk about and work out their "problems," and make no effort to relate to delinquents sympathetically in order to influence and change their outlook. What "help" probation officers do provide involves referral of the case to agencies that will perform this service: medical hospitals, psychiatric clinics, tutorial sessions, remedial speech programs. The probation officer sees his "helping" function as one of making referrals to outside treatment programs rather than directly undertaking any kind of personal counselling or casework.

Again, probation has little direct effect on the daily routine of the delinquent's life and activities. The attempt to reintegrate the delinquent into primary control institutions are one-sided and often doomed to failure. Inability to fit into the routines of these institutions in all likelihood brought the delinquent into court in the first place, and few efforts are made to smooth over the youth's troubled relations with these institutions. Probation officers, for example, do not consult with teachers, suggesting how to improve the behavior and performance of a delinquent in the classroom. Only rarely is some effort made to change the way parents relate to the youth, and more general factors disturbing family life—poor housing, lack of income, substandard living conditions—are never considered problematic. In general, probation officers adopt the perspective of these traditional institutions, seeking to readjust the delinquent to their ongoing routines *on their own terms*. Probation officers, therefore, only incidentally treat or rehabilitate delinquents. Rather their efforts assume as legitimate the operation of traditional child control institutions and seek to reassert their authority, as well as imposing a cursory surveillance on the youth's activities.

Finally, as the routine operations of control institutions are accepted uncritically, all efforts to implement change focus on the person of the delinquent. "Preaching," which assumes that the delinquent alone is responsible for avoiding future trouble, becomes the primary means of effecting change and "reform." In addition, probation officers come to operate on the assumption that mere verbal exhortation, combined with moralistic warnings, will reform the youth despite unchanged everyday life circumstances. As Cicourel notes:

> While the general policies or rules laid down are recognized by all as important (curfew, association with "bad" friends, etc.), the implementation is difficult because it presumes careful attention to particular problems that can arise and concerted action by others. It is much easier and convenient to assume that verbal discussions will somehow accomplish the same objective, that is, "it will only lead to more trouble," "you've got to change your attitude," and the like (1968, p. 223).

As Cicourel observes, court contact and probation do not change the delinquent's life "because no one is prepared to pay the price of altering their own daily existence as a condition for influencing or altering the juvenile's daily round of activities" (1968, p. 223). Probation officers simply do not make the commitment either to the delinquent personally or to those agencies dealing with the youth necessary to change this daily round of activity.[5] Cases are rather dealt with in a highly routinized, bureaucratic manner, with extra involvement and effort kept to an absolute minimum. Probation is stripped of any "rehabilitative" potential, leaving only relative leniency to recommend it. Probation represents merely another "break" for the delinquent, and a tenuous and chimerical one at that, since it leaves him exposed to the same circumstances and situations that previously led to delinquency. In the words of a Harlem delinquent, told by a juvenile court judge that he and his friends would receive "another chance" by being placed on probation: "Man, you not givin' us another chance. You givin' us the same chance we had before" (Brown, 1966, p. 123).

5. One Negro probation officer, a former street worker with strong ties in the Negro ghetto, did at least attempt to effect these kinds of changes. On call at any hour, he often worked late into the night, visiting delinquents and their families, helping and advising on immediate and recurring problems. However, even his efforts centered primarily on mediating between delinquents in trouble and officials, hence on trying to keep things from getting worse rather than on making improvements.

THE LIMITS OF AUTHORITY

While in his relations with delinquents the probation officer
tends to rely on his legal authority—particularly his right to
threaten or to invoke negative sanctions—his power over the delinquent is in practice somewhat restricted. First, the judge makes
all final dispositions of cases. Any threat to incarcerate a youth on
a surrender, for example, only becomes effective when the judge
is convinced that this is the appropriate course of action. Second,
both probation officer and judge are reluctant to invoke the ultimate sanction of incarceration except in extreme circumstances.
This means that the probation officer's ultimate sanction lies beyond routine use. Third, frequent attempts to incarcerate probationers tend to discredit the probation officer in the eyes of his
superior, the judge. Routine use of the surrender sanction suggests that the probation officer is not working conscientiously or
effectively with his charges.[6] But finally, reliance solely on threats
of negative sanctions inherently restricts the possibilities of influencing delinquent behavior. Adopting this kind of stance toward
probationers may be adequate where purposes are simply prohibitive and deterring, but it is ineffective where more positive influence is desired.

As a result, on occasion the probation officer must try to establish a "trust relationship" with the delinquent. This kind of relationship is not sought in each and every case. With delinquents
requiring minimal control the probation officer routinely maintains a distant and authority-laden relationship; here "trust"
exists only in the sense that the delinquent's conduct is viewed as
predictably normal (i.e., he is expected, and hence "trusted," to
stay out of trouble). Rather, trust becomes critical under circumstances where formal authority by itself is not adequate for dealing with the case. Here the probation officer, by developing more
personal ties with a delinquent, can exert a more basic and cer-

6. Cicourel has noted a similar tendency among the probation officers he
studied (1968, p. 229): "Few probation officers ever wish to recommend Youth
Authority commitment because it signifies they were unsuccessful in working
with the juvenile."

tain influence over his behavior. As Cicourel argues: "The P.O. must sustain some kind of trust relationship with the juvenile as a condition of obtaining compliance" (1968, p. 142).

The probation officer is most frequently driven beyond the routine, "let-it-go" approach to probation and toward increased involvement and trust when normal probation practices fail to prevent renewed trouble. In attempting to deal with such troublesome probationers, for example, the probation officer needs more detailed and intimate information about the youth, his family, background, outlook, and "problems" than he can possibly obtain through a purely negative relationship. Particularly where the probation officer must form some opinion of the youth's inner feelings and problems, something not necessary where ordinary control procedures work effectively, any minimally candid and open discussions are impossible unless the usual formal and authoritarian definition of the relationship can be modified. Similarly, the more committed the probation officer becomes to an active plan of "help" in a given case, the more dependent he becomes on enlisting at least some degree of cooperation from the youth. For example, in any "voluntary" placement, the child must be willing to go along with what is worked out or it will fall through. Although a threat (e.g., of incarceration at the Youth Correction Authority) may provide some incentive for a youth to cooperate, it alone will rarely be adequate, and the probation officer must consequently make some attempt to move beyond a strictly authoritarian relationship.

The underlying authoritarian nature of the probation officer's control, however, frequently thwarts his ability to establish and maintain this kind of personal, "trust" relationship.[7] Even when the probation officer tries to minimize his controlling power, delinquents often persist in viewing his attempts to "help" in authoritarian terms, reacting with distrust and suspicion. This

7. These problems and difficulties are emphasized by Ohlin *et al.* (1956, pp. 211–25) in their study of probation and parole workers. For example: "[The social worker in a parole or probation setting] . . . frequently attempts to play two roles. On the one hand, he tries to offer a caseworker's sympathetic understanding and help; on the other, he is the agent of law and respectability, attempting to explain one function as separate from the other" (p. 216).

resistance often reflects differing perceptions of probation "services," as delinquents and their families view as undeserved and unpleasant programs regarded by the court as in their best interests. Hence, many court attempts to provide "treatment" flounder on delinquents' resistance and lack of trust. Under these circumstances, the typical court response is to "reason" with the youth and his parents, presenting the proposal as for his own good and in his own best interests. But this plea to "let us help you" cloaks and ultimately gives way to the threat of coercive sanctions. Thus, many treatment proposals take the form: "You may think this is bad, but if you don't go along with it you'll end up somewhere much worse" (e.g., reform school). In the following case, for example, efforts to get two boys to cooperate in the attempt to obtain placements depart from the fundamental authority of the court over them:

> Two brothers, ages 9 and 11, who had been found neglected by the court, were held in detention while efforts were made to place them in boarding schools. The two had ruined all previous efforts in this direction, however, by telling school officials and Child Welfare Department workers that they would run away. They were brought into court in order to try to get them to be more cooperative. The judge confronted them, "Why do you tell those CWD workers that you've known so long that you'll run away? . . . You're blocking us from trying to do what we think is best for you." The workers have been trying to get you to visit the schools, and you keep on fighting them. "We're trying *not* to commit you, but that is exactly what is going to happen the way you two are behaving." After considerable lecturing and questioning, with major emphasis given to the fact that he would not allow them to go home, the judge got the two boys to promise that they would not say anything about running away from the schools.

This same threat of legal force underlies court helping efforts which rely on other agencies. For example, in transferring custody over a youth to the Child Welfare Department as a precondition to "placing" him, the child and/or his family is regularly pressured into signing a "voluntary referral" agreement. As a Child Welfare caseworker described this process:

> It's called "voluntary," but they're pretty much pushed into it. The probation officer will tell them, "If it weren't for Mr. Johnson [the present Child Welfare Department caseworker], we'd send you out to the Youth Correction Authority."

Thus, even where the court tries to get a delinquent to cooperate with the treatment efforts of another agency, its use of authority may undermine any possible "trust relationship" with that agency.

Finally, the continued existence of even an established personal working relationship may be extremely precarious. For example, an attempt to "crack down" and discipline the probationer may threaten to destroy it:

> A probation officer described the problems he had working with a boy, lamenting the fact that just as he began to get close to him he would be forced to discipline him. "I can let him go so far and then you have to snap him back. And this destroys any kind of relationship. . . . He just clams up. . . . Underneath it all, I think he's an angry boy."

Probation work routinely employs a number of techniques for bypassing or reducing this conflict between authoritative control and personal trust. In the first place, intermediaries are used to approach and work with the delinquent. At initial stages of contact with the court, for example, probation officers will routinely rely on lawyers to talk to and reason with the youth on matters that require some degree of trust (e.g., whether to appeal a finding or disposition). As issues affecting disposition arise, probation officers often refer cases to the court clinic in an attempt to obtain confidential and intimate material from the delinquent and family. But even more important, probation officers place great stress on working with and through the parents of the delinquent. If he can enlist the "cooperation" of the parents, obtaining their trust and support behind his controlling efforts, the probation officer can bypass many of the problems of maintaining the delinquent's trust. By getting the parents to confide in him and to support his "program" for the youth, the probation officer establishes indirect access to the youth that does not depend on the latter's trust. Thus the parents will provide the necessary information, will accept the probation officer's goals, and will try to convince the child to follow them, allowing the probation officer to sustain his authoritarian stance without his having to make any effort to establish a closer relationship.[8]

But again, the probation officer may effectively establish the same kind of working relationship with a sponsor of the delinquent youth (e.g., a priest or minister, a social worker). The sponsor will take over all "supportive" functions while the probation officer will carry on his more strictly controlling and disciplining functions.

Beyond the use of intermediaries, the probation officer seeks to lessen the conflict between authority and trust by personally obligating the delinquent to him. In this respect he acts as mediator between the youth and the court, committing himself to a recommendation for leniency as a way of obligating the delinquent to cooperate. Again, this strategy is more successful when the delinquent's sense of obligation is maximized. Hence, the need to obtain a delinquent's trust may lead the probation officer to emphasize the youth's vulnerability to legal sanctions even in these informal confrontations.

While cooperation may be initially obtained with this kind of implicit bargain over the recommendation, the probation officer must maintain the trust relationship throughout the supervisory period. Paradoxically, in this situation the probation officer's formal authority provides the easiest means of reaffirming the delinquent's sense of personal obligation. By ostentatiously failing to invoke his power to surrender a delinquent for violation of probation where this is clearly possible, the probation officer can not only establish closer rapport but also gain a hold over the youth with which he can be restrained in the future. Often this is done by suggesting knowledge of violations of rules or regulations laid down by the court as terms of probation, but tolerating or ignoring them by taking no formal action.[9] Rumored misconduct or

8. Elliot Studt has noted that parole agents' similar attempts to establish rapport with and gain information from the family or spouses of parolees increase the latter's problems of adjustment (1966, p. 14).

9. Blau, among others, has reported a similar strategy in obligating subordinates in a bureaucratic setting. Thus, minor rule infractions will be disregarded as a means of insuring compliance with more fundamental rules (Blau, 1963, pp. 213–17).

unconfirmed reports of delinquent behavior are particularly apt to be used in this way: indicating knowledge of incidents of misconduct, the probation officer demonstrates that he could surrender the youth if he were so inclined, but instead he seeks to obligate the delinquent by giving him a "break."

Nevertheless, there are serious limitations on the use of this strategy. This course of action involves tolerating exactly the kind of misconduct about which the probation officer has warned the youth. To ignore more than a few violations is to encourage the youth in the idea that he can "get away with it." One alternative here, of course, is the staged "saving" of the delinquent by the probation officer. But this kind of performance has to be carried out carefully if it is to create any sense of obligation and indebtedness on the part of the delinquent youth. In particular, the probation officer has to make it appear that he has no choice but to surrender the youth, for if it appears that the decision to go before the judge resulted from his own exercise of discretion, it is likely to impress the youth as a hostile act. The emphasis on formal probation rules reduces this danger, allowing the probation officer to present his decision as an objectively necessary response to violation.[10] Similarly, the misconduct may be presented as so serious and/or recurrent that he has no choice but to bring it to the attention of the judge.

PROBATION AND DISCREDITING OF CHARACTER

During probation, the moral character of a delinquent youth becomes highly vulnerable to discreditation. In the first place, almost constant surveillance renders information control, a crucial ca-

10. This quality of rules is also indicated at several points in Gouldner's analysis of the functions of bureaucratic rules in a gypsum plant (1954, pp. 157–80). Thus, Gouldner suggests the "the rules provide the foreman with an impersonal crutch for his authority, screening the superiority of his power which might otherwise violate the norm of equality" (p. 165).

In the case of the probation officer, rules are employed to screen power, but for the purpose of maintaining relatively close interpersonal ties. Disparities in the exercise of power need screening, in other words, not directly because of a general norm of equality, but because of the need to establish rapport and trust.

pacity for maintaining the version of character presented to others,[11] very difficult. Probation keying to reports of disturbance and trouble, irrespective of the more general prevalence of good behavior, accentuates this difficulty. In particular, a delinquent encounters problems in segregating misbehavior in the important realms of home and school from his relations with the court. In the face of such surveillance, delinquents can keep discrediting incidents secret only by chance and face constant threat of ruined character as a result.

Second, court reliance on authority as a means of control increases the delinquent's vulnerability to discrediting. Probation officers respond to renewed trouble by trying to increase their effective power over the case. On the one hand, this brings increased involvement in the youth's life, with regular inquiries to home and school about his behavior. This provides the court with greater access to evidence that the delinquent is "messing up," perhaps confirming the growing suspicion that he is not the kind of youth who can get along in an "open setting." On the other hand, the court will tighten its restraints on the youth, prescribing more minute regulations for his everyday behavior. This closer regulation increases both the likelihood and frequency of rule infractions, thereby speeding the movement toward total discrediting and incarceration. In general, renewed trouble escalates efforts to reestablish control and authority in such a way as to defile moral character and accelerate movement toward incarceration.

A crucial step toward this outcome occurs when the probation officer, seeking to maximize his control, places the delinquent on a suspended sentence. This not only procedurally facilitates commitment, but also provides objective evidence of dubious moral character, since a suspended sentence indicates the kind of delinquent who should be committed.

11. Goffman in particular emphasizes this as a critical aspect of interaction: "A basic problem for many performances . . . is that of information control; the audience must not acquire destructive information about the situation that is being defined for them" (1959, p. 141) . Also, Skolnick and Woodworth (1967, pp. 99–136) deal with the problem of information control in the face of interinstitutional communications in the enforcement of laws against statutory rape.

While this kind of "bad adjustment" to probation gradually discredits character, commission of a new offense rapidly and dramatically produces the same result. For example:

Leroy Lincoln, a 15-year-old Negro boy, had been given a suspended sentence for his involvement in a stolen car incident leading to the accidental death of one of the other boys involved. Less than two weeks after the final hearing on this case, Lincoln was surrendered by his probation officer, after the latter had received a report that the boy had been driving around in a stolen car. Probation officer reported these facts to the judge, emphasizing that this last incident had occurred after the boy had been in court on "a serious case just a month ago." Probation officer concluded: "He has not learned his lesson in this time about the danger and seriousness of [stealing] cars." He then recommended that the boy's suspended sentence be revoked and commitment to the Youth Correction Authority ordered. After brief conversation with the boy, the judge acted as had been requested.

The nature of discreditation reflects assumptions about moral character underlying court efforts to control delinquency through probationary supervision. Probation presupposes a delinquent of probable normal character and imposes a form of control structured to deal with this kind of actor. Consequently, probation serves in effect to test this normalcy. Routine probationary control assumes that a normal youth will be deterred by the probation officer's exercise of authority, intimidated by his lectures and warnings, and motivated to comply with the rules he sets down. The delinquent of essentially normal character, in other words, will be sufficiently intimidated by the authority and control of the probation officer to be dissuaded or deterred from all delinquent behavior and, to a lesser extent, from more general misconduct.

Beyond this, the probation relationship is so structured as to imply intent and responsibility for any such misconduct. The presumption of normality in child offenders derives largely from the belief that somehow the youth is too immature, impulsive, and unworldly to appreciate fully the meaning and consequences of delinquent behavior. Lack of responsibility is thus built into the common-sense conception of the ordinary child and carries over into the realm of delinquent activity. There is always some sense that the youthful delinquent "did not know what he was doing." Routine probation, particularly its preaching component, is structured exactly to create the conditions of responsibility: (a) the wrongful nature of the delinquent act or behavior is constantly driven home; (b) the actual or potential serious consequences of the act are emphasized; (c) the legal powers of court and probation officer are accentuated as a warning to the youth of what will be done to him for future misconduct. To have engaged in delinquency in the face of these cautions against it evidences responsibility: the delinquent can no longer claim that he did not know that the act was wrong, that it could have seriously injured others, or that he was risking incarceration by doing it. Further delinquent behavior, therefore, weakens the presumed childlike lack of intent for wrongful action and negates the imputation of normal character. As a result, the court comes to look on the delinquent as someone requiring constant and forceful restraint.

On another level, a bad adjustment to probation and renewed delinquency threaten the trust relationship between probation officer and delinquent. Such contradicting incidents make the probation officer unable or unwilling to sustain normal definitions of character and lead him toward incarcerating the youth. As Cicourel has described this process:

> . . . the P.O. expects the juvenile to control himself by direct reflection at the time of potentially troublesome acts so as to avoid their occurrence in a systematic way. The recurrence of incidents leaves the P.O. in a dilemma: either she must acknowledge her failure at maintaining the trust relationship as a form of control, claim that the juvenile's conduct is motivated by uncontrollable "underlying emotions," or "deep-rooted" criminal or character formation. In either case the recommendation then becomes one of incarceration (1968, p. 142) .

In the juvenile court studied here, however, trust relationships were not the routine technique of control. Thus, incarceration following the discrediting of character results from the probation officer's inability to establish a trust relationship with a delinquent, as well as from the violation of such a relationship. Without trust the probation officer will not sustain a definition of normal character. A trust relationship predisposes the probation officer to accept the delinquent's excuses, leading to toleration of new incidents as the inevitable product of trying circumstances or as expressions of some mental problem for which he should not be held responsible. If, however, the delinquent resists the probation officer's overtures, preventing development of a trust relationship, he is unlikely to weather successfully stricter controls and supervision. His probation officer will refuse to give him further "breaks," actively seek out confirmation of his discredited character, and generally try to bring about his incarceration.

Finally, probation officers are particularly apt to try to establish a trust relationship when they feel a youth is disturbed and needs special help. Resistance to efforts to provide "help" of this kind tends to undermine the trust relationship on which they are based and to spoil moral character. The following case, where a youth refuses to cooperate in a treatment plan, ruining character by messing up a hard-won placement, clearly illustrates this process:

> Ralph Robinson, a 16-year-old Negro boy, was brought to court for incorrigibility by his mother. Investigation revealed deep conflict between mother and son, and the probation officer on the case felt that both were somewhat crazy, noting the mother "is as disturbed as he is." Probation officer felt that the home situation was intolerable and that the boy had to be placed in a better environment, as well as separated from the mother. During the summer the boy was placed at a camp through the Child Welfare Department, and arrangements were completed to send him to the Roberts School, again with CWD financing.
>
> In early September, Ralph failed to report to the Roberts School as required. He was picked up by the police Monday night and brought to court but quickly ran away. Meanwhile, the Child Welfare Department worker agreed to cover for the court, telling the school that Ralph had been mixed up about when he was supposed to come. (The fact that he had refused to come to the school, plus the fact that he had been picked up by the police and held in detention, would have given the school second thoughts about taking him.) On Tuesday afternoon the probation officer went out and found the boy, gave him his "extra-special lecture," which ended with him turning his

back and walking back to his car, trusting Ralph to follow him there and thence to the school. But the boy disappeared.

That night he was again picked up by the police, and sent to detention. Wednesday in court the probation officer got the judge to put the boy on a suspended sentence and had another probation officer personally take him out to the school that afternoon. But by six that night, Ralph had run away from the school and was back in the city. Late Thursday the probation officer apprehended him again and again took him out to the detention center.

In court on Friday, the probation officer surrendered Ralph for violating his probation and recommended commitment to the Youth Correction Authority, explaining in some detail about the boy's escape from the school. He concluded: "We've gone as far as we can with him." After a lengthy confrontation with the boy, the judge ordered the commitment. (See pp. 187–88.)

After the hearing the probation officer commented to the observer: "There's no doubt in my mind that the kid is asking for it [i.e., commitment]. If he isn't he's giving a good show. . . . [Although he obviously is a bright kid] with this we just can't let it go."

When these efforts to insure cooperation—threats, lectures, pleas to "let us help you," and protestations of trust—fail, the moral character of the youth is dramatically reassessed. He is no longer a bright boy who is a "little crazy" coming out of a bad home; he is no longer the victim of circumstances who deserves special care and should be helped. His character has been totally spoiled as his situation has become redefined as one where there is "no choice" but incarceration. Moreover it was not the seriousness of the boy's original or subsequent offenses—incorrigible, running away from school—as much as his resistance to proffered help and his denial of court authority that made him incorrigible in the eyes of the court. In this way, the boy's inconsistent reaction to the dual authority-helping relationship with his probation officer both ruined his moral character and led to his commitment to reform school.

In summary, probation involves a form of authoritarian control that assumes the normal character of the person subordinate to that authority. Departures from the expected patterns of behavior suggest a delinquent of other than normal character. This fact transforms probation into a trial of moral character, a trial, moreover, the delinquent may easily fail. This may be the result, in the first place, where the delinquent either resists probation authority, or commits further offenses in the face of constant warnings of the consequences. But second, even the delinquent who can establish a trust relationship with the probation officer may ruin his character. Paradoxically, this frequently occurs when the probation officer undertakes an active "helping" program with a youth. Persistent reaction to the underlying authoritarian element in this program frustrates probation expectation of close cooperation and the trust relationship it assumes. This in turn will lead the court to rely on more nakedly coercive sanctions, beginning a vicious circle in which the youth's moral character becomes progressively defiled.

CONCLUSION: PROBATION AND SOCIAL CLASS

Cicourel has suggested that the middle class delinquent benefits from his capacity to fend off those processes in probation whereby moral character is discredited and incarceration recommended. This results from the middle-class prejudices of the probation officer: "The combination of middle class probation officer and middle or upper middle class family provides a more congenial atmosphere of interaction than, say, a lower class and less articulate family which may not be concerned with covering up difficulties in the family and embarrassment in the community" (1965, p. 39). Moreover, the middle class delinquent can more competently sustain the clinically oriented cooperation with the probation officer needed to preserve a trust relationship. The probation officer "tends to identify with the offender so long as the latter is cooperative, admits he needs help, and shows signs of altering his past conduct" (1965, p. 46). The middle class delinquent has greater inclination and capacity to adopt and maintain this attitude convincingly during his probation encounter than the lower class delinquent.

These findings must be modified in part when applied to this juvenile court. The juvenile court's model probationer is typically lower-middle class, not middle or upper-middle class, and the probation regime is organized to handle this kind of delinquent routinely. This reflects the lower-middle class background and outlook of its probation staff. This leads to strong identification with lower-middle class youths, particularly when from solid working class families of their own ethnic group. In contrast, youths from middle and upper-middle class families, often from suburbs, inhabit a world both alien and incomprehensible to the average probation officer.

Probation preference for the lower-middle class delinquent reflects the lack of professional training and identification among juvenile court staff. The clinically oriented probation regimes Cicourel has described had training in techniques that facilitate interaction with middle class delinquents who are "motivated" and have the "capacity" for treatment. Their prior training and experience provide juvenile court probation officers no techniques for managing interpersonal relations with delinquents in nonauthoritarian, persuasive ways. The result is to leave no viable alternative to the use of authority and discipline in dealing with delinquents.[12]

This reliance on authority and external rules to control behavior is particularly adapted to dealing with lower-middle class youth. Probation officers tend to develop a kind of hearty, authoritarian rapport with these delinquents. No such rapport appears in their relations with more distinctly lower class delinquents, who tend to resist their assertions of authority and whose parents often refuse to cooperate with the officer's efforts to "help." Lower-middle class youths are often easily intimidated by the probation officer's assertions of authority. They defer to his claims to obedience and respect and respond to his tough but sympathetic approach. Usually their parents firmly support the probation officer's control.

12. It should be emphasized that differences in interactional *style*, rather than any more substantive differences, underlie the contrast between the juvenile court's disciplinary probation regime and the more clinical approach to probation Cicourel observed. Fundamental to both regimes is a concern with trouble. Thus, although the probation officers described by Cicourel regularly employ casework techniques, seek to establish personal trust relations with delinquents, and rely more often on persuasion than on formal authority as a means of control, probationary supervision nevertheless focuses on preventing renewed trouble and on controlling immediate conduct.

Again, this authoritarian and disciplinarian stance fails to impress many middle and upper-middle class youths. These delinquents are apt to seem overly assertive and independent to probation staff. They appear "snobbish" and unrepentant, resisting the role of wrongdoer and the assertions of authority made by the probation officer. The following observation made at the Municipal Court provides an excellent example of the problems posed by such youths:

Three older teenaged boys, from middle class business families living in a nearby suburb, had been found delinquent and placed on probation for forging credit slips in a department store. They first reported to probation officer Biggs on a Saturday.

Mel Weissman first breezed into the office, cheerily greeting Biggs: "How's everything?" Biggs: "Fine." The boy then sat down, crossed his legs, relaxed, leaned back in the chair. Biggs did not quite seem to know what to do, but began to question the boy about items needed to complete the probation report card. After finishing this, he indicated that Weissman could leave. But as he reached the door, the boy requested: "Will you do me a favor? Leave a message for Dan Slotman when he comes in that I'll meet him at my old man's place?" At this Biggs looked incredulous, staring at Weissman for a second without comment, but then agreed with obvious reluctance to give the message to the other boy.

Later during the morning, Slotman and the third boy came in, behaving in the same cavalier and offhand manner. For example, Slotman told Biggs he was going into the army as soon as he got out of school. Biggs replied that the court would have to vacate the delinquency finding against him 'if he were to do this. But Slotman answered, "This is being wiped off the records," indicating that an agreement had already been reached with the judge by his lawyer and his father.

After the last of these boys had left, Biggs commented to me: "[These boys] are too uninhibited. They just don't know how to control their impulses. They walk in here and ask me how're things just like it was me that had done it. They're too aggressive. That's it. They just go around taking advantage of people."

Becker's study of public school teachers' reactions to different class students (1952) supports this correlation between disciplinary regime and preference for the lower-middle class youth.

Becker found that teachers preferred to teach children of the "middle group" (essentially lower-middle class) because of lack of discipline problems and conformity to teacher standards of moral acceptability. At bottom this preference seems to reflect the fact that such students acknowledged the teacher's authority. To quote from one of Becker's interviews:

> And they'll behave for you. . . . They can be frightened, they have fear in them. They're pliable, flexible, you can do things with them. They're afraid of their parents and what they'll do to them if they get into trouble at school. And they're afraid of the administration. They're afraid of being sent down to the principal. So that they can be handled (1952, p. 460).

In contrast, teachers experience greater problems with children from "slum schools" and those from the "upper" groups. The former present particularly difficult control problems, frequently offering direct challenges to teacher authority. The classroom regime thus becomes organized around maintaining respect and obedience, ultimately by means of physical force. The latter also pose discipline problems but these are interpreted more mildly as a consequence of weak control in the home:

> I mean, they're spoiled, you know. A great many of them are only children. Naturally, they're used to having their own way, and they don't like to be told what to do (Becker, 1952, p. 464).

Similarly, in the juvenile court, resistances to probation authority receive differential interpretations and hence differentially affect lower class and upper-middle class delinquents. Lower class youths appear more likely to resist probation authority openly and hence to risk fundamentally discrediting moral character. Moreover, they generally lack the family resources and support needed to counter moves toward incarceration effectively. In contrast, middle class misconduct is apt to be interpreted as disregard rather than as challenge of probation authority.[13] This re-

13. Becker provides this analysis of the reaction of teachers to the discipline problems posed by upper-middle class pupils:
> Children of the upper group often act in a way which may be interpreted as "misbehavior" but which does not represent a conscious attack on the teacher's authority. Many teachers are able to disregard such activity by interpreting it as a natural concomitant of the "brightness" and "intelligence" of such children (1952, p. 460).

flects not only the verbal and interactional skills of these delinquents, but also, as Cicourel suggests (1968, pp. 243 *ff*), possession of exactly those desirable social and moral qualities from which probation officers infer good moral character (e.g., a "good home," concern with proper appearances).

Furthermore, middle class delinquents suffer less drastic consequences from probation because probation officers tend to minimize contact with them. This occurs not only because their social characteristics indicate less need for control, but also because their problems tend to be defined as psychological in nature (Cicourel, 1968, p. 309). This frequently leads the probation department to transfer responsibility and primary contacts to the more permissive court clinic.

9
Character and the Court Practice of Psychiatry

The court clinic exercises an often decisive influence on the ultimate outcome of the court processing of delinquency cases. Derived largely from the professional competence of clinic psychiatrists, this influence is reflected in the consideration given psychiatric diagnoses and recommendations, and in the preference afforded psychiatric therapy in the court's treatment schema. This chapter describes the functions of psychiatry within the court, emphasizing the modification of conventional psychiatric practice resulting from accommodation to pressures of the court setting. It will then consider the ramifications for the clinic's handling of delinquency cases. Here, as in probation, several of the solutions available to delinquents confronted by the conflicting implications of "help" and control tend to create and perpetuate discredited versions of moral character.

USES OF THE COURT CLINIC

Cases are referred to the court clinic under two general circumstances. First, the court refers cases it feels fall within the clinic's distinctive professional competence—cases where the youth involved is judged of disturbed character. In cases of milder disturbance, court personnel generally hope that the clinic will decide to take the child into therapy. With more severe disturbance, the clinic is expected to transform this lay estimate of character into a professionally valid diagnosis. On the basis of such a diagnosis, whether "psychotic" or "retarded," the psychiatrist can negotiate with the appropriate institution for the child's placement in their program.

Second, referrals to the clinic may reflect uncertainty and conflict over the disposition of a case, and hence over the moral character of the delinquent involved. In this sense, the clinic confronts the questions: What kind of youth is this, and what should we do with him? Clinic referrals and psychiatric diagnoses thereby come to center on the relationship between conflicting proposals about what to do with a case and differing assessments of delinquent character. In any particular case, the range of possible alternatives framed by the court may cover a more or less extreme set of dispositions. And the range of possible versions of moral character may vary accordingly.

At the most lenient extreme, the "issue" presented to the clinic may center on whether to dismiss a complaint entirely as opposed to placing a youth on probation. For example, a probation officer, unable to convince the judge to "give the kid a break," may initiate a clinic referral in order to get the youth's character "cleared" as normal as justification for his lenient proposal:

> Probation officer had tried to give a break to two white boys from the suburbs in court for trying to steal a car. The probation officer wanted the case continued without a finding, but he had had no success: "I've been three weeks trying to get Rosie [Special Judge Rose] to let them off. But he just won't buy it." Finally, he had convinced the judge to refer the two boys to the clinic where they had been seen by a psychiatric resident new to the court. This psychiatrist had prepared reports that would be given to the judge later that morning, reports that went along with the probation officer's recommendation. Later that morning the boys actually were continued without a finding.

At the other extreme, the court often refers cases it considers criminally "hopeless." Moral character seems almost conclusively that of a hardened criminal and incarceration is pending. Under such circumstances, where a delinquent would usually be committed, the clinic is explicitly called on to make a psychiatric evaluation of the advisability of giving him a "last chance." For example:

In the course of an introductory meeting with the clinic staff, the judge emphasized the importance of the psychiatrist's recommendation, particularly with regard to the question of whether or not to commit a delinquent youth. It was especially important to recommend *not* to institutionalize cases where the child had a long record and the court was leaning heavily in that direction. Then "at least we have the opinion of an expert that he would not benefit from an institution." Otherwise, if the kid has been in court four or five times, "we'd generally say he's had it."

In effect, the clinic is being asked: Can you come up with any realistic and acceptable course of action as an alternative to commitment?

This right of review implies license to redefine moral character. The decision to seek out new alternatives requires rejecting the "hopeless" and criminal-like labels that already identify the delinquent. In such cases, therefore, referral is a final appeal, a provision for a last review that in practice, however, usually only confirms and legitimates the court's belief in the appropriateness of the impending incarceration.

The practice of routine appeal to the clinic to finalize proposed incarceration reflects several contingencies surrounding the court's assessment and processing of cases. In part, this practice results from the court's recognition of the momentous and often irreversible consequences of sending a youth to the custodial regime of the reform schools. To commit a delinquent to these institutions is equivalent to writing him off, and hence occurs only when the court feels absolutely convinced of the hopeless nature of the case. Consequently, the court wants to establish beyond doubt that to-be-incarcerated delinquents are fundamentally of such moral character that they should be committed. This requires professional elimination of any excusing conditions that could account for the youth's delinquency and thereby mitigate his responsibility for it. Furthermore, it demands psychiatric confirmation of the irrevocability of abnormal character. Both these requirements derive from the recognized possibility that even behavior that seems clearly and persistently criminal in nature and intent may be due to some inner emotional or psychological problem or conflict, requiring response other than commitment to reform school.[1] Hence, the ultimate question asked the clinic is prognostic: Are the criminal and dangerous tendencies of this youth so basically a part of his character and personality as to preclude change?

Psychiatric diagnoses in these cases also serve crucial functions for the judge in dealing with possible critics of court operation. The judge can use psychiatric diagnoses and findings to justify lenient handling of a delinquent with a prior record of numerous or serious offenses. Hence, he can use the psychiatrist's report to placate police, parole or school officials pressing for what he feels is premature or inappropriate commitment. The judge can also turn to the psychiatric report and its evidence where a decision not to commit backfires and comes to public attention. This report provides a professionally competent opinion to point to in justification of a decision under political or public criticism.

In conclusion, the court's expectations and pressures surrounding referrals to the clinic fundamentally constrain psychiatric practice in the court setting. Clinic referrals reflect certain kinds of organizational problems for the court and are accompanied by pressures to make evaluations on terms relevant to these court interests.

PROBLEMS OF PSYCHIATRIC PRACTICE IN THE COURT

Psychiatric diagnosis requires uncovering the "meaning" or significance of the delinquent offense with reference to the relationship between the act and the nature of the actor. Illegal behavior in general is held to be "pathological" and to reflect psychological conflicts which the psychiatrist can identify. To quote from a court clinic program leaflet intended to introduce new psychiatrists to the system:

1. The possibility that even serious criminal activity may "really" involve "mental illness" underlies the judge's threat concluding his confrontation with the young Italian car thief, recounted earlier: "He had better be psychotic because if he's not he's going (to the Youth Correction Authority) ."

The purpose of the Court Clinic diagnostic evaluation is to furnish understanding of the meaning of a particular offense in terms of the character structure of the particular individual, inasmuch as offenses in themselves do not necessarily have specific meanings.

The commission of an offense must, by its anti-social nature, indicate some breakdown, overpowering, or remission of that facility which human beings have, or are expected to have, to maintain their status as law-abiding citizens. In a sense, then, an offense may be seen as symptomatic of an inner conflict which the ego is not able to effectively deal with.[2]

This kind of interpretation must lean heavily on the delinquent's subjective account of and basic attitude toward his delinquency. Hence psychiatric diagnosis routinely involves inquiry into the offense and the child's explanations, feelings, and reactions associated with it.

Court pressures reinforce this tendency. The court expects the clinic to employ professional skills to elicit frank expressions of outlook and "problems." By uncovering and reporting the subjective attitudes and experiences of the delinquent, the clinic compensates for the court's alienating exercise of authority and control. Comments made by the judge to new clinic personnel during an orientation session reflect these concerns:

The judge discussed what the clinic could do for the court. "We're interested in the background you get," particularly since the psychiatrist can get more information from the child than can the probation officer. "We're interested in what you find his problems are." A little later he picked this up again: "If they form a relationship with a psychiatrist, many times you can give us more information than we can get."

Such "background" and "information" involve two basic dimensions: first, the general outlook and circumstances of the delinquent—his strengths and weaknesses, "problems," family situation, etc.; second, the events preceding and precipitating the de-

2. From a pamphlet entitled "Diagnosis of Offenders," by the director of the court clinic program.

linquency. In both instances, the psychiatrist seeks to serve the court by discovering and evaluating the youth's personal and sub-jective feelings, attitudes, and ideas.

To meet these court expectations, and to make professionally competent diagnoses, the clinic psychiatrist must gain the confi-dence of his delinquent patient. Authoritarian pressures imping-ing from the general court setting frequently hinder movement in this direction, however. In the first place, the manner of introduc-ing cases to the clinic increases the difficulty of establishing a close and trusting relationship with the delinquent. The delinquent and his family are explicitly told that cooperation with the clinic constitutes part of their legal obligation to the court. Probation officers always tell youth and parents that clinic attendance is compulsory, warning of severe repercussions if appointments are missed. Similarly, the court explicitly commands delinquents to cooperate in therapy efforts, presenting commitment to the Youth Correction Authority as the only alternative:

> A probation officer conferred with Dr. James about a boy he had ear-lier evaluated in the clinic. After some discussion, they agreed that Dr. James would see the boy in weekly sessions while the probation officer tried to work with him in the community. Probation officer then went and brought the boy and his mother into the room with the psychia-trist, lecturing the boy along the following lines: My inclination after hearing about this business with the stolen car [which he had smashed up in a serious accident] was to commit you on the spot. However, Dr. James and I have agreed to give you one more chance, if you follow this program. Come every week to see Dr. James, get a job und keep it, and report regularly to me. The probation officer then worked out the details on the clinic with the boy and his mother, again warning both: ". . . . if he should depart from what we lay down, that's it." He will be committed right away. "He fails to do anything and he'll be com-mitted straight to the Youth Correction Authority."

The delinquent's contact with the clinic, then, is consistently defined in authoritarian terms by court staff. Consequently, most youths are not predisposed toward openness and trust when they initially approach the clinic.

It should be noted that social class variations affect this initial encounter. Middle class youths and their families are more likely than lower and lower-middle class ones to take the initiative in suggesting psychiatric contact, and hence are frequently less distrustful and more cooperative in relations with psychiatrists. Even here, however, trust and cooperation may be only partial and expedient, since psychiatric self-referral often represents a strategy for avoiding other, more punitive outcomes.

If the delinquent realizes that what the psychiatrist reports to the court may determine its decisions about his fate, he may well persist in this initial distrustfulness. In the following case, for example, the psychiatrist encounters difficulty in completing his diagnosis when blamed for extending a stay in detention:

> A 12-year-old Negro boy, on parole from the Youth Correction Authority, was brought to court for stealing a handbag, and referred to the clinic, while being held at the detention center. The psychiatrist saw the boy for the first time somewhat later and had to decide whether to continue to detain the boy. He discussed this with the boy, who did not want to stay in detention for another two weeks. But the psychiatrist had felt he should be held in detention, and the court had gone along with this. When this decision was made in the courtroom, the boy began crying. As the psychiatrist explained his response to this: "I asked him about it and he could not say why. Probably it was anger toward me, but he did not know why. . . . He knows I was the one who sent him out there."

Similarly, the fact that the psychiatrist's recommendation will have an important influence on the court's permanent disposition of his case may induce reserve or evasiveness if not outright hostility on the part of the delinquent.

Psychiatrists practicing in the court setting encounter a variety of problems growing out of the suspiciousness and distrust of their delinquent patients. In the first place, psychiatrists report recurring difficulty in getting children to relate openly and frankly during interviews. As a clinic social worker succinctly noted: "Most of these kids don't talk." Second, as a consequence, psychiatrists often have to conduct two or three interviews with a delinquent before obtaining sufficient material and insight to commit themselves to a diagnosis. In the following case, for example, even after several interviews, the psychiatrist is unable to make a thorough diagnosis in the face of the persistent suspicion of her patient:

A psychiatrist new to the court reported on her efforts to diagnose the case of a 15-year-old Negro boy, Phil Johnson, who had been brought to the court by his mother on an incorrigible child complaint after she had discovered a note threatening suicide. During an initial, emergency interview, she had been unable to get anywhere with him: "I could not assess him . . . I got nothing from him." Subsequently the boy was held in detention and two more interviews were conducted in that setting. But he remained almost as "unresponsive" as previously. As the psychiatrist's report to the court noted: "He maintained a truculent uncommunicativeness and it was not possible to assess fully his mental state although it was determined that he was not psychotic or suicidally depressed." Despite these problems with diagnosis, however, the psychiatrist continued to see the boy in an effort to provide the treatment she felt he desperately needed. However, his initial bitterness and reticence continued unabated, and she could get nowhere with the case: "I was unable to reach him on any point and to help him in any way." Interviews had consistently been characterized by great "distance," as she had not been able to break down the boy's hostility and resentment. In later interviews, she had tried to get him to talk about things that had been noted in the case history (taken by the social worker from the mother). She would tell him, "I know about your tonsilectomy," but this would produce no reaction. "I had more and more the feeling that it was an interrogation on each point" (listed in the case history). The boy remained totally passive and uncooperative, even when she suggested that they could help him with his school work so he could get into the school he desired. (Mother had reported that he had been very upset when he had failed to do this previously.) In sum, she had been unable to accomplish a single thing with the case.

Finally, as the above case illustrates, reticence and distance characterize even those cases that are seen on a regular treatment basis. Thus, one recurring theme in conferences devoted to treatment cases was the superficiality of the therapeutic effort, at least in relation to the psychiatric ideal of getting down to unconscious processes. For example:

A psychiatrist who had treated a 16-year-old white girl for almost six months commented at the end of a conference devoted to the case that they had not gone into "anything deep," adding: "I think what she got out of it was the relationship."

A conference was held on the case of a 16-year-old white boy, a case considered by the court the great treatment "success" of the clinic. The boy had been in continuous trouble with the law and with his family but, after almost a year of visiting the clinic, had been reconciled with the latter and become somewhat more law-abiding. But recently the boy had begun to miss appointments, reflecting the fact that he had reached a "plateau" with his reintegration back into his family. The problem now, the therapist felt, was what to do: "How far do you go?" All agreed that the situation was still unhealthy; as the clinic director noted: "He has been reincorporated into the family still with a considerable degree of pathology." Another resident commented that he had been working on the "family interaction level," and in order to get any further would have to move on to "intra-psychic therapy." This would be too threatening to the parents, however, getting at things they did not want to face and hence increasing their resistance. Dr. James agreed, noting "there's no place to go except into intra-psychic." It was then decided that therapy should be terminated, but to still "leave the door open" in case of any kind of crisis.

In general, psychiatrists in the court clinic come to redefine the version of treatment learned during their analytic training. Therapy comes to focus on external behavior rather than personality change and development. Adjustment to current social conditions assumes priority over the ideal of increasing self-awareness and insight.

While the court practice of psychiatry redefines the nature of therapy, interpersonal skills and techniques fundamental to the routine practice of child psychiatry assume critical importance in allaying the suspicion and distrust of delinquents and their families. A warm and sympathetic personal stance, efforts to put the youth at ease, a nonjudgmental attitude toward the delinquent and his offense, are all employed to overcome the problems posed by evasive and suspicious patients.

Moreover, the court setting can itself be turned to advantage if the psychiatrist can establish himself as a sympathetic and trustworthy party in contrast to the disciplining and controlling probation official.[3]

However, success in establishing this definition of the relationship initially depends on how the psychiatrist introduces himself and explains his task to the youthful patient. The dominant approach, supported by both of the senior psychiatrists supervising residents who work at the court, plays down the psychiatrist's obligations to the court on the theory that to dwell on these unnecessarily creates barriers between psychiatrist and patient. As the director of the juvenile court clinic explained his handling of the issue:

> I don't tell him I'm a psychiatrist or go into what I will or will not report to the court, as some of them are doing. I'm against it. . . . No bargains. It sets up his guard. [RE: You don't tell them you're a psychiatrist?] No. . . . [If you do] the child wonders why you're making such a thing about it and what you're up to.

In contrast, in the minority position, expressed most explicitly by a psychiatric resident trained in another area who worked only temporarily at the juvenile court clinic, the psychiatrist clearly defines himself as an agent of the court, highlighting his official obligations in this direction:

> I asked a psychiatrist how he defined himself to the kids he interviewed. He replied: "I tell them I'm an agent of the court—," except not in those exact words. Rather he would reformulate it: "The court sent you to see me to find out more about you. I am going to report back to the court what you tell me. What you tell me may be held against you or it may not. You'll have to use your own judgment about that and what you tell me. Period. Oh—and I tell them I want to help them."

3. A similar tactic may well underlie the activities of professional helpers in other authoritarian settings. McCorkle and Korn, for example, point out that professionals in prisons are generally thrown into opposition to the regime of the custodians (1964, pp. 531–32). In light of the exigencies of psychiatric practice in the juvenile court, this may reflect not so much ideological conflict with the custodial regime as the need to elicit the trust and cooperation of inmates who stand opposed to this regime. Conflict with custodians therefore becomes a necessary condition for maintaining the trust of inmate-patients.

As both these quotations indicate, explanation of one's task inevitably leads into the area of confidentiality. In general, psychiatrists make no formal promises of confidentiality of information, at least during diagnostic interviews. Again, the degree to which this lack of confidentiality is made explicit to the patient varies, but the tendency is either to avoid the issue completely or to handle it more indirectly:

> I asked Dr. James whether he told his patients that he would report to the court things that they told him. He answered: "No. . . . But I do tell them, 'Mr. Manello [assistant chief probation officer]—or the judge—is worried about finding out more about your problems.' "

Similarly, in trying to get the youth to talk about the delinquent offense, psychiatrists generally avoid direct mention of confidentiality. Instead, the offense will frequently be introduced in natural and neutral terms, implicitly suggesting that the psychiatrist is open to what the youth has to say and perhaps will even take his part:

> A psychiatrist reported that he did sometimes meet reluctance on the part of children to talk about the offense, but he tried to get around this by approaching the topic with the question, "What brings you in here?" This seemed to work, and children were generally willing to talk openly about their problems.

This avoidance strategy at best prevents the authority issue from becoming central to the relationship. It also, however, may deprive the psychiatrist of one of the most essential tools he possesses for establishing conditions of trust. He cannot make the kind of *bargain* basic to the psychiatric relationship, that is, the revelation of secret and soiling details of one's life in return for the promise that they will not be disclosed (and will receive sympathetic consideration). The resulting difficulties of making a diagnosis are brought out by the following comment:

> ["Do you explain to any of your patients here what you will and will not report to the court?"]
> Dr. Becker: "If he and I were in therapy I might do that. . . . While

doing an evaluation I would not make deals with him." But this created just the dilemma he was facing with this boy: the boy did not
trust him, was not sure of him and yet he [Becker] needed more information from the boy in order to make his decision. In order to obtain
this trust he would have to make commitments he neither wanted nor
could keep. This is the dilemma of the conflicting demands of diagnostic versus treatment situations: "You've got to get them to give you
the information you need to form a working framework to evaluate
the case. To do this you need to have them trust you. But you cannot
make a commitment you can't keep. . . . You try to get them to feel
you'll do what's in their best interests. . . . [As a psychiatrist] the
most we can give is our interest and our experience. This is what I try
to do. . . . I'm still trying to work it out."

While the psychiatrist here interprets the difficulties in establishing rapport as one aspect of the general problem of diagnosis,
these difficulties reflect the influence of the court setting in several
ways. The commitment a psychiatrist can make to a case is restricted by the limited amount of time he can devote to therapy,
this in turn reflecting the heavily diagnostic pressure on the court
clinic. But the development of rapport and trust is inhibited by
the authoritarian nature of the court operation and by the psychiatrist's dual obligations within it, as discussed previously.

THE FATE OF CLINIC REFERRALS

While a delinquent may reasonably react to his referral to the
clinic with suspicion and distrust, this kind of reaction will damage clinic handling of his case and hence impair his ultimate fate
in the juvenile court. On the one hand, hostile behavior in contacts with the clinic directly discourages favorable consideration
of the case by clinic personnel. On the other, such behavior forces
clinic staff to rely on strategies to circumvent this lack of cooperation that tend to perpetuate prior discrediting definitions of
character and disadvantageous programs of action.

Evasiveness, lack of cooperation, and hostility discourage psychiatrists from supporting and "saving" many of the "last chance"
cases referred to them. If the delinquent patient reacts to the

psychiatrist primarily as an authoritarian figure, exhibiting distrust and reticence, he significantly decreases the possibility that the clinic will try to obtain a favorable disposition of his case. First, the psychiatrist is apt to feel that placement is inappropriate for the delinquent who behaves in this way. Psychiatrists tend to assess reticent youths who express open distrust and who repulse all sympathetic overtures as lacking in those fundamental "character strengths" held prerequisite to normal personality development, perhaps even making a diagnosis of "character disorder." Either evaluation will quickly rule out the desirability of placement. Furthermore, the psychiatrist is unlikely to involve himself in such a case sufficiently to carry through the negotiations necessary to effect such a disposition. The extra commitment—leading the psychiatrist to extend his professional prestige and contacts in working out a placement—simply will not be forthcoming in these cases of overt distrust and suspiciousness.

Second, the clinic will not "save" the delinquent who reacts in this way by taking him on as a treatment case. The few available therapy slots are allocated to patients who seem cooperative, communicative, and generally responsive to the psychiatrist's proffered help. Discouraging accounts of cases taken on for therapy despite initial and continuing resistance reinforce the priority psychiatrists give patients showing these qualities.[4] Furthermore, the clinic prefers to treat patients whose pathology is not too deep-rooted, where a minimum amount of psychiatric care will produce tangible results. On both counts, the distrustful and uncooperative delinquent will be considered a bad risk for therapy.[5]

The frequent lack of cooperation and reticence shown by de-

4. This was clearly the impact of the case conference report on Phil Johnson, described earlier in this chapter.

5. David Mechanic has described a similar process within a mental hospital in the following terms:

[The psychiatrist] realizes that he must convince the patient that he is indeed "sick" and in serious need of treatment. . . . Should the patient refuse to accept the patient-role and deny his illness, this resistance is viewed as a further symptom of the "illness," and he is told that if he is to get well, he must recognize the fact that he is ill.

Should the patient continue to reject the psychiatric definition of his illness, the psychiatrist is likely to report that the patient is a poor treatment risk (1967, p. 31) .

linquents referred to the clinic has a number of less direct consequences for the functioning of psychiatry in the juvenile court. When the delinquent patient evades or resists clinic overtures, the psychiatrist is compelled to turn to diagnostic strategies that circumvent this uncooperativeness. These strategies have great impact on how the psychiatrist and clinic operate, for they increase routine dependence on probation officers and hence fundamentally restrict the clinic's ability and inclination to redefine prior assessments of moral character and to advocate new courses of action for handling cases.

As a general rule, clinic psychiatrists are heavily dependent on the court and its probation staff in deciding on recommendations for those cases referred to them. Lacking any prior involvement in the case, psychiatrists routinely function by first ascertaining the probation officer's views about what "reasonable" courses of action are open. Subsequent clinic evaluation is constrained within these limits. In this way, learning what are "reasonable" and expected recommendations in various sorts of cases is fundamental to a psychiatrist's socialization into the workings of the court. Often such expectations are explicitly sought from the probation staff:

> A psychiatric resident new to the court was talking to a probation officer about a boy who had been sent to the clinic for evaluation. This boy had been brought into court for an offense while already on parole from the Youth Correction Authority. At one point in the conversation, the psychiatrist asked the probation officer: "What do you think will happen [when the case is decided in court]?" The probation officer replied that "cases like this usually go back," i.e., the youth would probably be returned to the Youth Correction Authority for violation of his parole.

In this way the psychiatrist gradually builds up a body of knowledge concerning recommendations the court considers "realistic" for various sorts of cases.

But even within the limits of what is considered "reasonable" by the court, clinic psychiatrists regularly function by specifically basing their recommendations on the courses of action suggested by the probation staff:

> A new resident psychiatrist commented about his contacts with the probation department: "My approach is to go along with the probation officer unless there's some good reason against it." Usually he tries to find out what the probation officer wants and will generally go along with it: "I let the probation officer handle it."

This psychiatrist—one of the most highly respected and trusted by the court staff, it might be added—thus routinely probes into what the court anticipates doing and "goes along" with the indicated course of action unless contradicting evidence appears.

But in learning what is considered "reasonable" in various kinds of cases, the psychiatrist learns and accepts both court standards for assessing moral character and court application of the standards in specific cases. (Learning how the court groups "cases of this kind" means learning how it assesses moral character.) Again, in routinely "going along" with probation preferences, the psychiatrist also comes to take over probation assessments of moral character. Thus, in discovering that the probation officer expects to commit a particular youth, the psychiatrist also learns to anticipate that this is the kind of youth who *should* be committed. His evaluation, then, will be premised on this kind of judgment: it will seek to determine whether or not this is the case, rather than making a more open assessment of character. Any signs of criminal-like character, therefore, will confirm this anticipated version of the youth's character.

In general, then, to the extent that the psychiatrist routinely "goes along" with the probation officer's desired disposition of the case, he is led to accept and therefore validate previously established assessments of the delinquent's moral character. Delinquent distrust and hostility can strongly reinforce these tendencies. This stance denies the psychiatrist access to a variety of material from and about the delinquent himself. This in turn insures the probation officer a near monopoly on information relevant to the case. The probation officer's initial description of the noteworthy features of the offense, the youth's background, and prior court contacts, and hence the court's perception of moral character and the desirable outcome, remain unchallenged. In addition, as noted previously, this kind of stance tends to confirm the court version of discredited moral character. Finally, it forces the psychiatrist to rely on the probation officer's informal channels of communication about the child, his offense, and his background. In this way, for example, versions of particular incidents, or judgments of moral character, may be passed on from the police, family, or other enforcement agency, through the probation officer to the psychiatrist. This means that the psychiatrist has regular although indirect access to opinions and information from sources in whose eyes the delinquent may be completely discredited.

Furthermore, patient resistance may force the psychiatrist to turn to the probation officer to resolve problems and issues that arise in the course of his evaluation. In the following instance, for example, the psychiatrist calls upon a probation officer to provide information concerning local institutions and their functioning of which he has little or no knowledge:

> A psychiatrist wondered why a boy he was currently diagnosing had been committed to the Youth Correction Authority on his second offense, both of which had been "use without's." He went up to the probation officer working on the case and asked him about this commitment, feeling perhaps there was something involved that did not appear on the formal record. Probation officer called a probation officer at the court that had committed the boy and then reported that this was the regular practice over there (to commit on the second "use without") and there was nothing else involved.

Again, the psychiatrist relies on the probation officer and his ties to informal channels of communication to substantiate many of the claims and accounts he does receive from delinquent patients. For example:

> Dr. Becker talked about a boy who was charged with assault and battery on a police officer. The boy told a story very different from the official one, which described him attacking the policeman with a screwdriver. The boy claimed he had been picked up and put in the patrol wagon, finding the screwdriver there and throwing it at the policeman in anger, after being roughed up. Dr. Becker was uncertain about which was true, whether the boy was making it up or whether he had really been pushed around as claimed. He then checked with the

probation officer on the case, asking whether the police would be rough with a kid like this and whether they would make such a complaint without reason. "He told me that the police don't really bring that kind of serious charge without good reason. . . . He convinced me that this is not the kind of thing people are just going to throw on a kid."

In this case, an inconsistency between the youth's version and the official version of the offense is resolved by consulting the probation officer. When the probation officer validates the official version, the delinquent is discredited not only by association with the offense, but also by the fact that he is judged to be lying. Moreover, the psychiatrist avoids a fundamental reevaluation of the case by accepting the official accounts of the incident handed down from the police. In general, psychiatrists treat the accounts and interpretations provided by probation officers as valid on their face, thereby confirming and perpetuating established perceptions and evaluations.

Several other forces make the psychiatrist dependent on the probation officer in his routine operations, strengthening his tendency to "go along" with both the court's intended course of action and the implicit version of moral character associated with it. In the first place, in cases where the court is at least tentatively committed to incarcerating the youth, to go against this expectation requires more investment in the case by the psychiatrist than merely "playing along." As one more experienced clinic staff member noted:

> "You don't want to make a recommendation they are going to think is ridiculous." But if you do want to do something with a case that the court does not want, you have to put special effort into it. "If you want to do something out of the ordinary you just can't drop it in their laps and let it go at that." Rather you have to start working on those involved before the case went back into court, getting things arranged before the recommendation is formally made. "You have to justify it, work on it, keep after them." Otherwise, the unusual recommendation would not be accepted.

In order to go against court expectations, the clinic must take the initiative, deciding on new plans and beginning to implement the necessary arrangements. Particularly for an overly scheduled psychiatrist, the ensuing requirements of extra time and effort may become prohibitive. Clinic work proceeds more smoothly the more exactly one follows the expected course of events, relying on what the probation officer has worked out previously and leaving primary responsibility in his hands.

The limited amount of treatment time available to the clinic further constrains its freedom of action. Under most circumstances, the recommendation not to institutionalize a likely candidate leaves the probation officer with total responsibility for the case. For this reason, the recommendation not to commit will often be accompanied by an expression of willingness to take the youth involved into treatment. In this way, the psychiatrist shows that he is willing to commit himself to the case and thereby gains a greater right to determine what disposition should be made. The limited amount of time that can be devoted to treatment cases, therefore, effectively limits the number of cases the psychiatrist can save. Similarly, in those cases he is not willing to treat, the psychiatrist is under greater pressure to defer to the wishes of the probation officer, who retains the responsibility and liability for the case.

Again, where cases are presented to the clinic in terms of commitment, so that positive and assertive action is required to "save" them, the failure to make or agree to such assertive actions will often lead to commitment. For example, in the following case, a boy is committed when the psychiatrist avoids implicit pressures to come forward and work with the case in an active way:

A 15-year-old boy of Italian-Filipino background, James Basilio, was the subject of a conference the day before his case was due in court for decision. He was charged with truancy and runaway. He lived with a foster mother, continually resisting both her efforts and those of the probation officer to get him to go to school. Psychiatrist reported that in an interview the boy had initially been very reserved, had then opened up some, only to withdraw once again. Also emphasized that the boy had been rejected by his mother at a very early age, and showed basic feelings of rejection. Probation officer underlined the fact that he could do no more with the case, unless something opened up in the way of treatment or a placement. "He will be committed

tomorrow, unless something comes up before then." Psychiatrist refused to take the boy for therapy, arguing: "I think the same thing
would happen. He would come a little way and then back off. He
would not come." The next day the boy was in fact committed.

Finally, even where the clinic does "save" delinquents and redefine character, such saving and redefinition is extremely precarious, as prior court perceptions and expectations are quickly re-
asserted with any kind of "trouble":

> A 16-year-old parolee from the Youth Correction Authority, Dan
> Bucher, was charged with use without authority and assault with a
> dangerous weapon on a police officer during the course of his appre-
> hension. His case was referred to the clinic because he "had never
> been evaluated before," and he was seen twice by a psychiatrist. The
> psychiatrist was impressed by the boy's apparent passivity, reflected in
> the "way he handles aggressive impulses". The assault on the police
> officer took place, he felt, only because the boy had been drinking.
> Thus the psychiatrist concluded in his report: "I could find little to
> make me suspect that assaultiveness is typical of his usual style and
> behavior." He then recommended sending the boy to the Boys' Train-
> ing Program, thereby keeping him on the streets, and indicated that
> he would consider taking the case on for treatment.
>
> The court accepted this recommendation, but clearly was somewhat
> surprised at it. A probation officer commented to me about the case:
> "It's amazing how he [psychiatrist] pulled that one out." The reason
> for this is that parolees are almost automatically returned to the
> Youth Correction Authority for violating their parole, and are gener-
> ally returned to reform school by its decision-making board. The
> judge later commented how he had gone out on a limb with the Youth
> Correction Authority in keeping a parolee like this on the street after
> another offense.
>
> Two days after this disposition had been made the boy was brought
> to court again, this time for another incident involving a stolen car
> and a minor assault on a police officer. The boy was quickly returned
> to detention, and was eventually surrendered by his parole offi-
> cer. In later conversations, the psychiatrist was somewhat upset by the
> outcome of this case, commenting: "This is the first case that backfired
> this quickly in this way." He saw it as a "mistake," and felt that his
> diagnosis had been way off base, in most likelihood manipulated by
> the boy: "I would say—except that it's too pejorative—he conned us.
> He conned me."

In this case, the psychiatrist knowingly made a recommendation that strongly countered the expectations and routine practices of the court. The fact that the youth "messed up" almost immediately consequently not only ended the psychiatrist's efforts to keep the boy out of reform school, but also invalidated his diagnosis of the boy's problems and character. This occurred despite the presence of fairly strong extenuating circumstances—the boy had argued with his mother and been kicked out of the house just prior to the offense. The new incident dramatically reconfirmed the prior court evaluation of the youth's moral character, leading the psychiatrist to disregard these extenuating circumstances and to cast around for an appropriate accounting of the incident and of the youth's character. As the psychiatrist commented after the new offense:

> "Why he's doing this is just not clear to me. . . . At some level he must want to get caught or punished or something." You would think that a boy given a break like this would watch out and behave himself, for a while anyway. But he had messed up only two days after the court hearing: "The court had given him a kind of chance and he screwed up. The little bastard!"

These comments suggest how the psychiatrist, in "saving" delinquents, operates with a very low tolerance for any subsequent delinquencies. In this way he comes to share the court's view of renewed trouble as basically discrediting moral character, assuming that a normal child would be deterred from further offenses by the intimidating effect of the court experience. In such cases, therefore, court assessments of moral character are reaffirmed following any disturbing incident.

Finally, as the case illustrates, subsequent delinquencies discredit the psychiatrist as well as the delinquent he has saved. The psychiatrist makes an implicit bargain with the court that youths he saves will stay out of trouble. Since he is in no position to guarantee this bargain, he faces great uncertainty in making any such recommendation. This uncertainty makes him extremely cautious in using his power to save. The psychiatrist, in other words, in order to avoid a reputation for unreliability and overleniency, a reputation that would lead the court to disregard many of his recommendations, must conserve his credibility with court personnel. He must make "realistic" and credible diagnoses and recommendations. In doing this, he tends to avoid taking a "chance" on delinquents considered hopeless by court personnel. Instead, he comes to exercise his discretionary power to save on the court's standards, closely conforming his recommendations to court expectations. The psychiatrist thus takes smaller "gambles," saving delinquents the court sees some hope for, shunting "parolees" or other confirmed hardcore cases into the correctional system. In general, the psychiatrist is under pressure to conserve his *credibility* with the court in a way that limits his inclination to save delinquents from incarceration.

CONCLUSION

The contingencies surrounding the practice of psychiatry in the juvenile court setting undermine the independence of the clinic. Diagnoses tend to reflect prior assessments of delinquent character communicated to the psychiatrist by probation officers. The clinic's ability and inclination to resist the momentum generated by prior court involvement in cases are eroded by dependence on court personnel incurred in carrying out daily clinic operations. The psychiatrist's recommendations are consequently pulled in a conservative direction, coming to conform to prevailing court standards of what is reasonable and to eschew risk-taking. These factors severely restrict psychiatric reassessment and redefinition of criminal-like character, and hence psychiatric "saving" of hardcore delinquents from incarceration. Only occasionally does the clinic perform its "last chance" function.

In addition, the delinquent's reaction to his referral to the clinic may contribute to this confirmation of his discredited character and thus further his own incarceration. The delinquent may define the clinic as part of the authoritarian court setting and respond evasively or hostilely to the clinic's efforts to "help" him. If he maintains this stance, the clinic will evaluate him as unfeeling, secretive, and anti-social. Moreover, clinic personnel will ascertain neither his inner feelings nor his subjective accounts for his behavior. This ruins the psychiatric assessment of his character and leads to unfavorable recommendations to the court. In this way, the suspicious and uncooperative delinquent helps destroy his "last chance" to escape incarceration and hence possible permanent stigmatization at the hands of the court.

10

Conclusion

This book has attempted to describe the process by which a juvenile court judges and manages delinquency cases. Early chapters presented the background of this process, emphasizing the nature and consequences of the court's relations with environing institutions. Through a series of exchange relationships, the court develops a system of working ties with local enforcement and welfare institutions. These ties and the pressures they entail underlie the court's fundamental concern with controlling juvenile behavior and with preventing serious delinquent activity. These concerns are reflected in court procedures for identifying cases of "trouble." Trouble cases are those felt to require special attention and measures of control.

In determining how to deal with trouble cases, the court comes to study and assess the moral character of delinquents. Indeed, the assessment of moral character can be seen as the characteristic court activity. Attention centered particularly on procedures for assessing character during the courtroom hearing, including the ways in which agents can present, discredit, or build up a delinquent's character, in which the delinquent can defend character against the discrediting implications of misconduct and denunciation, and in which the delinquent reveals character within the ceremonial structure of the courtroom event. It was argued that these procedures fundamentally shape case outcomes, and hence delineate critical dimensions of the labeling process in the juvenile court.

In the last two chapters, attention shifted to the delinquent's continuing relations with court personnel while on probation or with referral to the court clinic. Here the delinquent often finds himself in a bind: he is expected to cooperate with and confide in persons who exercise authority over his immediate behavior and ultimate fate. Character may well be discredited if the delinquent persists in responding to the overtures of court staff as essentially authoritarian measures.

This analysis has implicitly touched on several underlying functions of the juvenile court. In this brief conclusion I would like to make some of these explicit.

THE JUVENILE COURT AS A BACK-UP INSTITUTION

From the viewpoint of its users the juvenile court should serve as a *back-up institution.* I mean "back-up" in two closely related senses: first, the court is expected to support the users' official actions and programs; second, the court is expected to support their authority and general legitimacy.

In general, the juvenile court is subject to strong pressure to back up and legitimate the internal control regimes and practices of agents dealing with troublesome youths. As noted earlier, delinquency complaints are not simply abstract allegations of illegal conduct, but products of the practical work contingencies of these control agents and trouble specialists. Each complaint represents a demand that the court "do something" about some organizationally determined trouble case. The court is expected to back these institutions up by making decisions that support and reinforce practical work difficulties arising out of their controlling efforts. With the police, these difficulties generally reflect efforts to "keep the peace" in the local community. With other controllers, such as school agents, welfare workers, and parents, the problem generally centers on the support and maintenance of an internal system of control.

Support and "backing up" of these internal control practices take two general forms. First, in the case of the police, the expectation is that the court use its authority to sanction and intimidate those delinquent troublemakers who have been "disturbing the peace" in the local community. That is, the police bring into court delinquents they have had difficulty in controlling and pressure the court to supplement their controlling efforts with its own supervision and authority. In this way, the police expect the court to find the youth delinquent, give him a stiff lecture, put him on probation or a suspended sentence, and supervise and control his activities in such a way as to discourage him from making more trouble.

Similarly, with other users of the court, cases are brought with the expectation that the court will support and reinforce internal institutional efforts to deal wih troublemakers. Hence truant officers appeal to the court to use its authority and its threatened sanctions to get truants to attend school; school officials to discipline and control in-school "behavior problems"; the Child Welfare Department to augment caseworker and group home control over troublesome youths; and parents to support efforts to deal with their recalcitrant children.

Second, where both internal control measures and the threat of court sanction fail (or are felt to be too costly), pressure is exerted to have the court remove from these institutions those persistent troublemakers who have come to be regarded as "uncontrollable" and hopeless. Thus the police pressure the court to incarcerate the delinquent who has committed a large number of offenses or who has committed a particularly vicious and serious one. Similarly, schools, welfare agencies, group homes, and sometimes parents ask the court to incarcerate youths who have become intolerable because of continually disruptive and often dramatic resistance to the control regime.

If the court in fact carries out this "dumping," it not only validates and ensures the continued viability of internal institutional norms by punishing those who have violated them. But it also reestablishes institutional control over those who remain by demonstrating what happens to those who challenge it and by depriving them of possible leaders in rebellion.

A second kind of back-up pressure on the juvenile court focuses on the support and legitimation of the authority of those who use it and of the institutional norms upon which they operate. Here it is important to note that in appealing to the court to back up a particular institutional decision by taking out a delinquency complaint, the complainant runs an inherent risk that it will be turned down. This in turn threatens the complainant's authority. For example, to request that a delinquent be placed on probation or in reform school, and then have the court refuse to grant the request, means that the agent has publicly failed to achieve a threatened sanction. In contrast, by "going along" with the proposed course of action, the court both supports the authority of the agent who initiated it, and validates the judgments and norms underlying and justifying the proposal.

Again, this kind of legitimating backing-up extends beyond the court's ultimate disposing and sanctioning of the case. The police, for example, placing heavy reliance on maintaining their authority in carrying out their tasks, expect the court to sanction all violations of this authority. Thus the police pressure the court to punish those who resist arrest and are hostile and "uncooperative," not only by finding them delinquent, but also by consistently sanctioning them, e.g., by setting high bail, by holding them in the adult jail rather than the juvenile detention center.

THE JUVENILE COURT AS RELUCTANT LABELER

From the viewpoint of the court itself, institutional demands to be "backed up" must be met within the limits imposed by its own distinctive problem relevances and institutional constraints. These relevances and constraints differ from those of the initiators of delinquency complaints, if only because the court must meet numerous demands from a variety of controlling institutions. In this respect the court is fundamentally constrained by the scarcity of resources available to it—in terms both of "placements" and commitments and of the direct use of its own sanctioning and supervisory powers. As a result, in order to conserve its limited resources and to allocate its efforts properly, the court tends to at least partially resist the pressures of client institutions. Seeking to conserve its exercises of control, the court becomes more tolerant of delinquency than many of the agencies bringing cases before it. Under constant pressure to intervene with its controlling power, and hence to "label" youths delinquent through such intervention, the court in fact tends to intervene and label only reluctantly and conservatively. Because of its distinctive institutional position and interests, then, the court tends to operate with a kind of inherent self-restraint.

To cite only a few of the more striking expressions of this kind of self-restraint: First, the court is extremely reluctant to incarcerate any delinquent (feeling that to commit any youth to reform school is to write him off as hopeless) despite persistent pressure from various primary institutions to dispose of cases in this way. Second, the court is inclined to resist what it feels are excessive demands upon its authority. It is established probation policy, for example, not to inform Catholic school officials about students on probation at the court. This resulted from court feeling that these school officials were overly harsh and restrictive toward such "delinquents," trying to dump them back on the court with the first recurrence of "trouble," however minor in the eyes of the court.

Again, the court is acutely aware of its own stigmatizing effects and tries not to become involved in cases where it feels there is no pressing need to do so. One expression of this is the "cooling out" of what are regarded as inappropriate complaints. Another is regular use of the "continued without a finding" disposition; this keeps court involvement to a minimum and produces no official record for delinquency.

Finally, where it is difficult to resist complainant pressures, the court may seek to deflect them. The court clinic may play a crucial role in this process, serving to recast cases within a psychiatric framework in such a way as to initiate and justify more lenient courses of action. The handling of "serious cases" illustrate these processes. Serious cases mobilize strong institutional and community pressures that "something be done." Moreover, the serious offense strongly indicates "dangerousness" to the court, and court personnel presume such a delinquent to be of criminal-like character. However, serious cases are routinely referred to the court clinic for expert evaluation of this dangerous and criminal potential. Here, the psychiatrist can deflect punitive pressures by presenting evidence that despite the serious offense, the youth's character is such that he is not really dangerous; that "it is not likely to happen again." In general, when the serious act can be separated from the actor's true character, the court can justify "treating" the delinquent rather than handling him as a criminal.

However, while the court tries to use its powers conservatively and with restraint, its ability to do so is at least partially undermined by its dependence on those institutions demanding backing up. The court's decision on whether to honor a particular back-up request depends largely on its assessment of the moral character of the delinquent. The court tries to hold its intervention to a minimum where it feels a delinquent is of normal character, but will concede that severe, restrictive measures are necessary for hard-core delinquents of criminal character. However, the court's acceptance of the standards and indicators of moral character held by controlling institutions means that in practice it will generally feel that restrictive measures are appropriate. In this way, for example, the court tends to accept police standards regarding the seriousness of offenses, presuming that a youth who steals a handbag will be a hard-core delinquent. Moreover, court personnel come to share the indices of moral character used by the police. For example, "uncooperativeness" and resistance to police authority are accepted indicators of criminal-like moral character. Similarly, court staff feel that a youth in trouble at school, as defined by school officials, has a high potential for serious delinquency. In general, in backing up trouble specialists the court tends to honor their standards for judging delinquency, standards that reflect the distinctive problems and contingencies of their work situations.

Finally, while the court will always question requests to back-up the actions of its users and will often refuse such requests, it is always careful to back up the authority and legitimacy of those making such requests. The court actively protects the moral character of these institutions and their agents in confrontations with delinquents: not only are personal attacks on individual motives and actions penalized by the court, but also the integrity of institutional programs is defended against criticism and questioning. In fact, this kind of back-up protection of authority and institutional legitimacy is most crucial exactly when the court refuses to support and validate the particular request of the complainant. Court handling of police complaints provides the most dramatic case in point. The court will support the police officer's authority even when it dismisses his particular complaint. For example, in cases of illegal search and seizure, the judge may commend the officer for doing the best he could under the circumstances while still dismissing the complaint. Similarly, where the accused is found not delinquent, the judge will routinely lecture him along the lines: "You may have been found not delinquent, but we still know you did it." This emphasis on the distinction between legal and actual innocence supports police authority while refusing to support their specific request for action.

In conclusion, this persistent backing-up of complainants' authority and standards actually allows the court more latitude to refuse their requests for specific actions. It blunts and glosses over the rebuke implicit in a refusal to accept and validate such requests.

THE LIMITS OF "JUDICIOUS NON-INTERVENTION"

A recent critique of the juvenile court (Lemert, 1967b) has underscored the *stigmatizing* consequences of court intervention in delinquency cases. In "helping" delinquents, the court tends to label them as such, in this way becoming "a connecting or intervening link of a vicious circle in which delinquency causes delinquency". To minimize such stigmatization, Lemert proposes reconstitution of the juvenile court on the principle of "judicious non-intervention":

> [The juvenile court] is properly an agency of last resort for children, holding to a doctrine analogous to that of appeal courts which require that all other remedies be exhausted before a case will be considered. This means that problems accepted for action by the juvenile court will be demonstrably serious by testable evidence ordinarily distinguished by a history of repeated failures at solutions by parents, schools, and community agencies (Lemert, 1967b, pp. 96–97).

However, as Lemert implicitly recognizes and as the previous pages have suggested, the juvenile court's actions and "labels" cannot be viewed in isolation from the reasons for court referral. In part the juvenile court produces delinquents by validating the prior judgments and demands for action of local institutions encountering problems of control from troublesome youths. The juvenile court's label represents the end product of the efforts to such institutions to deal with troublesome cases. From this perspective, the juvenile court not only labels delinquents, but it also *resists labeling* by refusing to validate complainant's judgments and to follow their proposed course of action. This suggests that the goal of minimizing court stigmatization requires not only limiting court jurisdiction and power by holding it to a doctrine of "judicious non-intervention," but also maximizing its power and inclination to resist and change established definitions and proscriptions about delinquents and their situations.

Moreover, the concrete thrust of judicious nonintervention is toward keeping minor and trivial delinquency cases out of the juvenile court. In this sense, this strategy would actually prevent court stigmatization of the *marginally delinquent* (i.e., youths who are not "really" delinquents, such as the neglected, the incorrigible, the truant). But as this study has suggested, the juvenile court tends to resist most strongly pressures to intervene in cases of marginal delinquency. The court deals leniently with such marginal delinquents and consciously tries to avoid stigmatizing them. The real threat of stigmatization centers on juvenile court handling of "hardcore" cases—Lemert's cases of "last resort." It is the hardcore delinquent, the youth who causes trouble for enforcement and control institutions, who feels the brunt of court sanctions and who is most apt to suffer incarceration and fundamental stigmatization. From this perspective, the tragedy of the juvenile court lies not in its stigmatizing so many, but in its "saving" so few. Yet the principle of judicious nonintervention would not seem to change the juvenile court's handling of such hardcore, discredited delinquents most in need of salvaging.

Appendix

Table 1: Disposition of All Complaints, Juvenile Court, 1966

	NUMBER	PER CENT	
Adjudicated:			
Found not delinquent	99	7%	
Found delinquent	828	57%	
Total			927
Not Adjudicated:			
Dismissed without finding	478	33%	
Dismissed, turned over to criminal authorities for prosecution	50	3%	
Total			528
Total complaints		100%	1455

Table 2: Disposition of Cases Found Delinquent, Juvenile Court, 1966

	NUMBER	PER CENT		
Appealed cases	36	4%		
Filed or dismissed after adjudication of delinquent	384	46%		
Probation	313	38%		
Ordinary probation			186	22%
Suspended sentence			127	16%
Committed to Youth Correction Authority or County Training School	66	8%		
Cases pending	29	4%		
Total	828	100%		

276

The figures in the preceding tables are taken from the juvenile court's own statistics, which are compiled in terms of individual complaints and their ultimate disposition. The fact that the basic unit here is not the individual delinquent must be born in mind when interpreting these statistics.

Table 1 supports the conclusion that very few cases are found not delinquent, at least when an adjudication is formally made. Thus, only 99 out of 927 adjudicated complaints (10.7%) were found not delinquent.

However, somewhat more than one third of all complaints were dismissed without formal adjudication. For the most part, such actions are not equivalent to "not delinquent" findings. In the first place, fifty complaints were dismissed as a prerequisite to taking criminal action against the juvenile involved. Second, the remainder of the complaints dismissed without formal adjudication include: (1) Complaints dismissed for lack of evidence, hence equivalent to the finding of "not delinquent"; (2) Complaints dismissed only in conjunction with an adjudication of "delinquent" on a separate complaint. For example, if a youth faces a number of complaints, either from several incidents or from several charges arising out of one incident, he might be found delinquent on just one complaint while the rest are dismissed. This occurred in a case described in Chapter 5 (p. 137), where two reform school escapees were charged with a total of thirteen counts of "use without authority" and two of larceny; they were eventually found delinquent on one complaint each and returned to the Youth Correction Authority, while the remaining thirteen complaints were dismissed. (3) Complaints dismissed after successful completion of unofficial probation when the case has been continued without a finding. This category, then, includes cases that have effectively been under court supervision for a period of several months.

A second general point that can be made about these figures is that they obscure the full significance of "probation" as the routine disposition employed by the juvenile court. As mentioned above, a significant number of complaints dismissed without adjudication in fact involved informal probation under the "continued without a finding" disposition. Similarly, in Table 2, a large proportion of those cases which were filed or dismissed after adjudication involved delinquents who had successfully completed probation and had their delinquent record cleared.

Table 3: Types of Offenses, Juvenile Court, 1966

Category of Offense	NUMBER	PER CENT
Assaults (including one manslaughter)	152	9%
Offenses involving sex (including prostitution, fornication, indecent assault, unnatural acts, etc.)	46	3%
Narcotics offenses	8	0.5%
Robbery (armed, unarmed, attempted)	47	3%
Breaking and entering	117	7%
Larceny from a person	46	3%
Larceny (largely shoplifting)	375	23%
Using motor vehicle without authority	174	11%
Offenses against public order (destruction of property, trespassing, idle and disorderly, disturbing the peace, etc.)	105	6.5%
Drunkenness	46	3%
Runaway	148	9%
Incorrigible	96	6%
Truant	60	4%
Other	192	12%
Total	1612[a]	100%

[a] This figure includes 157 complaints pending at the end of the year excluded from Table 1.

Bibliography

ALLEN, FRANCIS A. 1964. *The borderland of criminal justice: essays in law and criminology.* Chicago: University of Chicago Press.

AUBERT, VILHELM. 1965. *The hidden society.* Totowa, N.J.: Bedminster Press.

BALL, DONALD W. 1967. An abortion clinic ethnography. *Social Problems,* 14 (3) : 293–301.

BANTON, MICHAEL. 1964. *The policeman in the community.* New York: Basic Books.

BECKER, HOWARD S. 1952. Social class variations in the teacher-pupil relationship. *Journal of Educational Sociology,* 25: 451–65.

———. 1953. The teacher in the authority system of the public school. *Journal of Educational Sociology,* 27: 128–41.

———. 1963. *Outsiders: studies in the sociology of deviance.* New York: The Free Press.

BITTNER, EGON A. 1967a. Police discretion in emergency apprehension of mentally ill persons. *Social Problems,* 14 (3) : 278–92.

———. 1967b. The police on skid-row: a study of peace keeping. *American Sociological Review,* 32 (5) : 699–715.

BLAU, PETER M. 1963. *The dynamics of bureaucracy: a study of interpersonal relations in two government agencies.* (Rev. ed.) Chicago: University of Chicago Press.

BLUMBERG, ABRAHAM S. 1967a. The practice of law as a confidence game. *Law and Society Review,* 1 (2) : 15–39.

———. 1967b. *Criminal justice.* Chicago: Quadrangle Books.

BOHANNAN, PAUL. 1965. The differing realms of the law. In Laura Nader (Ed.), *The ethnography of law.* Special publication of the *American Anthropologist,* Part 2, 67 (6) : 33–42.

———, AND KARAN HUCKLEBERRY. 1967. Institutions of divorce, family and the law. *Law and Society Review,* 1 (2) : 81–102.

BROWN, CLAUDE. 1966. *Manchild in the promised land.* New York: New American Library.

BURKE, KENNETH. 1954. *Permanence and change: an anatomy of purpose.* Indianapolis: Bobbs-Merrill.

CAMERON, MARY OWEN. 1964. *The booster and the snitch: department store shoplifting.* Glencoe, Ill.: Free Press.

CAVAN, SHERRI. 1966. *Liquor license: an ethnography of bar behavior.* Chicago: Aldine Publishing Company.

CICOUREL, AARON V. 1965. Social class, family structure and the administration of juvenile justice. *Estudios de Sociologia,* 9: 27–49.

———. 1968. *The social organization of juvenile justice.* New York: John Wiley.

———, AND JOHN I. KITSUSE. 1963. *The educational decision-makers.* Indianapolis: Bobbs-Merrill.

CLOWARD, RICHARD A., AND IRWIN EPSTEIN. 1965. Private social welfare's disengagement from the poor: the case of the family adjustment agencies. In Mayer N. Zald (Ed.), *Social welfare institutions: a sociological reader.* New York: John Wiley.

CUMMING, ELAINE, IAN M. CUMMING, AND LAURA EDELL. 1965. Policeman as philosopher, guide and friend. *Social Problems,* 12 (3) : 276–86.

DANIELS, ARLENE K. 1966. The exigencies of labeling deviants for psychiatrists in the military setting. Paper presented at the meetings of the American Orthopsychiatric Association, San Francisco.

DONNELLY, RICHARD C., JOSEPH GOLDSTEIN, AND RICHARD D. SCHWARTZ. 1962. *Criminal law.* New York: Free Press.

DUNHAM, H. WARREN. 1958. The juvenile court: contradictory orientations in processing offenders. *Law and Contemporary Problems,* 23: 512–25.

ERIKSON, KAI T. 1964. Notes on the sociology of deviance. In Howard S. Becker (Ed.), *The other side: Perspectives on deviance.* New York: Free Press.

FREIDSON, ELIOT. 1966. Disability as social deviance. In Marvin B. Sussman (Ed.), *Sociology and rehabilitation.* Cleveland: American Sociological Association.

GARFINKEL, HAROLD. 1956. Conditions of successful degradation ceremonies. *American Journal of Sociology,* 61: 420–24.

———. 1967. *Studies in ethnomethodology.* Englewood Cliffs, N.J.: Prentice-Hall.

GERVER, ISRAEL. 1957. The social psychology of witness behavior with special reference to the criminal courts. *Journal of Social Issues,* 13: 23–29.

GIBBS, JACK P. 1966. Conceptions of deviant behavior: the old and the new. *Pacific Sociological Review,* 9 (1) : 9–14.

GLUCKMAN, MAX. 1955. *The judicial process among the Barotse of Northern Rhodesia.* Manchester: Manchester University Press.

GOFFMAN, ERVING. 1952. On cooling the mark out: some aspects of adaptation to failure. *Psychiatry,* 15 (4) : 451–63.

——. 1959. *The presentation of self in everyday life.* Garden City, N.Y.: Doubleday & Company.

——. 1961a. *Asylums: essays on the social situation of mental patients and other inmates.* Chicago: Aldine Publishing Company.

——. 1961b. *Encounters: two studies in the sociology of interaction.* Indianapolis: Bobbs-Merrill.

——. 1963a. *Behavior in public places: notes on the social organization of gatherings.* New York: Free Press.

——. 1963b. *Stigma: notes on the management of spoiled identity.* Englewood Cliffs, N.J.: Prentice-Hall.

——. 1967. *Interaction ritual: essays on face-to-face behavior.* Chicago: Aldine Publishing Company.

GOLDMAN, NATHAN. 1963. *The differential selection of juvenile offenders for court appearance.* New York: National Council on Crime and Delinquency.

GOULDNER, ALVIN W. 1954. *Patterns of industrial bureaucracy.* Glencoe, Ill.: Free Press.

Harvard Law Review. 1966. Juvenile delinquents: the police, state courts, and individualized justice. 79 (4) : 775–810.

HAZARD, JOHN N. 1962. Furniture arrangement as a symbol of judicial roles. *Etcetera,* 19 (2) : 181–88.

HUGHES, EVERETT C. 1958. *Men and their work.* Glencoe, Ill.: Free Press.

KESSLER, ROBERT A. 1962. The psychological effects of the judicial robe. *American Imago,* 19: 35–66.

KITSUSE, JOHN I. 1964. Societal reaction to deviant behavior: problems of theory and method. In Howard S. Becker (Ed.), *The other side: perspectives on deviance.* New York: Free Press.

KORN, RICHARD. 1964. The private citizen, the social expert, and the social problem: an excursion through an unacknowledged utopia. In Bernard Rosenberg, Israel Gerver, and F. William Howton (Eds.), *Mass society in crisis: social problems and social pathology.* New York: Macmillan.

LEMERT, EDWIN M. 1967a. *Human deviance, social problems, and social control.* Englewood Cliffs, N.J.: Prentice-Hall.

——. 1967b. The juvenile court—quest and realities. In President's Commission on Law Enforcement and Administration of Justice, *Task force report: juvenile delinquency and youth crime.* Washington, D.C.: U.S. Government Printing Office.

LEVINE, SOL, AND PAUL E. WHITE. 1961. Exchange as a conceptual framework for the study of interorganizational relationships. *Administrative Science Quarterly,* 5: 583–97.

LINTON, N. K. 1965. The witness and cross-examination. *Berkeley Journal of Sociology,* 10: 1–12.

LLEWELLYN, KARL N., AND E. ADAMSON HOEBEL. 1941. *The Cheyenne way: conflict and case law in primitive jurisprudence.* Norman: University of Oklahoma Press.

LORBER, JUDITH. 1967. Deviance as performance: the case of illness. *Social Problems,* 14 (3) : 302–310.

MCCORKLE, LLOYD W., AND RICHARD KORN. 1964. Resocialization within walls. In David Dressler (Ed.) , *Readings in criminology and penology.* New York: Columbia University Press.

MATZA, DAVID. 1964. *Delinquency and drift.* New York: John Wiley.

——. 1966. The disreputable poor. In Reinhard Bendix and Seymour M. Lipset (Eds.) , *Class, status and power.* (Rev. ed.) New York: Free Press.

——. n.d. On early warning systems. Ms. Center for the Study of Law and Society.

MECHANIC, DAVID. 1967. Some factors in identifying and defining mental illness. In Thomas J. Scheff (Ed.) , *Mental illness and social processes.* New York: Harper and Row.

MESSINGER, SHELDON L., AND VILHELM AUBERT. 1958. The criminal and the sick. *Inquiry,* 1: 137–60.

——, HAROLD SAMPSON, AND ROBERT D. TOWNE. 1962a. Life as theater: some notes on the dramaturgic approach to social reality. *Sociometry,* 25 (1) : 98–110.

——, ——, ——. 1962b. Family processes and becoming a mental patient. *American Journal of Sociology,* 68 (1) : 88–96.

MILLER, DOROTHY, AND MICHAEL SCHWARTZ. 1966. County lunacy commission hearings: some observations of commitments to a state mental hospital. *Social Problems,* 14 (1) : 26–35.

MILLER, WALTER B. 1958. Inter-institutional conflict as a major impediment to delinquency prevention. *Human Organization,* 17 (3) : 20–23.

NADER, LAURA. 1965. The anthropological study of law. In Laura Nader

(Ed.), *The ethnography of law*. Special Publication of the *American Anthropologist*, Part 2, 67 (6) : 3–32.

OHLIN, LLOYD E., HERMAN PIVEN, AND DONNELL M. PAPPENFORT. 1956. Major dilemmas of the social worker in probation and parole. *National Probation and Parole Association Journal*, 2 (3) : 211–25.

PARSONS, TALCOTT. 1951. *The social system*. Glencoe, Ill.: Free Press.

PAULSEN, MONRAD G. 1962. The delinquency, neglect and dependency jurisdiction of the juvenile court. In Margaret K. Rosenheim (Ed.), *Justice for the child*. New York: Free Press.

PILIAVIN, IRVING, AND SCOTT BRIAR. 1964. Police encounters with juveniles. *American Journal of Sociology*, 70 (2) : 206–214.

PLATT, ANTHONY. 1969. *The child-savers: the invention of delinquency*. Chicago: University of Chicago Press.

———, HOWARD SCHECHTER, AND PHYLLIS TIFFANY. 1968. In defense of youth: a case study of the public defender in juvenile court. *Indiana Law Journal*, 43 (3) : 619–40.

REICHSTEIN, KENNETH J., AND RONALD M. PIPKIN. n.d. Appeals day: a study in the use of conduct defenses in a judicial process handling academic failure. MS. Center for the Study of Law and Society.

REISS, ALBERT J., JR., AND DAVID J. BORDUA. 1967. Environment and organization: a perspective on the police. In David J. Bordua (Ed.), *The police*. New York: John Wiley.

ROSENHEIM, MARGARET K. (ed.). 1962. *Justice for the child: the juvenile court in transition*. New York: Free Press.

SACKS, HARVEY. n.d. Methods in use for the production of a social order: a method for warrantably inferring moral character. Ms. Center for the Study of Law and Society.

———. 1967. The search for help: no one to turn to. In Edwin Shneidman (ed.), *Essays in self-destruction*. New York: Science House.

SCHEFF, THOMAS J. 1966. *Being mentally ill: a sociological theory*. Chicago: Aldine Publishing Company.

———. 1968. Negotiating reality: notes on power in the assessment of responsibility. *Social Problems*, 16 (1) : 3–17.

SCHUTZ, ALFRED. 1962. *Collected papers, vol. I: the problem of social reality*. Ed. by Maurice Natanson. The Hague: Martinus Nijhoff.

———. 1964. *Collected papers, vol. II: studies in social theory*. Ed. by Maurice Natanson. The Hague: Martinus Nijhoff.

SCHWARTZ, CHARLOTTE GREEN. 1957. Perspectives on deviance—wives' definitions of their husbands' mental illness. *Psychiatry*, 20 (3) : 275–91.

SCHWARTZ, RICHARD D., AND JEROME H. SKOLNICK. 1962. Two studies of legal stigma. *Social Problems*, 10 (2) : 133–42.

SCOTT, MARVIN B., AND STANFORD M. LYMAN. 1968. Accounts. *American Sociological Review*, 33 (1) : 46–62.

SKOLNICK, JEROME H. 1966. *Justice without trial: law enforcement in democratic society*. New York: John Wiley.

———. 1967. Social control in the adversary system. *Journal of Conflict Resolution*, 11 (1) : 52–70.

———, AND J. RICHARD WOODWORTH. 1967. Bureaucracy, information, and social control: a study of a morals detail. In David J. Bordua (Ed.), *The Police*. New York: John Wiley.

STRAUSS, ANSELM, LEONARD SCHATZMAN, RUE BUCHER, DANUTA EHRLICH, AND MELVIN SABSHIN. 1964. *Psychiatric ideologies and institutions*. New York: Free Press.

STUDT, ELLIOT. 1966. The reentry of the offender into the community. Ms. Center for the Study of Law and Society,.

SUDNOW, DAVID. 1965. Normal crimes: sociological features of the penal code in a public defender office. *Social Problems*, 12 (3) : 255–76.

———. 1967. *Passing on: the social organization of dying*. Englewood Cliffs, N.J.: Prentice-Hall.

SYKES, GRESHAM M., AND DAVID MATZA. 1957. Techniques of neutralization: a theory of delinquency. *American Sociological Review*, 22: 664–70.

WERTHMAN, CARL. 1964. *Delinquency and authority*. Unpublished M.A. thesis, Department of Sociology, University of California, Berkeley.

———. 1967. The function of social definitions in the development of delinquent careers. Appendix J, *Task force report: juvenile delinquency and youth crime*. Task Force on Juvenile Delinquency, The President's Commission on Law Enforcement and Administration of Justice. Washington, D.C.: U.S. Government Printing Office.

———, AND IRVING PILIAVIN. 1967. Gang members and the police. In David J. Bordua (Ed.), *The police*. New York: John Wiley.

WESTLEY, WILLIAM A. 1953. Violence and the police. *American Journal of Sociology*, 59: 34–41.

WHEELER, STANTON, AND MARTHA BAUM. 1968. Becoming an inmate. In Stanton Wheeler (Ed.), *Controlling delinquents*. New York: John Wiley.

———, EDNA BONACICH, M. RICHARD CRAMER, AND IRVING K. ZOLA. 1968. Agents of delinquency control. In Stanton Wheeler (Ed.), *Controlling delinquents*. New York: John Wiley.

WILSON, JAMES Q. 1968. The police and the delinquent in two cities. In Stanton Wheeler (Ed.), *Controlling delinquents*. New York: John Wiley.

WOLFGANG, MARVIN E. 1957. Victim-precipitated criminal homicide. *Journal of Criminal Law, Criminology and Police Science*, 48 (1) : 1–11.

Yale Law Journal. 1956. The influence of the defendant's plea on judicial determination of sentence. 66 (2) : 204–222.

Index